Lessons Learned

Volume 3

Practical Advice for the
Teaching of Psychology

Editors:

Baron Perlman
Lee I. McCann
Susan H. McFadden

ASSOCIATION FOR
PSYCHOLOGICAL SCIENCE

©2008 by the Association for Psychological Science
All rights reserved.
Printed in the United States of America
Second Printing 2010

Published by
Association for Psychological Science
1133 15th Street, NW Suite 1000
Washington, DC 20005

International Standard Book Number: 0-9626884-5-2
Library of Congress Control Number: 99-62277

To order copies of *Lessons Learned* Vol. 1, Vol. 2, or Vol. 3
go to www.psychologicalscience.org/books

**ASSOCIATION FOR
PSYCHOLOGICAL SCIENCE**

Acknowledgments

The Association of Psychological Science's dedication to **Teaching Tips** and its staff's attention to its place in the **Observer**, our authors, and ourselves has been professional, ongoing, and exemplary. Without the hard work and constancy of APS, **Teaching Tips** would not be what it has been. We thank Alan Kraut for APS's engagement with teaching through **Teaching Tips** and for his commitment to us, its editors. We thank Ann Conkle, Eric Jaffe, Patrick McHugh, and Brian Weaver for their expertise which provides the foundation for the publication of **Teaching Tips** month after month. We cannot imagine editors in other venues having greater support and assistance than we have received.

As always, we acknowledge our authors whose ideas we have edited with respect. Their patience with us has been extraordinary, their abilities and willingness to stretch and think about their ideas admirable. It is through our authors that we are able to assist those who teach psychology. Whereas **Teaching Tips** never strays far or long from concrete, useful ideas of what and how to teach students in and out of the classroom, its readers tell us it also assists them in thinking more globally, critically, and speculatively about teaching. For these outcomes, we thank our authors as well.

Lastly, we thank our colleagues both in and out of our department. We appreciate their patience with and assistance to us as we ask for writings relevant to teaching topics, bounce ideas off of them, and inquire about a specific area of teaching.

Baron Perlman
Lee I. McCann
Susan H. McFadden

Contents

Part III Tests and Grading

Part IV Teaching Challenges

Part V   Themes Across Psychology

Part VI Beyond the Text and Classroom

Part VII Coda

Preface

Teaching is an exceedingly personal activity, and anyone who presumes to advise anyone else on how to go about it does so at his or her own risk (Gleitman, 1984, p. 421)

As this, the third volume of **Teaching Tips** columns opens to you, the reader, with all of its wonderful and helpful ideas, the chapter in our life of being the stewards of **Teaching Tips**, closes for us. After 15 years and over 100 **Teaching Tips** columns, we are calling it a day. We conclude our work as editors, honoring the commitment, risks, and hard work of the many teachers who have presented their ideas to us and to you. And we end our work knowing that, as editors, we have learned more about teaching than we ever expected. **Teaching Tips** — if it has influenced anyone as a teacher and anyone's teaching, changed it, improved it, caused one to ponder—has also influenced us.

What began in 1994 as an unknown has evolved into three volumes, in which we take a modest pride. Over the years, **Teaching Tips** has emphasized more ideas and aspects of teaching than we realized existed. Our anxieties about running out of ideas gave way to the knowledge that there more ideas about teaching than there is space in the APS **Observer** to publish them.

This third volume of **Teaching Tips** columns reflects the evolving nature of teaching. For example, for the first time, we have integrated our two columns about technology into other sections. Computer and internet technology as it relates to teaching has become so commonplace that it is no longer "special." The book's major sections begin with The Act of Teaching and move to Enhancing Student Learning, Performance, and Participation. The book then presents Tests and Grading before presenting some Teaching Challenges. Once again there are several chapters on Themes across Psychology. Ours is a discipline that lends itself to a myriad of approaches and ideas we can place in our courses. We again emphasize Beyond the Text and Classroom, knowing from our authors' and our own experiences that fine teaching and much of our influence takes place outside of formal course meetings. We end with a Coda reflecting on the 15 years of **Teaching Tips** columns and the three volumes of **Lessons Learned**. We have endeavored to distill the most important themes and ideas of our authors about teaching over this decade and a half.

"In the final analysis, teachers teach. And good teachers teach well because they have thought deeply about what they do and why they do it, about their students, and about their commitment." (Perlman, 2007). We will be pleased if this volume of **Lessons Learned** helps you to think more deeply about your teaching and your students. We hope that it sustains you as a teacher, maintaining your commitment to your profession, art, and craft, and that we and our authors are not presumptuous or too audacious in putting forth these ideas on the teaching of psychology.

Teaching Tips will continue with Raymond Green as editor and Jennifer Schroeder-Steward and Mary Hendrix as his coeditors. We wish them the very best in their editorship and smile with pleasure when we think of the road they are walking.

Baron Perlman
Lee I. McCann
Susan H. McFadden

References and Recommended Readings

Gleitman, H. (1984). Introducing psychology. *American Psychologist, 39*, 421-427.

Perlman, B. (2007, August). *Thoughts from a think house: Reflections on teaching.* Paper presented at the 115th Annual Convention of the American Psychological Association, San Francisco, CA.

About the Editors

BARON PERLMAN is a Rosebush and Endowed Professor, a Distinguished Teacher in the Department of Psychology at the University of Wisconsin-Oshkosh, and a Fellow in APA's Society for the Teaching of Psychology. He has a long-standing interest and involvement in the development of faculty. He also is senior editor of **Teaching Tips** in the APS **Observer**, available in book form, **Lessons Learned: Practical Advice for the Teaching of Psychology** (Perlman, McCann, & McFadden, Eds., Volume 1, 1999; Volume 2, 2004) published by the Association for Psychological Science.

LEE I. McCANN is a professor of psychology, a Rosebush and University Professor at the University of Wisconsin-Oshkosh; and a Fellow of the American Psychological Association and the Society for the Teaching of Psychology. He is the coauthor (with Baron Perlman) of *Recruiting Good College Faculty: Practical Advice for a Successful Search* (1996, Anker), coeditor (with Baron Perlman and Susan McFadden) of **Lessons Learned: Practical Advice for the Teaching of Psychology: Vol. 1** (1999, Association for Psychological Science), **Lessons Learned: Practical Advice for the Teaching of Psychology: Vol. 2** (2004, Association for Psychological Science), and the **Teaching Tips** column in the APS **Observer**, and coeditor (with Baron Perlman and William Buskist) of **Voices of Experience: Memorable Talks From the National Institute on the Teaching of Psychology** (2005, Association for Psychological Science).

SUSAN H. McFADDEN is a Rosebush and Endowed Professor, a University of Wisonsin System Distinguished Professor and a professor at University of Wisconsin-Oshkosh. She has taught psychology for 35 years, and is coeditor (with Baron Perlman and Lee I. McCann) of **Lessons Learned: Practical Advice for the Teaching of Psychology: Vol. 1** (1999, Association for Psychological Science), **Lessons Learned: Practical Advice for the Teaching of Psychology: Vol. 2** (2004, Association for Psychological Science), and the **Teaching Tips** column in the APS **Observer**.

Part I

The Act of Teaching

Teaching Tips From Experienced Teachers

Dᴀᴠɪᴅ G. Mʏᴇʀs
Hope College

TEACHERS WANTING TO take their game to a new level are hungry for what this *Observer* page offers: tips for effective teaching, tips for teaching that informs, stimulates, energizes, and even entertains.

My favorite teaching tips, presented here, have been gleaned from the collected advice of master teachers and seasoned with my own experience. Some years ago, my collection began to extend beyond Bill McKeachie's classic *Teaching Tips* (2002). During an extended discussion of teaching tips for new teachers, experienced teachers participating in Bill Southerly's Teaching in the Psychological Sciences listserv (http://faculty.frostburg.edu/psyc/southerly/tips) offered their secrets of success. Here are my 10 favorites from that discussion, with my own reflections:

- ♦ *Be positive.* Correcting mistakes is important, but so is catching students doing something right and reinforcing them. Poet Jack Ridl, a revered professor on my campus and Michigan's Carnegie Professor of the Year, harnesses this principle in his teaching of writing (as I can vouch from Jack's mentoring me with his feedback on several thousand pages of my writing). Jack offers not only specific wisdom — "Your point will have most impact if not buried mid sentence" — but also his delight when catching peak moments: "Dave, can you feel your rhythm here? The cadence is lovely."
- ♦ *Give frequent and fast feedback.* It takes no more time to read papers and exams immediately — and to return them the next class period. Students welcome the

immediate feedback and instructors are glad to have the chore behind them.

♦ *Be enthusiastic.* As Nalini Ambady and Robert Rosenthal (1992, 1993) have found, it takes but a few seconds for observers to "read" a teacher's warmth and enthusiasm and thus to predict their course evaluations. Some people are naturally expressive (and therefore talented at pantomime and charades); others are less expressive (and therefore better poker players). Bella DePaulo and her colleagues (1992) have shown that even inexpressive people, when feigning expressiveness, are less expressive than expressive people acting naturally. Bill Clinton and Dick Cheney could not imitate each other's styles for more than a few moments. The moral: If you're a low-key person who needs to express more enthusiasm, don't worry about overdoing it. What's more, fake it and you may make it.

♦ *Don't expect them to be as enthusiastic.* Chronically sleep-deprived and sometimes self-conscious collegians may not visibly reciprocate our energy, warmth, and enthusiasm. Nevertheless, energy, warmth, and enthusiasm help awaken minds. And as alumni memories of a class sometimes indicate, the mind behind the blank face may register more than we're aware.

♦ *Give lots of practical examples.* My first textbook editor offered this advice in response to my first submitted draft chapter: "Remember, Dave, for every abstract point you must have a concrete example." This principle of good writing is also a principle of good teaching.

♦ *Make questions concrete.* After showing a video, I used to ask, "Comments anyone?" and suffer the silence. But then a colleague modeled a more effective strategy for me: "How did you react to the argument that ... ?" An easily engaged, specific question can unleash a discussion.

♦ *Have patience awaiting answers.* Don't answer your own question. Allow a few moments of calm silence, and a hand, or perhaps an expressive face, may signal someone's willingness to answer. As a further step, inviting students first to *write* an answer virtually ensures that they will then have something to say.

♦ *Do say, "I don't know" and entertain ideas about how to answer a question.* We show our humanity and humility when acknowledging our ignorance. And we can use such times to engage students in thinking like scientist-detectives — by brainstorming how one might go about answering the question.

♦ *Assume your introductory students will never take another course in your field.* Focus on the big questions. What from this course should an educated person know? What are the big lessons you hope they will never forget?

♦ *Realize that in teaching, as in life, two things are certain: You're going to make a fool of yourself at some point, and you're going to have your heart broken.* Although teaching for me has been rewarding, even the best of semesters has offered at least one student evaluation that has seized my attention like a bee sting, as in these answers from one of my students: "What did you find beneficial about this course?" "Nothing!" "What could be improved?" "End the course." "What advice would you give a friend who is planning to take this course?" "Don't."

In hopes of harvesting the teaching tips of our master psychology teachers, several years ago, Bill Buskist (2002) interviewed award-winning psychology professors, asking them for secrets of their success. Buskist and his colleagues confirmed some of the highlights (see listing on the following page) in a follow-up study that asked community college faculty and students what they perceived as the qualities or behaviors of effective teachers (Schaeffer, Epting, Zinn, & Buskist, 2003). Both groups agreed that these qualities were among the top 10: being approachable, being creative and interesting, being encouraging and caring, being enthusiastic, being flexible and open-minded, being knowledgeable, having realistic expectations and being fair, and being respectful.

During his dozen years on university teaching award committees, Dean Keith Simonton (2003) has also observed the qualities of great teachers. And he has observed the qualities of scandalously bad teaching — the sort of bad teaching that brings faculty to the attention of personnel committees or leads to their being denied promotion and tenure. Behaviors related to the Big Five personality traits are the key to success, he observes (see Table 1). Great teaching is marked by behaviors associated with high extraversion, agreeableness, conscientiousness, and openness and by behaviors associated with low neuroticism.

To these teaching tips and marks of master teachers, I add but six more, drawn from my own experience of what has worked best while teaching dozens of sections of introductory and social psychology.

Advice for Teachers From Award-Winning Teachers (Gathered by William Buskist)

1. First, know the content
2. Study the science and art of teaching
3. Observe great teaching and reflect on what might work for you
4. Meet with people who value teaching
5. Be willing to experiment
6. View tests as learning, not just testing opportunities
7. You won't always be effective, but strive to give your best daily
8. Be enthusiastic!
9. Demand the best, with patience
10. Genuinely care about students
11. Talk with students outside class
12. Get to know your students
13. Remember being a student
14. Focus on students with varying needs and skills
15. Always ask for feedback; be grateful for criticism
16. When the passion ends, quit; if your humor is gone, become an administrator

1. Learn Students' Names Immediately

"Remember that a [person's] name is to [that person] the sweetest and most important," advised Dale Carnegie (1937, p. 103) in *How to Win Friends and Influence People*, as one of his six "ways to make people like you." (The other five also are applicable to teaching: Become genuinely interested in other people. Smile. Be a good listener; encourage others to talk about themselves. Talk in terms of the other person's interests. Make the other person feel important — and do it sincerely.) At various times, I have used three strategies for mastering students' names.

Rehearsal Exercise

In classes of 35, I have simply invited the first person to say his or her first and last name, the second person to repeat that name and to add their own, the third person to repeat the first two names and add their own ... concluding with my repeating all 35 names, followed by my own. I would tell students that "we're here to help each other when names are forgotten — someone's forgetting provides our opportunity to learn and remember." Still, forgetting happened less often than I expected. Moreover, memory lapses — often for the name immediately before one's own, for which there had been no rehearsal — provided opportunities for a preview of memory principles. Likewise, my noting the contrasting relaxed and tense body postures of students who had completed or were awaiting the task provided both humorous relief and a preview of stress and physiological arousal. Even so, the exercise, which also breaks the ice by engaging every student in saying something, takes but half an hour. (Obviously, though, Jim Maas, who has taught 65,000 introductory psychology students at Cornell University, could not have done this in one of his student sections of 1,700.)

Photo Lineups

Needing more help as the years went by, I next turned to photographing each class. To create a panoramic sweep, three or four pictures can be stapled to a sheet on which students have written their names according to that day's seating. With a half hour of study at home, plus occasional retrieval practice — often just before class — their names become accessible during class discussion.

Flash Visits

Perhaps I have more capacity for anxiety than most faculty. Starting a new class has always provoked excitement but (while facing new students whose friendship and enthusiasm has not yet been won) also feelings of threat. To jump-start the friendship formation (as well as the name learning), I have dedicated one day within the first week to scheduling students for five-minute get-acquainted conversations in my office. Meeting, say, 10 students an hour, I could talk with the 70 students in two sections of introductory psychology (well, the 60 that remember to show up) during seven intense but enjoyable hours. After some easy questions — Where are you from? What drew you to Hope College? What interests do you have? Have you any questions I could answer? — I thank them for coming by and invite them to come back anytime. When next meeting the class, I have found myself noticeably more comfortable, as if surrounded by friends.

2. Minimize Exam-Related Disagreements

I suspect we all dislike handing back exams, and dislike even more taking class time to be publicly challenged regarding the interpretation of multiple choice questions or points awarded on essay questions. To preclude such hassle, I have asked students to speak to me about their exam-related questions after class. This also, I have explained, spares the rest of the class having to sit through my dealing with individuals' problems.

I have also given students an option when they confront a seemingly ambiguous question. The option is to not answer the multiple choice question and instead to write a short essay that answers the question. If they can display an accurate understanding, they receive full credit. If not, they don't (and they will have passed up their chance to guess the right answer). Out of 35 students, a half dozen typically have elected this option in responding to one or two questions. Their doing so virtually eliminates complaints about unfair questions. Sometimes it also alerts me to a question that does have a valid alternative interpretation. (Other faculty achieve the same ends by allowing students to skip a question or to complete a form on which they can challenge a teacher's answer.)

3. Create the Space

Theater directors and sports fans appreciate that a "good house" is a full house. As social facilitation research reminds us, the presence of others is arousing. It intensifies reactions. Some years ago, Jonathan Freedman and his coworkers (1979) had an accomplice listen to a humorous tape or watch a movie with others. The accomplice could more readily induce fellow audience members to laugh or clap when they all sat close together. Likewise, a class of 35 students feels more warm and lively in a room that seats just 35 than when those 35 students are scattered around a room that seats 100. With heightened arousal and more awareness of one another's responses, jokes become funnier and discussion more animated.

To create a "good house" for our classes, we can create optimal classroom ecology. If possible, schedule the class for a room barely big enough to contain it. Arrange chairs in an arc so people can see one another's faces, while still orienting toward the instructor. Arrive early, stack extra chairs in a back corner, and group the others close together (or rope off the back rows).

The Best Teachers Exhibit	The Worst Teachers Exhibit
High extraversion	Low extraversion
Before-class chats/enthusiasm/interaction (e.g., shows of hands)	Arrive late/leave early/avoid eye contact/inaudible
High agreeableness	Low agreeableness
Learn names/liberal office hours	Dislike Q's/minimal office hours
High conscientiousness	Low conscientiousness
Read text/complete syllabi	Unprepared/bad syllabi/dated
Low neuroticism	High neuroticism
Relaxed/easy-going/flexible	Anxious/defensive/inflexible
High openness to experience	Low openness to experience

Table 1: Big Five Personality/Behavior Differences Between Best and Worst Teachers (Observed by Dean Keith Simonton)

4. Beware the Curse of Knowledge

Technology developers, authors, and teachers often find it irresistibly tempting to assume that what is clear to them will be clear to others. We realize that others lack our expertise, yet, after teaching a class 25 times, we underestimate how confusing an explanation can be. I may feel certain that I have clearly explained "negative reinforcement" and so am astonished when nearly half the class persists in thinking it is punishment.

"The curse of knowledge" describes our egocentric inability to see the world as it looks to those without our knowledge. Ask someone, "How long do you think it takes the average person to solve this anagram — to see that *grabe* can be unscrambled into *barge*?" Knowing the answer, it seems easy, perhaps a 10-second task. But as Colleen Kelley and Larry Jacoby (1996) have shown, if given similar anagrams without knowing the answer (*wreat*), the task proves surprisingly difficult.

Likewise, Boaz Keysar and Anne Henly (2002) have shown that speakers readily overestimate their effectiveness in communicating meaning. They asked speakers to read an ambiguous sentence (such as "Angela shot the man with the gun") in a way that communicated one of its two possible meanings. The speakers routinely overestimated their listeners' accuracy in perceiving the intended message. They presumed that what was obvious to them would be similarly obvious to their audience. This curse of knowledge is surely a source of much miscommunication not only among friends and lovers, but also between teachers and students, and authors and readers. Whatever can be misunderstood will be. Once we know something, it becomes difficult to appreciate what it's like not to know. But we can, by restraining our assumptions, better enable students to cross the bridge from ignorance to knowledge.

5. Lecture Less

After authoring my own text — which stole my best lecture material — I was motivated to subdue my talking head and to offer students briefer synopses of key or difficult concepts interwoven with experiences that more actively engaged them (see below). The resulting student evaluations proved gratifying, and without any performance decline on exams that covered all text chapters.

In hindsight, this makes sense. Given that even average readers can absorb words at double the speed of a teacher's speaking — and can pause to reread difficult material — lecture is an inefficient means of transferring words from one head to another. I believe I speak for fellow text authors in suggesting that, in comparison to lecture-based teaching, learning from textbooks can offer broader, less idiosyncratic, more representative, and more carefully checked coverage of a discipline. And I am confident I speak for the community of text authors in saying that all introductory texts are superior to their authors' pre-text lectures. Thanks to the magnitude of effort and the extensive quality controls, the resulting teaching package is more comprehensive, tightly organized, carefully reviewed, painstakingly edited, efficiently presented, and attractively packaged than any instructor could home brew. In the spirit of Winston Churchill's remark about democracy, textbooks are the worst way to present information, except for all the others.

6. Activate Students

Writing for this column a decade ago on "The Merits of Classroom Demonstrations," Doug Bernstein (1994) observed that "my 27 years of teaching have left me convinced that the best use of class time is not so much to teach things as to do things — tell stories, give examples, present new concepts, and of course offer demonstrations — in ways that motivate the students to read the book, ask important questions, and learn for themselves. ... Classroom demonstrations, like other breaks from the straight lecture mode, can provide highlights that make teaching more enjoyable for you as well as the students." (25)

I concur, and have devised or gleaned from others a series of demonstrations that are fairly quick, utterly reliable, dramatic (it doesn't take a statistical caliper to see the effect), pedagogically effective, and just plain fun. Thus, at different times of the semester my students have, for example, been found to be:

- Groaning, grinning, and laughing — after virtually 100 percent have labeled "unsurprising" a seemingly common sense finding that is actually opposite to what the people on either side of them also claim, in hindsight, to have known all along.
- Squeezing each others' shoulders and ankles in a human chain — demonstrating psychological measurement principles while measuring the speed of neural transmission.
- Befuddled by pseudoparanormal ESP tricks.
- Experiencing perceptual adaptation with special glasses that displace the visual field.
- Displaying dramatically greater memory for visually than acoustically encoded sentences.
- Exhibiting common illusory thinking tendencies.
- Illustrating group polarization after discussion in small groups.

All these demonstrations (Bolt, 2004) are fun and games — but with a purpose that links to a basic principle and makes it memorable.

Nearly 20 years ago, Colorado State psychologist Frank Vattano and I sat down with a Corporation for Public Broadcasting executive, hoping to persuade her to allow highlights of the PBS series, "The Brain," to be made available to psychology teachers as affordable brief clips (rather than expensive 60-minute programs). To our delight, she did commission Frank to repackage the series in teaching-friendly modules and then invited him to do the same with "The Mind" series. Thanks to these and to subsequent resources, in nearly every class period we can now offer one or more brief video clips that enliven lecture and stimulate discussion. If we have been considering split-brain research, we can display a split-brain patient being tested. If we have been demonstrating illusory thinking principles, we can meet Daniel Kahneman and Amos Tversky on screen. Judging by the response of my students, this simple innovation — replacing long films and videos with vivid three- to 10- minute clips that are directly pertinent to the topic at hand — has been a boon to the teaching of psychology.

Finally, I have engaged my students in active processing through out-of-class computer simulations. The best of today's interactive programs can engage students as experimenters (as when training a rat), as subjects (as when being tested on a memory or perceptual illusion task), and as learners in a dynamic tutorial (as when harnessing dynamic computer graphics to teach concepts such as neurotransmission).

So, learn names and make friends, minimize exam hassles, create the space, beware the curse of knowledge, lecture less, and activate students — those are my echoes to the accumulated wisdom of master teachers of psychology.

References and Recommended Readings

Ambady, N., & Rosenthal, R. (1992). Thin slices of expressive behavior as predictors of interpersonal consequences: A meta-analysis. *Psychological Bulletin, 111*, 256-274.

Ambady, N., & Rosenthal, R. (1993). Half a minute: Predicting teacher evaluations from thin slices of nonverbal behavior and physical attractiveness. *Journal of Personality and Social Psychology, 64*, 431-441.

Bernstein, D. (1994, July/August). Tell and show: The merits of classroom demonstrations. *APS Observer*, pp. 24-25, 27.

Bolt, M. (2004). *Instructor's resources and lecture guides.* New York: Worth Publishers.

Buskist, W. (2002). Effective teaching: Perspectives and insights from Division Two's 2- and 4-year awardees. *Teaching of Psychology, 29*, 188-193.

Carnegie, D. (1937). *How to win friends and influence people.* New York: Simon & Schuster.

DePaulo, B. M., Blank, A. L., Swaim, G. W., & Hairfield, J. G. 1992). Expressiveness and expressive control. *Personality and Social Psychology Bulletin, 18*, 276-285.

Freedman, J. L., & Perlick, D. (1979). Crowding, contagion, and laughter. *Journal of Experimental Social Psychology, 15*, 295-303.

Kelley, C. M., & Jacoby, L. L. (1996). Adult egocentrism: Subjective experience versus analytic bases for judgment. *Journal of Memory and Language, 35*, 157–175.

Keysar, B., & Henly, A. S. (2002). Speakers' overestimation of their effectiveness. *Psychological Science, 13*, 207-212.

McKeachie, W. J. (2002). *McKeachie's teaching tips: Strategies, research, and theory for college and university teachers* (11th ed.). Boston: Houghton Mifflin.

Schaeffer, G., Epting, K., Zinn, T., & Buskist, W. (2003). Student and faculty perceptions of effective teaching: A successful replication. *Teaching of Psychology, 30,* 133-136.

Simonton, D. K. (2003). *Teaching and the Big Five: Or what I've learned from a dozen years on teaching award committees.* Presentation to the Society of Personality and Social Psychology teaching workshop, Los Angeles, CA.

Preparing for a Class Session

Baron Perlman
Lee I. McCann
University of Wisconsin-Oshkosh

*"When the task is done beforehand, then it is easy. If you
do it hurriedly and carelessly, it must be hard."*
(Cleary, 1989, p. 5)

THERE IS MUCH TO BE
gained from preparing for a class session by meditatively contemplating what works well, previous mistakes made, the nature
and needs of your students, and your goals for the session. This
process is separate and different from the usual content preparation. We recognize, however, that the realities of academe often
preclude this process, and we do not fault teachers who cannot
prepare before each class session, ideal as that may be. Often,
faculty have rushed from a meeting, were delayed getting to campus by family matters, or were engrossed in writing and looked
at the clock a bit late. They now have a class to teach, and in the
few minutes that remain, if any, "best" preparation is difficult.
Some teachers might think about their classes only once a week,
and others might think about them even less frequently.

To encourage and help such efforts, we present the types of
preparation teachers might do before a class session. Interestingly, we found nothing in the teaching literature on preparation
for individual class sessions.

Intellectual Content: Findings, Ideas, Theory, Methodology, People, and the Like

Whether the class session involves a lecture, discussion, or
small group work, a teacher must be familiar with the day's

intellectual content. New teachers often work harder at this, whereas experienced teachers may need minimal review. Nonetheless, a close reading of the day's lecture notes or discussion points may illuminate nuances previously overlooked or forgotten. We recommend this practice, regardless of the teacher's experience level.

Equally important, we believe, are the purposes to which the content will be put. Questions such as the following should be con-sidered and prioritized, and decisions should be made.

- Why am I addressing this material at this juncture of the semester? Where are we in the semester and in the course's progression or module? What "...links, umbrellas, and frameworks..." (Gleitman, 1984, p. 425) can be emphasized? How will I provide transitions between this content and what went before and what will follow?

- How does this day's class help students move closer to meeting course goals as stated in the syllabus? What course themes might be touched on or discussed?

- Why is this day's content important and how will I convince students? Do I want to ask them about its importance, and how long should I spend doing so?

- What is the single most important point I will make today? Second most important? How can I best communicate the importance of these ideas?

- Is there an emotional component to the upcoming class? How do I expect students to feel, and how do I want to go about entering their affective world?

- How does the class relate to students' lives? Are there topics that should be especially relevant to what they and their friends, family, and peers experience?

- Is this a good class in which to have students generate examples or metaphors? Both are powerful ways of anchoring course materials. What success have I had in the past in asking students to do this? How much and what kinds of preparation will they need to develop good examples?

- How will I conclude the class and prepare students for the next one?

Making Class Fresh – The "In the Moment" Teacher

You will be more focused and energized if you focus on today. "...When you think you will be on the job forever, then trouble starts" (Cleary, 1999, p. 86). Fatigue vanishes and distractions disappear when teachers are mindful only of the present.

There is an applicable adage from psychotherapy: "If the therapist is dead or not present psychologically, treatment does not go well." What can teachers do to stay fresh, focus their attention on the task at hand, and communicate enthusiasm to their students? How many times can a teacher teach about Milgram, Pavlov, Asch, or Erikson before going brain dead? If you are bored, what can you expect from your students? Pretend you are a student in your own class and that this is the first time you are exposed to today's material. What would you expect? What would "grab" you or confuse you?

- Pretend you are teaching today's class for the first time. Keep in touch with the "wonder" of psychology. Remember the awe, satisfaction, hope, appreciation, and revelation you felt when you first taught. It should not be "work" to teach the upcoming class, nor should it be a problem or drudgery (Carroll, 2004). Such thoughts and feelings take away teachers' purpose and resolve.

- If you were engaging in peer review of teaching, what would you advise or think about today's class period if you were the reviewer? What would be its strengths and weaknesses?

- Remind yourself that in class no one can email you and there are no phone calls — your only obligation is to teach. It may not only be the most important task of the day, but it may be the most focused and the least interrupted, and, for a change, you will only be doing one thing at a time.

- Vitalize yourself. Go outside, even if just to walk around your building for a few minutes. Aren't you tired of your office anyway? It is amazing how seeing things from a different physical perspective changes one's mood. If you have energy, you will bring it to your students. If time is short, a few brief exercises (push-ups, deep knee bends, etc.) can get your blood flowing before class.

- Depending on how your day has gone, you may want to compose yourself. Turn off the lights in your office for a few minutes. Do some slow, deep breathing, meditate, and think of nothing. Luxuriate in the stillness. Teaching asks us to give a lot to others; we need to give something to ourselves. Try to be still at least once a day at work.

♦ Exercise your voice, especially for a large class.

Learning From Experience

Recall your previous experiences teaching this topic and try to repeat the good ones.

♦ If the class has gone "well" in the past, what made that happen? If you or the students were unhappy with the class session, what was not working? What might have worked?

♦ Are you doing anything different today than in the past? If so, pay special attention to how students respond and ask several for their opinions after class.

♦ Do you need to slow down? Are you rushing? Remember that more is not necessarily better and that rushed material may not provide the depth or foundation you hope for.

♦ Have you previously experienced this classroom as depressing or ill-suited to your teaching? Can you be assigned a different room?

Beware of Habituation

Most teachers teach to their strengths. The entertainer tells stories and lectures to an enthralled class; the cheerleader uses group discussion, moving from group to group of students, supporting their work and urging them on; and the perfectionist spends hours on brilliant, detailed (usually too much so) PowerPoint slides. No matter how you teach, keep in mind that students will habituate to your presentation method. Variety is the spice of good teaching. Change the pace and your teaching style.

♦ If you typically use PowerPoint, do something else for a class period once in a while.

♦ If you always stand in the front center of the room, move somewhere else

♦ If you use an overhead projector, sit somewhere in the class and have one of your students write important points on the overhead as you get to them. (Students love this and a friend can take notes for them.)

♦ Tell a relevant story from your own life that might evoke students' stories as well.

- If you are a lecturer, mix in some group work once in a while.
- Is it time for a demonstration, perhaps including students?
- Seize the moment. If the weather is getting nicer and students are wearing shorts, does their behavior relate in any way to course content (e.g., conformity, hopefulness)? Once, when teaching about anorexia, one of us asked a female student athlete what she weighed. She would not answer. Every man in the class volunteered to publicly state his weight. Her refusal led to a discussion of the cultural pressures women experience about the power and privacy of weight and body measurements, making it clearer how eating disorders may arise and be maintained.

Students

Classes have the tendency to blend and blur together. One class goes well, whereas another is not as much fun to teach as usual. What often gets lost is the audience (Gleitman, 1984): the students we are teaching, who are individuals with differing needs, problems, and successes.

- Which students that day may need attention? Who is a member of an athletic team, for example, who merits recognition for the team's performance?
- Which students say little or nothing at all in class? Is there someone in particular you want to ask, "How is the semester going?" before class?
- Is there an issue that must be dealt with directly (e.g., student performance on an exam, class attendance, students' lack of preparation for class or lack of questions)?
- Have any students come to office hours to talk about their academic performance? Do any of these students need feedback or support as you pass back exams or papers? Are kudos called for?
- Have students approached you about personal matters — their own or a family member's illness, a friend who recently attempted suicide, family problems, and so forth? Do you need to check on how they are doing and see if they need to talk with you more?
- Have you ever gotten to class early and sat in the last row to talk with the students who are always the furthest

away during class sessions? Entering their physical world is interesting and is often gratifying to them.

♦ Do you begin the class period with course content or other matters? Do you need to ask the students as a whole how the course is going? Are there ways you could establish a sense of common purpose and "togetherness" in the course (i.e., a sense of community)?

Teach Within the Rhythms of the Semester

Semesters may be likened to military campaigns. "At the beginning ...morale is high, after a while it begins to flag, and in the end it is gone" (Tzu, 2003, p. 65). Semesters also are like a musical composition. They have different rhythms and energy throughout their course. If you can stay attuned to a semester's rhythms, you can conduct your teaching accordingly. For example:

♦ If you are tired, then your students probably are as well. Is there something you can do that day that is especially fun or requires less intellective work, what Duffy and Jones (1995) call "beating the doldrums" (p. 159)?

♦ If the weather is gorgeous, especially when that is unusual (e.g., spring semester in Wisconsin, when it sometimes snows until the last week of the semester), then respond to a beautiful day. Call class off early (remember, content after a certain point may be the biggest road block to good teaching), hold class outside, bring each student a flower, open the classroom windows wide (assuming you have them and they can be opened!), or acknowledge the day in some other way.

♦ Attend to how you have designed your course. Is the most important material presented when students are at their lowest ebb? Move something around or make a note that something has to be changed for the next semester.

♦ Is this the right day to seek the student feedback (e.g., one-minute paper) you had planned? If students are anxious about an upcoming exam, perhaps you should talk about the exam and their preparation instead, saving something you had planned for another day.

The Details Are Important

For all of the emphasis on content, presence, emotion, seizing the moment, and the like, good teaching also lies in the details.

These minutia are best attended to directly before class. Consider and pay attention to the following:

- Do not forget to take fluids with you to ease a dry throat while speaking.
- Remember your flash drive, extra batteries, and other technological supports.
- Always bring extra copies of the course syllabus, assignment descriptions, and other handouts. It is much easier to give one to a student than to remember to email them one later or to bring it to the next class.
- Bring a small pad of lined paper to every class. Consider it a "real-time list" on which you keep track of 1) things to bring students (e.g., journal articles, books); 2) students who came for office hours or spoke about needing a tutor, wanting to do better in the course, or missing an exam; and 3) a host of other requests and information about and from students. Reviewing this real-time list before class allows you to talk with students about their studies, week, semester, and lives. Even in a large class of hundreds of students, teachers can achieve a more personal relationship and can better care for their students.
- Get to class early to check that your technology is working and to talk with the students.

Conclusion

Preparation for class sessions is a habit worth cultivating. We hope it serves you as well as it has served us.

References and Recommended Readings

Carroll, M. (2004). *Awake at work: Facing the challenges of life on the job*. Boston: Shambhala.

Cleary, T. (Trans.). (1989). *Zen lessons: The art of leadership*. Boston: Shambhala.

Cleary, T. (Trans.). (1999). *Code of the Samurai: A modern translation of the Bushido Shoshinshu of Taira Shigesuke*. Boston: Tuttle Publishing.

Duffy, D. K., & Jones, J.W. (1995). *Teaching within the rhythms of the semester*. San Francisco: Jossey-Bass.

Gleitman, H. (1984). Introductory psychology. *American Psychologist, 39*, 429–437.

Prégent, R. (1994). *Charting your course: How to prepare to teach more effectively.* Madison, WI: Magna Publications.

Tzu, S. (2003). *The art of war.* San Francisco: Long River Press.

The Professor's Voice: A Resource and a Risk

CATHY SARGENT MESTER
Penn State-Erie

WHAT DO MOST COLLEGE professors have in common with Billy Joel, Reverend Billy Graham, Bill Murray, and Bill Clinton? Few of us are named "Bill," so that's not it. Rather, it is our occupational dependence on our voices. Like politicians, singers, actors, and preachers, teachers rely on their voices as a rich resource, capable of conveying, clarifying, and emphasizing ideas and feelings.

The nature of our daily work, like that of politicians and singers, also puts our voices at risk. We speak for hours at a time, often in rooms with poor air quality, and we must project our voices to the depths of lecture halls with poor acoustics. There are a number of steps that any of us can take to strengthen our voices and be the James Earl Jones of our classrooms, speaking in vigorous, resonant tones that hold students' attention and enlarge their comprehension.

Biomechanics of Voice

Variations in voice production are often within our deliberate control. By consciously controlling specific muscle groups, we can create a more richly expressive voice with plenty of carrying power.

Pitch

Speech scientists tell us that we each are physically able to use about a two-octave range when we speak. Naturally, we rarely use the full range, typically speaking within a few notes of our optimum pitch.

Being fairly elastic, the vocal bands can be stretched and relaxed, causing pitch variations. The mass of each person's vocal bands is genetically determined, making us each "natural" baritones, altos, tenors, or sopranos. However, by changing the tension on the bands, we can create a wide array of varying tones within that natural range.

Rate, Volume, and Timbre

Our typical speech rate, volume, and timbre likewise result from genetic predisposition, but they are also subject to consciously created variations. Volume and timbre, for instance, are strongly affected by the size, shape, and sound-absorbing quality of the resonating cavities in our heads, the largest being the mouth. Each mouth is a certain size, but by dropping the lower jaw slightly and opening the lips wider, the size of the oral cavity and its subsequent resonating power are drastically changed.

Such capabilities lead many voice experts to assert that the human voice is more expressive than any musical instrument. Because of its enormous ability to be varied, the voice can convey the excitability of the piccolo, the mournfulness of the sax, the ponderousness of the bass, or the lighthearted glee of the tympani. We can each "play" our vocal instrument more skillfully with certain types of care and practice.

With this background in mind, let us now consider the ways and means to develop classroom voices that are both athletic enough to bear the strain of talking all day and vigorous enough to provide plentiful nonverbal cues to meaning.

The Athletic Voice

As speaking comes from proper use of several muscle groups, experts rightly refer to speaking as an "athletic" activity. As such, we can make best use of our voices if we use the same practices of preparation and exercise that the athlete does. Doing so should provide the speaker with a voice that has endurance, power, and flexibility while avoiding overexertion.

Tips for Fitness

Warm up regularly. Begin the day with vocal stretching exercises. Appropriate exercises include deep-breathing work to relax the chest and abdominal muscles that will control the flow of breath needed for speaking. Do a few neck rolls as well to stretch the neck muscles. By warming up physically for the challenge of speaking, the muscle groups controlling respiration, phonation, and resonation should be relaxed enough to allow you to achieve varied expression.

- *Practice diaphragmatic breathing.* The energy for speaking needs to come from the diaphragm, both to reduce strain on the voice box and to provide the power needed to carry your voice effectively. If your shoulders rise and fall as you speak, you are using clavicular, not diaphragmatic breathing. Switching the breathing power to the diaphragm takes considerable practice but will reduce vocal strain noticeably.

- *Employ optimum posture and vocal exertion.* Standing up straight allows the diaphragm to be fully supported, the resonating cavities to be properly aligned, and breathing to be unimpeded. Trying to speak emphatically while sitting usually involves leaning forward at the waist and jutting out the jaw. Such exertion constrains diaphragmatic breathing and stretches the muscles controlling vocalization, risking damage. Remember that variations of expression to suit your meaning can be achieved with just slight changes in tension on the vocal folds or a well-placed pause: Screaming and shouting are not necessary.

- *Proper hydration.* Teachers who speak for an hour or more should keep water bottles handy. Water or citrus juices are best for vocal fold hydration — coffee actually hinders your ability to sustain a strong speaking voice. Switch to water with a little squirt of lemon, and you will speak comfortably and longer. As we grow older, the vocal folds are naturally drier and less flexible, so hydration becomes especially important.

- *Avoid smoking.* Smoking is a bad habit for anyone but especially for those who need to sustain healthy voices. Smoke dries out the vocal folds, making them less flexible and therefore less expressive and more susceptible to injury.

- *Avoid throat clearing.* Note the frequency with which you "clear" your throat. That little semicough makes the vocal folds smack roughly together. A better response to a perceived throat tickle or phlegm buildup is to take a sip of water and a deep, cleansing breath.

Sore Throats and Laryngitis

Despite all our best efforts, we do occasionally develop sore throats or full-fledged laryngitis. The result can be disastrous. Clinton lost his voice at a crucial point in his 1992 presidential campaign, leading to a disruptive hiatus in his travels. Similarly, John Kerry lost a crucial day of campaigning in Iowa during the January 2004 primary election due to laryngitis. In 1998, Joel incurred serious damage to his vocal folds and had to cancel a six-month tour. Can you imagine if a teacher had to stop talking for that long! Even going silent for a day is hard to abide.

If struck with laryngitis, silence is absolutely the best therapy. Even whispering can damage the vocal folds. Do not just talk in class, choosing silence only when convenient: Go completely silent. This calls for some real creativity if you must still teach, but it is necessary for long-term vocal health. Write out some discussion questions for the class, show a film, and let students actually do the teaching — anything, as long as you do not vocalize for a day or two.

The Vigorous Voice

The literature on teacher effectiveness references vocal expressiveness as a factor perceived as beneficial. By varying our expression, we clarify for students the distinctions between important and peripheral points in our lecture; we hold their attention; and we convey to them that this material is interesting, perhaps even incredibly fascinating.

Our vocal expression, however, is very much a matter of habit. Those who are accustomed to speaking relatively blandly will have to work harder to achieve dynamic expression. And old habits are hard to break.

Breaking the Monotone Habit

If students have told you that you speak in a monotone, you will first need to learn to recognize that tendency in yourself. Audio or videotaping is the best mechanism for such self-monitoring. Tape yourself in a couple of classes. Look at your notes to identify the most important points you intended to emphasize in each class. Then, listen to the tape at those emphatic points to determine if your vocal expression changed accordingly. Was there a perceptibly lower or higher or more varied pitch used? Was the idea set off with significant pauses? Was the most important idea spoken more slowly or more resonantly? If none of

Association for Psychological Science

these devices are regularly apparent in the taped lectures, then the students were right.

You can modify monotonal habits by planning changes in vocal pitch, rate, volume, or timbre for each lecture. However, that is likely to result in a delivery that seems awkwardly choreographed. President Gerald Ford, for instance, once planned specific changes in delivery to enliven a key televised speech; however, he appeared so marionette-like that one of his sons called him later that night to tell him how badly he had done.

The better approach is a more systemic revision of vocal use. Start by critically listening to voices that you admire or recognize as more expressive than your own. Listen closely, identifying emphatic moments and the vocal cues alerting the listeners to that emphasis. Try to commit the flow of that model's speech to your aural memory, gradually emulating it in your own speaking. Be sure to emulate, not imitate. Try to capture the rhythmic flow of the more expressive voice within your own pitch range and personality. With time and persistence, you will become more "multitonal."

Exercising Your Way to Expressiveness

Following the tape-assisted analysis of your voice, you are ready to undertake some exercises to achieve desirable vocal modifications. Several of the references provided at the end of this column include vocal exercises to expand pitch range, modify speech speed, and enhance vocal resonance, among other things.

To improve speed, swimmers wear ankle or arm weights during practice, so that they'll have more strength to meet the unweighted demands of normal competition. Likewise, if we want to improve our use of our full pitch range, we should do exercises demanding extreme reach within our range. One exercise is to speak the sentence, "Who was that masked man?" with at least four different meanings.* Doing so requires fairly dramatic pitch and rate changes to emphasize distinctly different parts of the message. There are exercises to enhance resonation,

---

* Still wondering about four different meanings for, "Who was that masked man?" Here are some possibilities:
1. The one over there, not here.
2. The one with the mask, not the hat.
3. The one who was soooo handsome!
4. The one whose name is "Who."

improve speaking rate, reduce timbre problems, increase vocal projection, etc. Here are a couple of examples to illustrate the possibilities:

- *Rate:* For those who speak at an unchanging rate with few meaningful pauses, try reciting the final stanza of "The Twelve Days of Christmas," deliberately saying each day's gift at a slower or faster pace than its predecessor. Be sure to pause enough between days to get a breath and to readjust your mental pace.

- *Resonation:* Those who speak at a higher pitch than preferred, or whose voices do not carry well, should try exercises that enhance oral resonation, such as the classic, "How now brown cow?" The goal here is to open the mouth wider on the "ow" sounds, creating a more resonant oral cavity.

- *Timbre:* There are a variety of exercises designed to increase vocal quality (timbre), depending on the particular quality you want to modify. Those whose voices tend to be too breathy, for instance, can work on controlling that excess by reciting the "Husbandless Hannah Hughes" monologue, which requires sustaining 10 or 12 words littered with the breath-wasting "H" phoneme.

None of these exercises are a quick fix. A regular regimen of such exercises will, however, produce a much-improved range of natural vocal expression over time.

Richness Without Risk

The human voice is a treasure whose potential we hear realized in the singing of Placido Domingo, the poetry of Maya Angelou, and the acting of Anthony Hopkins. We also have heard it in the teaching of those instructors who are enthusiastic about their subject and who work at developing healthy habits of vocal expression, allowing their enthusiasm to be obvious. Any of us can join that pantheon by practicing sensible habits of vocal care and exercise.

As long as there are no preexisting physiological problems, anyone can break the monotone habit with patient and dedicated effort. The effort will be rewarded with new or enhanced skills that help attract and hold student attention, place clarifying emphasis, and establish the instructor's credibility.

References and Recommended Readings

Eisenson, J., & Eisenson, A. (1996). *Voice and diction: A program for improvement.* New York: Macmillan.

Hahner, J.C., Sokoloff, M., & Salisa, S. (2002). *Speaking clearly: Improving voice and diction.* New York: McGraw-Hill.

Mayer, L.V. (2004). *Fundamentals of voice and articulation.* New York: McGraw-Hill.

Sataloff, R. T. (August 5, 2001). *Common medical diagnoses and treatments in professional voice use.* Retrieved August, 12, 2007,from http://www.emedicine.com/ent/topic695.htm

University of Pittsburgh Voice Center. (2001). *Frequently asked questions regarding voice problems.* Retrieved August 12, 2007, from http://voicecenter.upmc.com

Technology Is Not a Toy!

CATHY SARGENT MESTER
Penn State-Erie

STAR WARS PRODUCER George Lucas and former Illinois Governor and presidential candidate Adlai Stevenson would surely have had a lively conversation if able to discuss the place of technology in education! They would be at opposite ends of the love-hate relationship that teachers of all levels experience as they try to incorporate the newest technological innovations in their classrooms. Lucas, by virtue of his colossal Hollywood success and his dedication to utilizing the best of that world in the world of education, has contributed enormous amounts of money and resources to schools interested in enhancing learning with technology. Stevenson, on the other hand, was so averse to technology that in a 1954 speech at Columbia University, he once described it this way: "Technology, while adding to our physical ease, throws daily another loop of fine wire around our souls" (1955, p. 156).

Even the most common educational technology, presentation software, yields similarly mixed reviews. Increasingly a staple in the college classroom, Power Point and its cousins are perceived both as exciting opportunities and as wearying attacks on students' "souls." I will consider the controversy here and suggest concrete tips to capitalize on the software's strengths for those who choose to use it.

Changes in technology are so swift and constant that it is difficult to keep up with new capabilities. We are encouraged to continue using the technology even though not all of us have been given instructions in those new capabilities. I hope to "catch everyone up" with the suggestions noted here.

Bane or Boon?

Research on presentation software's impact on students suggests two reasons why it may be an asset to learning. First, the dynamism of the visual image accompanying the instructor's voice can help capture and focus student attention. Although this is true of all visual aids, the advantage is magnified when the visual is as sophisticated and complex as presentation software.

The second advantage is more unique to the specific nature of presentation software: its ability to incorporate a variety of extraordinarily clarifying images within the visual aid. By adding film clips, diagram close-ups, sound, and 3-D images, it can take students to a new level of content comprehension. We experience this advantage every time we hear the collective "aah" of students as they literally see brain function or statistics broken out into meaningful segments.

At the opposite end of the spectrum, we find anecdotal evidence of the narcotic impact of slideshow abuse. Students complain of being overloaded with onscreen information. As their natural tendency is to write down whatever appears on the screen, students often find themselves frantically copying information from a slide and thus blocking out the sound of the instructor's voice. Students also complain that so much of the class period is devoted to watching slide after slide in a semidarkened room that their physical alertness is actually diminished. In other words, they fall asleep!

One final complaint about presentation software's impact comes not from students, but from educators and researchers who suggest that bullet points discourage critical thought. The best slides, visually, are those that are succinct. However, in their brevity lies an implied simplicity that often fools the viewer/learner into an unchallenging mindset. NASA recently "blamed" Power Point for some of their mission failures. They reported that engineers who received research reports via software presentations often failed to grasp the complex seriousness of the data being presented.

So, where does this diversity of opinion lead us? Put simply, presentation technology is not a toy. It is still so relatively new that many of us are taking to it like we did the hula-hoop — with lots of enthusiasm and not much technique. To capitalize on the advantages of the technology and not be victimized by its playful allure, we should learn from those who are finding that it is a device that actually benefits student attention and comprehension.

We know that various classroom props should always be used to enhance clarity of message as well as to sustain teacher-student immediacy (Mester & Tauber, 2004). As research on immediacy has concluded, students' trust of and respect for the teacher increases their likelihood of learning, and teachers' presentation styles can increase that trust and respect. So, the recommendations noted here are intended to contribute to an immediacy-enhancing presentation style. We can take steps both in how we prepare a slidewear-assisted class and in how we actually present it to accomplish that aim, thus increasing student learning.

While Preparing

Preparation Rule #1: Minimize the Content of a Single Slide

As the basic function of anything presented visually in class is to clarify and emphasize, each slide should provide a minimal amount of verbiage. The slides are not speaker notes, nor are they complete explanations. They are "highlights" that will help the students grasp the most important point of whatever the instructor is explaining. A highlight can be quickly jotted down in students' notes, allowing them to be more attentive to the instructor than to the screen, adding to their brief note as the explanation progresses.

For instance, a slide of the explanation presented here would probably look like this:

> **Minimize the content of a single slide.**
>
> One two three four five six
> One two three four five six
> One two three four five six
> One two three four five six
> One two three four five six
> One two three four five six

This sample slide contains only the briefest of information and allows me to introduce the "6 x 6" rule without writing it out in an unnecessarily boring essay form. The "6 x 6" rule derives from the research of a number of vision scholars who concluded that six words or numbers across the field and six down is the maximum that a viewer can grasp in a single look. Anything over that number requires so much concentrated visual attention that accompanying speech is ignored. Naturally, part of the reason for this rule is that the more figures on a screen, the smaller the font will need to be. Small fonts cannot be read beyond the front row of class.

This minimalist guideline is especially important when including charts in your presentation. Even if the research being presented references ten variables over two-year increments of a twenty-year span, the table created for a single slide should include no more than six rows and six columns, not ten and ten. Consequently, in creating the table, you will select the most important variables or the most meaningful time periods. Such a compression of data has the benefit of forcing the instructor into framing a narrow focus for the explanation that will be more readily understood by the students. NASA would remind us, however, to be careful of oversimplifying in the interest of succinctness of data.

Preparation Rule #2: Select Uncomplicated Images

The best use of Power Point slides is their provision of visual images that clarify the instructor's spoken words. We can include diagrams, models, photographs, and video either reproduced from another source or of our own creation. As the old adage suggests, these "pictures" speak volumes.

At a recent technology conference, a speaker who teaches speech pathology explained a new technique in stuttering therapy. After a brief orientation, she segued to a series of video slides showing the progress of one patient treated with the procedure, ending with a split screen showing before and after images of the patient. The illustration was quite striking and left the audience with a much clearer image of the procedure and its benefits than the speaker's own words could possibly have done.

There is one "downside" to incorporating such complex video into a Power Point program – the size of the file needed to handle it. For the above presentation, the speaker had to dump quite a bit of material from other files to create space for the video.

The benefit, however, was the clarity created by these sharply contrasting images. It worked because the images were simple: one person seated at an empty table and speaking a few sentences. There were no distracting images of the therapist or other persons — no busy backgrounds or irrelevant sounds.

Such simplicity should mark all visual images seen in presentation programs. Black and white line drawings on a plain background are easy for the viewer to see and understand and provide the narrow focus needed for learning. Images should be large enough that everyone in the room can see their detail and know what they are looking at. Like a good map, slide images have high contrast, and clear labels and are big enough to read without a magnifying glass.

Keeping the image simple also applies to the slide backgrounds and font selection. There are many beautiful and graphically striking backgrounds available. Choose one that will help your students' eyes focus on the slide's substantive content, not the pretty background. The font, like the drawings or pictures, should be large enough for all to see and read at a glance — not like this one! Lucida, Bookman, Times New Roman, Franklin Gothic, and even Comic fit the bill quite nicely, especially if used in bold.

Simplicity of format also applies to audio features available in the software. Although there are plenty of fun sounds available to add flair to transitions, the best advice is not to use any of them. The sounds do not clarify or emphasize content. They serve no pedagogical function and constitute a distraction. Some students even report getting annoyed by the repeated "bells and whistles." Annoyance deters learning. Only use sound for imported video clips, not just to "decorate" the basic informational slides.

Some well-crafted slides may be available as supplements for textbooks. Feel free to use them if permitted under the book's copyright and if they meet the standards of clarity and simplicity as outlined here.

Preparation Rule #3: Keep the Room Well Lit

Prior to lecturing with presentation slides, try showing them in the room in which you will speak. Experiment with different light switches to determine the combination that will allow greatest visibility of the on-screen images without plunging the students into darkness.

Think about it. For learning to happen, students must be engaged in the process. At the very least, this means that they must be awake! More than that, they must be drawn into a sense of dialogue with the instructor. Therefore, the instructor must be visible, the students must be able to take notes, and both need to see and respond to feedback from the other. So the room in which we learn must be relatively well lit. The use of presentation slides that are more visible in low lighting does not change that fundamental standard. Trying to teach in a completely darkened room with the only light coming from the screen virtually insures that learning will not happen!

The best arrangement, then, is to dim the bank of lights immediately in front of the screen and leave all other room lights on as normal. If the slides are only part of your lecture, return all lights to full brightness immediately after the slide presentation is completed. Do not continue to stand and speak in a dimly lit area. This brings us to presenting the finished product.

While Presenting

Presentation Rule #1: Synchronize Visual Images With the Spoken Word

Presentation technology allows several options relating to the pace at which the slides and their component parts are revealed. Overall, the slide show can be manually advanced or can operate on a timed advance. In addition, each slide can be fully or gradually revealed. To be most useful to your students, the best combination of options is the use of manual advance and gradual reveal.

Manual advance allows you to stand anywhere in the room (with a remote mouse) and reveal the slide only when you are actually talking about the specific point it states or clarifies. Doing so means that your students will receive a coordinated message, making learning more likely. Additionally, manual advance allows you to spend as much or as little time on a single slide as circumstances dictate, pausing for questions or to add detail should students appear confused.

That same reasoning applies to gradually revealing the content of a single slide. Students will dutifully write whatever appears on the screen; so only show the specific point you want to address. A single slide may, for instance, list the five symptoms of Attention Deficit Disorder, but you plan to explain each in some detail. If you show all five symptoms at once, the students will be so busy writing down #2-5 that they will not even hear your explanation of #1. That "attention deficit" can be remedied by revealing just one symptom, explaining it, then revealing the next, etc.

Presentation Rule #2: Use Optional Features as Needed

Synchronizing your spoken words with the visual images is easily achievable by using optional features built into the software. By selecting options, you can highlight certain points, clarify references, and temporarily blank the screen while you speak.

Options can be accessed several different ways. The fastest may be to click on the pale arrow that will automatically appear in the bottom left hand corner of each slide. Doing so takes you to imbedded pointers, highlighting options and avenues for moving through the program in different directions. Just click on the arrow or pencil and then move it by dragging the mouse as you draw the students' attention to a particular part of a diagram or an especially important point. Similar emphasis can be accomplished by using the highlighter or underlining options.

Another option that is very valuable but rarely used is the blank screen. If your progress through the program needs to be interrupted, make the screen blank rather than leaving the preceding slide in view. Again — remember the students — they will pay attention to what is on the screen, not to you. So, get rid of that image by hitting "w" or "b" on your keyboard to switch temporarily to an all-white or all-black screen. Hit the button again when you are ready to return to the show.

Presentation Rule #3: Speak to the Students, Not the Screen

This is an important one! The most common mistake is the instructor speaking while looking at the screen instead of at the students. It is naturally tempting to turn back to look at what is on the screen — after all, it is huge, it is bright, it is interesting. However, you put the words and images up there. You know what it says. You do not need to look at it as you speak.

Of course, you will want to take a quick glance to make sure that the correct image is appearing. Sometimes, one can inadvertently tap the mouse a little too much and cause the program to skip ahead. A quick peek at the monitor or the screen should suffice to provide that assurance. Turning your back on the students to read from the screen, on the other hand, is disastrous for two reasons.

Reading from the screen causes students to wonder why we are not familiar enough with the material to talk about it without using the screen images as cue card. If they have that suspicion, then we have damaged the vital teacher immediacy referenced earlier.

Turning your back to read from the screen has the additional disadvantage of cutting off eye contact with the students. Anytime that happens in a classroom, there are negative results: a diminishing of student attention, an increase in student misbehavior, and a reduced sense of trust between students and instructor.

Occasionally, instructors turn their backs on the students, not to read from the screen, but to point at something on it. Big mistake! As you walk in front of the projected image, it is now projected on you. So, trying to point at something with your hand actually decreases clarity since the image shows up on the creased, three-dimensional surface of your hand, instead of on the smooth screen. Instead, use a pointer. The imbedded pointers work fine as do hand-held laser pointers. Use the pointer only when you need to reference a particular concept or diagrammatic feature; do not let it roam around the screen idly while you speak.

Presentation Rule #4: Be Prepared for "Mechanical Difficulties"

Contrary to what some of us have been told, computers do make mistakes! Now and then, a well-prepared slidewear presentation will not cooperate with the instructor. It may not be accessible from the classroom computer, may have succumbed to a virus, or the hardware may be compromised — any number of things can go wrong. Be prepared! Faculty need to arrive at class early to ensure necessary equipment is working properly, but beware of focusing so much on the technology that you ignore your students. After all, the usual purpose of coming early to class is to create rapport, answer student questions, and the like. If you do encounter problems, the best response is to switch to "back-up" visual aids such as transparencies or handouts. These can be easily prepared at the same time as the creation of the slideware show and should always be kept handy.

Conclusion

Like any new strategies that become available to us as teachers, presentation software is fun to play with. There are so many things it can do, and it will be able to do more with each passing year. We should experiment with it. We should consider that this technology might help to present difficult material in a way that holds student attention and assists meaningful learning. What we should not do is play with it in the classroom. That is, adopt it selectively instead of using fancy slide shows just because we can.

Once you have made the decision to learn how and where the presentation software could assist your class, pledge to use it correctly. Create slides that are clear, nondistracting, and purposeful. Use them with sensitivity to the reality of student attention. Finally, be prepared to fine-tune your use of this new tool, not just play with it!

References and Recommended Readings

Brooks, S., & Bylo, B. (2004) *Using PowerPoint.* Retrieved July 1, 2005, from http://www.internet4classrooms.com

Chickering, A.W., & Ehrman, S.C. (1996). Implementing the seven principles: Technology as lever. *American Association for Higher Education/Teaching and Learning with Technology Group.* Retrieved June 1, 2005, from http://www.tltgroup.org/programs/seven.html

Daniel, D.B. (2005). How to ruin a perfectly good lecture: Presentation software as a teaching tool. In B. Perlman, L.I. McCann, & W. Buskist (Eds.), *Voices of Experience: Memorable talks from the National Institute on the Teaching of Psychology* (pp. 119-130). Washington, DC: Association for Psychological Science.

Mayer, R.E. (2001). *Multimedia learning.* New York: Cambridge University Press.

Mester, C.S., & Tauber, R.T. (2004). Acting lessons for teachers:Using performance skills in the classroom. In B. Perlman, L.I. McCann, & S.H. McFadden (Eds.), *Lessons learned: Practical advice for the teaching of psychology* (Vol. 2, pp.157-164). Washington, DC: Association for Psychological Science.

Microsoft PowerPoint for Windows Support Home Page (August, 12, 2007). Retrieved August 12, 2007, from http://www.microsoft.com/MSPowerPointSupport

Stevenson, A.E. (1955, October). My faith in democratic capitalism, *Fortune,* 126-127, 156, 160, 162, 167-168.

Tufte, E. (2003, November 9). Power corrupts, PowerPoint corrupts absolutely. *Wired, 118.* Retrieved from http://www. wired.com/wired/archive/11.09/ppt2.html

Zhu, E., & Kaplan, M. (2001) Technology for teaching. In W. J. McKeachie (Ed.), *McKeachie's teaching tips: Strategies, research and theory for college and university teachers.* (pp. 204-224). Boston: Houghton-Mifflin.

Asking Questions: Promoting Student-Faculty Interchange in the Classroom

JUDITH E. LARKIN
HARVEY A. PINES
Canisius College

REMEMBER HOW, AS A student listening to a lecture, your attention drifted between the words of the professor and sundry personal thoughts? A particular class might have been uneventful had not the speaker suddenly changed pace and begun directing questions at the class. If silence prevailed, the teacher, intent on gaining a response, often resorted to a favorite weapon for class participation: "calling on" students.

How Students Feel About Being Called On

We can remember feelings of dread while waiting and hoping that we would not be the one singled out when teachers initiated direct questioning. To find out whether students today feel the way we once did, we surveyed our introductory psychology students about their reactions to a number of common teacher behaviors. What we learned was that more than half of the nearly 200 students either disliked or strongly disliked being called upon, and only 12 percent liked it. We also found negative responses for other teacher practices such as returning exams in order of highest to lowest grade (84 percent negative), not returning exams face down (66 percent negative), and posting name and grade (65 percent negative). Each of these behaviors directs attention to a particular student and publicly reveals the person's level of performance, but the one with the greatest potential for embarrassment is calling upon students when their hand is not raised.

Why Do Teachers Call On Students?

There are undoubtedly dozens of reasons teachers call upon students, but the most obvious ones are to get their attention and to elicit participation. Still, we should distinguish between reasons for asking questions in general and reasons for asking questions of particular students. Some questions are motivated by teachers' concerns that they are (or are not) getting the material across and their need for feedback. Teachers may also seek to facilitate learning by getting students to think at a deeper level about the topic (e.g., explain or apply a concept) or to seek diverse perspectives on an issue.

Sometimes, however, we pointedly focus on particular students. For example, we may call upon quiet students in hopes of gaining participation from someone other than the usual "talkers." We may also try to encourage a student to speak whom we think might know the answer. Less lofty reasons, of course, are to confront (and possibly embarrass) those who are talking to others and not paying attention to us, or those who have not read the material or done the homework or who have annoyed us in some other way. Alternatively, we may be just plain bored with the class (it happens) and decide to adopt a change of pace to get everyone including ourselves interested again.

Is Being Called On Really Aversive?

Regardless of our motivation, if students perceive being called on as punitive, they may engage in actions to prevent us from being successful. With the help of several student "experts" who had previously told us about their reluctance to speak in class, we developed a behavior checklist to find out what students do to avoid being called on in class.

The "top five" behaviors that 125 introductory psychology students said they use to avoid being called on (each endorsed by over 50 percent of the sample) included:

- ◆ Avoid eye contact.
- ◆ Look like you are thinking of the answer (but have not come up with it yet).
- ◆ Act like you are looking for the answer in your notes.
- ◆ Act like you are writing in your notes.
- ◆ Pretend to be reading something course-related.

Other responses included dropping a pen or notebook to look busy, hiding behind the person in front of you, and even a write-in response: pretend to be asleep. Constructive, preemptive participatory behaviors — such as raising one's hand to say something related to the topic or to ask a question about the topic — were endorsed by less than 20 percent of students.

That active participation promotes learning is a fundamental belief among educators, and one can hardly fault teachers for seeking ways to encourage interchange with students in class. However, the attention and energy students direct towards avoiding being called on suggests that this teacher behavior may not be the best way to engage them. At the very least, it is counterproductive when the students we want to reach instead become defensively motivated to direct their energy and mental activities into avoidance behavior. At worst, feelings of shame and embarrassment drain cognitive resources that students might otherwise direct towards learning. To avert these negative consequences, we offer a sample of alternative teacher behaviors that may increase student participation and decrease their avoidance behavior.

Setting the Stage for Voluntary Participation

Create an Environment Conducive to Participation

To achieve student participation without calling upon them, the teacher needs to create an environment where students feel psychologically safe in taking the risk of asking a question that may make them look ignorant or volunteering an answer that may turn out to be wrong. Class size is not the essential factor in creating an environment supportive of participation. We can all think of small classes we have attended (or taught) where teachers had difficulty getting student participation. And even in a large class, the instructor who is motivated to do so can produce active interchange with students. More important than class size, teachers' desire for interaction with students, the nature of the questions teachers ask, and the way they respond to students' questions and answers play a critical role in determining whether communication in the classroom blossoms or dies on the vine. The suggestions we offer below can be adapted for either large or small classes.

Establish a Norm of Participation

♦ Have students interact during the very first class. A two-minute ice breaker (e.g., "Get to know the persons around you") changes the whole atmosphere in the classroom from passive to active.

♦ Let students know, through your words and actions, that you expect to hear from everyone at least once within the first three weeks of class.

♦ Learn students' names and use them when responding to reinforce participation. To help you learn their names quickly, bring a digital camera to class and photograph students in small groups.

♦ Consider asking students to keep a record of their contributions — what questions they answered or asked — and collect the logs periodically. One student we know created a daily participation chart for all of her classes. The act of record keeping sensitizes students to their participatory behavior.

Safe Questions Break the Ice

A simple way to get some sign of life is to ask students for a non-verbal response:

♦ "Let's have a show of hands ... how many of you think that . . . ?" You can then follow up with, "Okay, let's hear some reasons people think that ..." Other safe questions and processes include:

♦ A planned pairing of a closed ended question requiring a single fixed answer (e.g., "Have you ever observed ... ?"), followed by an open-ended question ("Why do you think that happens?") starts an interchange.

♦ Questions that ask for factual answers, or for answers called out in unison, signal to students that you want their involvement. This level of question serves as an attention-getting precursor to questions requiring a higher level of mental processing.

♦ Rapid brainstorming (without commenting) can generate numerous ideas with minimal personal threat to the contributors. Jotting them on the board gives students time to think. Keep saying, "Okay, what else?" to keep things going.

♦ Nonthreatening questions help get participation started. A good example is "How do you feel about ...?" To encourage a wide range of responses, set the stage by stating that you expect to hear some opposing or "far out" views.

Increasing Student-Faculty Interchange

Monitor Your PPQ Ratio

How much participation per question (PPQ) do you get in class? When many students offer answers to a question, the ratio is high. A consistent pattern of stony silence lowers the PPQ ratio but, more importantly, leaves teachers feeling frustrated at the very least and possibly vindictive at worst. The absence of student response may well be the most common stimulus for initiating "calling on" behavior. Adopting the do's and don'ts below will increase the participation quotient and stimulate student-faculty interchange.

When Nobody Volunteers an Answer

What is your most effective weapon when students do not volunteer an answer to your question? Silence. Meet their silence with your silence. Wait . . . A common teacher communication failure is not to wait long enough for students to respond. Good (and bad) questions often require a few moments of reflection for students to make connections or retrieve prior learning. Count to yourself (one thousand one, one thousand two...) for five seconds until students fill the gap. It may seem like forever but be assured that if you are feeling pressure, your students are feeling it even more. Someone will eventually break the silence, and after one person speaks, another usually quickly follows.

Instructors who do not wait long enough for a response may compound the problem in several nonfacilitating ways (Napell, 1976). One self-defeating teacher reaction is to answer the question they just asked. Besides being personally unsatisfying, answering your own question sends a message to students that they do not have to respond. The tactic may also reinforce teacher misgivings about student motivation and ability. Better to wait for a hand to go up.

Another ineffective tactic is to immediately ask another question, or restate the first one, in rapid succession. Rather than facilitating thinking, however, asking multiple questions is more likely to confuse students who may still be thinking about the original question.

Get Maximum Mileage Per Question

To increase your PPQ, experiment with the student activities below:

- Turn to the person next to you. If you call on one student, only that student is involved, not the rest of the class. Many others will undoubtedly choose to engage in one or more of the avoidance behaviors described above. Instead, have students turn to the person next to them to answer the question. In less than two minutes, you will have engaged the full class and can elicit varied responses from students throughout the room.
- Jot down your answers. Before beginning a discussion, ask students to jot down their answers to one or two questions. Writing primes the pump and may produce a greater variety of answers. More students will volunteer answers when they have something written in front of them.
- Summarize key points. Near the end of class or the end of a topic or discussion, ask students to write down the key points they would tell others if they had to teach the material to them. Going rapidly around the room afterward with students stating what they think was important provides a quick review of the material covered and, in addition, gives you the opportunity to fill in any serious gaps.

Other teacher activities that will increase PPQ are to:
- *Hand out questions in advance.* Or tell students ahead of time what you are going to ask. Especially for shy students, having the opportunity to prepare their response makes them feel more comfortable about volunteering an answer. Another beneficial effect is that more students will have done the reading before coming to class. The quality of the questions you ask may also benefit from the forethought.
- *Forecast questions before playing a video.* Write discussion questions on the board before showing a video. The questions focus students' attention as they watch and will produce more active mental processing of the information and a greater readiness to respond afterwards.
- *Design small group activity.* Even a large lecture class can benefit from the change of pace that occasional small group interaction provides. Although group activity can be time consuming, a teacher who carefully structures a task for students sitting near each other to

work on creates a high degree of engagement. Enhance student-to-student interchange by asking groups to report out and to respond directly to each other. Kramer and Korn (1999) offer useful suggestions on how to form groups and implement the fish-bowl technique in large classes.

Responding to Students' Answers in Ways That Promote Interchange

Traditional teacher questioning follows a repeated IRE pattern: teacher Initiates with a question, student Responds, and teacher Evaluates (Van Zee & Minstrell, 1997). No instructor who assigns grades to students would argue that evaluation is not a significant part of the teacher's role. Yet evaluation, as Carl Rogers once said, is the single greatest obstacle to interpersonal communication, and so it is in the classroom. Students' fears of negative evaluation and thoughts about potential negative social consequences drive their defensive behavior and underlie their avoidance of risking participation.

To their credit, most instructors are sensitive to student vulnerability and tactfully correct a wrong answer. Still, if one thinks in terms of learning principles, the teacher's implied or actual criticism functions like punishment, decreasing students' subsequent question-answering behavior. Some techniques, however, encourage continued participation and avoid the negative consequences of evaluation:

- *Acknowledge without evaluation.* If you ask an open-ended question that has no single predetermined "right" answer, you can accept each contribution neutrally and quickly move on to the next one. Nod your head and say, for example, "Okay," "Thank you for that contribution," "I see," "That's an idea," etc. Deliver praise for the act of contributing, not for the correctness of the answer. You can always discuss "incorrect" answers later, independent of the persons who suggested them.

- *Do not reinforce the first "right" answer* (even if it is a good one). Continue eliciting and acknowledging contributions. It is easy to become excited when the first student's response is the one you were hoping for, but reinforcing that first response may actually serve as a participation-stopper. As Napell explained, other students turn off their interest ("Why bother?") when they believe teachers have already received the answer they were seeking.

- *Apply active listening techniques.* Nothing is quite as reinforcing as when the teacher paraphrases and accurately reflects back what a student said. Similarly, teachers validate a student when they refer to an earlier remark a student made and credit the person by name.

- *Deal with "the talkers."* They are the students who raise their hand too often to answer questions and make it easy for the rest of the class to sit back and passively observe. This is one time when it is good to avoid eye contact! Look out towards others in the room and say, "Let's hear from people who haven't spoken yet," or "We haven't heard from people in the back of the room." Move around the room so that more students than just front row dwellers will experience the physical proximity to you that makes it easier to ask and answer questions.

- *Practice the "Reflective Toss."* The reflective toss is a metaphor for the discussion process in which the teacher "catches the meaning" of a student's statement and "tosses" responsibility back to the student and to the whole class (Van Zee & Minstrell, 1997). Unlike the IRE (teacher-student-teacher) sequence, the reflective toss shifts the focus one turn, to sequences of student-teacher-student interactions and promotes open discussion in the process.

At its simplest level, an instructor uses the reflective toss by responding, "What do you (or the class) think?" in response to a student question. By encouraging students to respond to each other, and to elaborate on their own and each other's thinking, teachers maintain the interchange by keeping the ball in the students' court. Providing training in discussion skills, as Kramer and Korn (1999) suggest, can improve the quality of the discussion.

Helping Students Ask Questions

To become active participants in their learning, students must ask as well as answer questions. Yet, the act of asking a question also entails risk. Some ways instructors may facilitate the process:

- *"Any questions?"* Asking for questions this way may

not be the best way to signal interest in hearing from students. However, a simple change in wording invites students to respond. "What questions do you have?" or "Okay, let's hear some questions" conveys your expectation that students do have questions and your desire to hear them. Nothing is quite so disheartening, however, as when after explaining (brilliantly) a difficult concept, a student asks, "Will that be on the test?" To lessen the frequency of the nonsequitur question, ask for procedural questions at the beginning of class (West & Pearson, 1994). Answering questions on students' minds about assignments, due dates, etc., will free up their cognitive resources for better use during class.

♦ *"No dumb questions."* No matter how many times students have heard "there are no dumb questions," many continue to withhold questions. To make it easier for them to ask, a teacher might say, "Lots of people have questions they think are 'dumb' — let's hear some dumb questions...." We have been surprised at the results when students feel that it really is all right to ask the "dumb" questions on their minds.

Still, many students need "permission" to ask, and need knowledge about different kinds of questions. In a recent convocation address to students, Perlman (2003) urged them to risk questioning and to learn how to phrase questions to produce a positive interchange. He suggests some types of questions below:

♦ *Simple process questions.* Faculty can assist students by encouraging them to ask simple process questions like "Could you please give an example?" or "Could you please go over that again" when something is unclear. We can also illustrate the importance of phrasing by relating the often-told tale about the student who returns to class after an absence and asks, "Did I miss anything important?" — rather than "What did I miss?" In this way, students also develop social skills as part of the student-faculty interchange process.

♦ *Intellectual questions.* It may seem obvious to us, but some students need to be told that we want them to ask questions. Encourage questions about ideas and concepts they find interesting or confusing — or that relate to topics covered in other classes.

- *Personal questions.* Teachers who feel comfortable bringing aspects of their personal life into class may invite student questions about their lives and experiences. This type of interchange develops relationships that produce a sense of community and gives meaningfulness to students' education.

Questions That Develop Cognitive Skills

To improve the quality of participation — and importantly, develop students' cognitive skills — it is worth becoming familiar with the ways that different kinds of questions can elicit different levels of thinking. We recommend entering the phrase "Bloom's taxonomy" in Google to discover a wealth of useful information about model questions and key words to stimulate questions and responses appropriate to students' cognitive level.

The "Bad" Class

Sooner or later we all experience a "bad class." Nothing works; students sit there, responding grudgingly at best. When that happens, the worst thing to do is develop an adversarial relationship with the class. Just as you know that things are not going well, so do the students. It is often wise to acknowledge the reality and take a proactive approach towards change. A good opening is "Let's talk about how the class is going . . . what can I do to make this class a better experience for you?" — followed by your paraphrasing their feedback. Alternatively, some teachers (and students) may prefer anonymous written comments. In either case, an open, flexible, and nondefensive approach to a difficult class is the best way we have found to win students over.

Finally, Still Desperate for a Response ...

One popular statistics teacher we know tackled the problem of nonparticipation through the blatant use of behavior modification techniques. Armed with a bowl of wrapped candies, she tossed one out for each correct answer volunteered. Needless to say, students' rate of response increased dramatically — as did her evaluations!

Your Suggestions

How do you increase participation in class? If you introduce (or adapt) any of these ideas, we would like to learn about your experiences. Please e-mail us, and we will compile and disseminate the results.

References and Recommended Readings

Forsyth, D.R. (2003). *The professor's guide to teaching: Psychological principles and practices.* Washington, DC: American Psychological Association.

Kramer, T.J., & Korn, J.H. (1999). Class discussions: Promoting participation and preventing problems. In B. Perlman, L.I. McCann, & S.H. McFadden (Eds.), *Lessons learned: Practical advice for the teaching of psychology* (pp. 99-104). Washington,DC: Association for Psychological Science.

Napell, S.M. (1976). Six common non-facilitating teacher behaviors. *Contemporary Education, 47,* 79-83.

Perlman, B. (2003, September). *Questions and relationships.* Address given at UW Oshkosh Honors Program Convocation. Available by e-mail from perlman@uwosh.edu

Van Zee, E., & Minstrell, J. (1997). Using questioning to guide student thinking. *Journal of the Learning Sciences, 6,* 227-269.

West, R., & Pearson, J.C. (1994). Antecedent and consequent conditions of student questioning: An analysis of classroom discourse across the university. *Communication Education, 43,* 299-311.

Engaging Students With Humor

TED POWERS
Parkland College

HE WANTED TO BE called Lunch Box instead of his proper name. When I finished writing something on the board, I would usually turn to see him making a comment to a classmate with a devious smile on his face. Lunch Box was enrolled in an intersession class that met five days a week for three hours with a break in the middle. A little over a week into the class I returned to find my markers and eraser missing. I calmly asked the class, "Would anyone happen to know where the markers and eraser are?" At first nobody said a word, but there were a few giggles and some anxious looks. Lunch Box, smiling like the cat that ate the canary, said, "Oh they're still in here. You just need to find them."

So what would you do in this situation? I was frustrated and could easily understand how an instructor could become angry and demand the location of the items immediately. Luckily for me, we had just covered the learning section, and I took this opportunity to do a variation of shaping. I asked the students to say "hot" or "cold" as I moved closer to or away from the items.

Students started to laugh and the tension was broken. Eventually they led me to the items on a shelf underneath the overhead projector. When I picked up the items, the class cheered and applauded. The discussion that followed was fantastic. We talked about how difficult shaping can be. Examples ranged from training animals to treating individuals with disorders.

That evening I received an e-mail from Lunch Box. He apologized for what had "seemed like a fun idea at the moment." He also wrote, "It was cool how you turned the hot-cold thing into a lesson." His level of activity and engagement increased for the rest of the semester, and he performed well on the remaining assignments and exams.

I believe occasional, appropriate use of humor can increase student attention and maintain focus. Along with others (Bobek, 2002; Friedman, Halpern, & Salb, 1999; McLaughlin, 2001), I have found that humor can help create a more open atmosphere and can aid in classroom management. Students report they retain more information from humorous lectures and class discussions (Berk, 2000) and that humor can reduce the anxiety produced by taking a test or quiz (Berk, 2000; McMorris et al, 1997), and it is generally fun for all concerned, including the instructor.

I define humor broadly as an event that elicits laughter. It is not limited to jokes or humorous stories but can include props, puns, short stories, anecdotes, riddles, or cartoons. It can be anything that creates a positive feeling in students and makes them smile and laugh. Humor captures their attention and is memorable.

Guidelines for Teaching With Humor
Humor Should Not Be Hurtful or Offensive

Humor that furthers teaching is "constructive humor" (Tauber & Mester, 1994, p. 64) — humor that is nonhostile and nonderisive of others. When considering the use of humor an instructor needs to consider "1) the subject, 2) the tone, 3) the intent, and 4) the situation, including the teller and the audience" (Nilsen, 1994, p. 930). Humor is something that everyone can laugh at.

The Subject

Common sense and consideration of what your students may have experienced can help you decide what subject matter lends itself to appropriate humor. I have taught students struggling with eating disorders, those who have been stalked, been in abusive relationships, survived rape and incest, been forced to have abortions, been assaulted, had a loved one unexpectedly die, conquered or fallen victim to substance abuse, and one who died. There are subjects that are off-limits for humor.

Tone

Some of you have probably overheard students talking about another instructor saying something like, "S/he think s/he's being funny, but s/he comes off as a jerk." There is no simple recipe for the correct delivery of humor (if there were, there would not be so many horrible stand-up comics). However, teachers need to be conscious of their level of sarcasm as too much sarcasm may turn off students who believe the instructor is being too negative. If they cannot distinguish between sarcasm and seriousness, students may become confused or offended. A simple "and folks, I was being sarcastic," may help create a more positive tone.

Intent

Like most everything else a teacher does, the intent of adding humor is to facilitate learning. An example of what not to do was related by a colleague:

In a night class, a student had fallen asleep. The instructor told the rest of the class to scream loudly at the count of three. The instructor then turned off the lights and counted to three. The sleeping student awoke in a panic and couldn't see a thing. Apparently the instructor and several students got a good laugh out of the situation, but the sleeping student did not attend another class.

Before using humor, it is wise to ask, "Will this use of humor alienate or embarrass any of my students?" If the answer is "yes," try a different strategy to get the point across.

The Situation

Be aware of the dynamics between your personality and your use of humor, and the personalities of your students. A night class can react differently than a mid-day class. Summer and inter-session classes can be quite different from full-semester classes. If an instructor feels uneasy about use of humor, then it is a good idea to find an alternate strategy for presenting that topic (see Sev'er & Ungar, 1997, for discussion on considerations of an audience).

Events outside the classroom also can change use of humor. I had used a story about a plane being hijacked in a telephone-like memory demonstration for years without a problem. After 9-11, I needed a new story. Having said all that...

Don't Be Afraid to Be Funny

When I was learning to teach in graduate school, I was told that effective teachers do not fear making fools of themselves in front of their students, and I believe it. In fact, the professor who taught me this lesson made sure every teaching assistant he had lost all fear of embarrassment. During my time on his staff, I had to play a bit of information in the information-processing model of memory and run around a lecture hall to where sensory, working, and long term memories were located. Another teaching assistant and I had to wear Halloween masks of Beavis and Butthead (from MTV fame) and sit in the back of the class and model inappropriate student behavior. I also beat up a Bobo Doll during the discussion of social learning.

Students often resist asking questions because they fear embarrassment. If the instructor shows no fear of embarrassment and models that learning the information is paramount, he or she will create an atmosphere where students will take a chance and get involved. The suggestions in the "Act It Out" and "Use Yourself as an Example" sections that follow directly relate to this topic.

Make Humor Relevant

Humor in the classroom is most effective when linked to concepts being studied. Humor for the sake of humor might make you a "cooler" teacher in the eyes of some students, but humor that educates will help you become a more effective instructor for all students.

If a class is inattentive and an instructor tells a joke like, "Did you hear about the termite who walked into the saloon? The first thing he asked was, 'Where's the bar tender?'" that instructor may have regained the attention of the students, but no learning occurred. On the other hand, if an instructor tells that joke and follows it with a discussion of the role of top-down processing and context in communication (bar tender and bartender sound alike – how do we know when it is two words and when it is one?), then the humor facilitates learning.

A three-step method exists for delivering content-relevant humor (Pollio, 2002; Ziv, 1988). The instructor first explains the content information without humor. The humorous example, demonstration or activity then follows the explanation. Finally, the instructor summarizes the information and how it relates to the humorous event. Ziv (1988) found his method resulted in a measurable increase in the final exam scores of his students.

Act It Out

Good teachers all face the problem of important course content for which no good visual (film, video, DVD) or audio examples exist. Often they stand in front of the class and explain the research, concept, or disorder. Another strategy is to engage your students by "acting it out." When I teach abnormal psychology, I sometimes demonstrate different therapy techniques for the class by portraying both therapist and client. The content of the demonstration will not be particularly funny, but seeing the instructor flip-flop between chairs and roles often makes students smile or laugh.

A benefit of acting out a concept, disorder, or piece of research is the ability to stop at any moment and ask questions like: "What do you think will happen next?", "How do you think this person will respond?", or "What would you be thinking if you were this person?" My experience is that students are more willing to take a chance and respond, as I have risked embarrassment by acting something out, not merely talking about it.

Use Clips From Movies or Television Shows

You can facilitate learning by using funny movie or television clips to bring to life course concepts or by asking students if the example was accurate or not and in what ways. Students often enroll in psychology courses expecting to see clips from *A Beautiful Mind*, *Silence of the Lambs*, *One Flew Over the Cuckoo's Nest*, and *Rainman*. Why not show them clips from *Me, Myself, & Irene* (Dissociative Identity Disorder), *Monk* (Obsessive-Compulsive Disorder), and *Deuce Bigalo: Male Gigolo* (Narcolepsy)? Sometimes merely referring to a funny show can recapture students' attention. For example, during a discussion of brain structures you could note that anyone who has seen *The Waterboy* (a slapstick comedy about a simpleton who works for a college football coach as his waterboy and is found to be an excellent defensive player; he is then added to the team and must attend class) should be familiar with the medulla oblongata. If you could say it like Adam Sandler, the film's star, you may have students laughing out loud.

By linking course information to popular, fun shows, you show students that course concepts exist in the world in which they live. When watching these shows at some later time, the students may be reminded of the course information and have better retention. You can also ask your students to bring examples of the concepts you are discussing in class that they have found in their favorite shows and movies.

Try Music

Many classrooms today are equipped with computers for multimedia presentations allowing instructors to introduce topics with music as well as movie clips. Choose something unexpected or funny from time to time. Most instructors' favorite songs are ones with which students are unfamiliar. Here is a list of songs you may not have heard, but might want to use after you hear them: "Uncorrected Personality Traits" by Robyn Hitchcock, "Institutionalized" by Suicidal Tendencies, "Paranoid" by Black Sabbath, "Basket Case" by Green Day, "Entangled" by Genesis, "No Self-Control" by Peter Gabriel, "Your Racist Friend" by They Might Be Giants.

Classroom Management

Most teachers become annoyed when students talk during class or their cell phone rings during a lecture or discussion. I have found using humor can stop the disruptive behavior while maintaining a positive classroom atmosphere. Instead of saying something like, "There is code of conduct for our students and I expect you to follow it," try something like, "Are you going to make me write your name(s) on the board?" After making that statement, I usually pause then say in a very serious voice, "And you know what will happen to you if you get a check by your name."

I have tried something new to combat the ever-growing problem with cell phones. As most cell phones play music instead of ringing, I will stop lecturing and dance until the phone is turned off (it usually happens quickly since I am a horrible dancer and I usually try to disco dance). This behavior may not be appropriate for you, but for me, after one dancing episode, students are quick to admonish each other when a cell phone goes off, "Turn it off quickly or he'll start dancing again!" One instructor I know begs students to let him talk to whoever is calling and actually has done so on several occasions.

Tests and Quizzes

Some teachers find no place for humor in testing because, for example, they believe it may be distracting to students (Renner & Renner, 1999). I am not one of them. I believe a humorous item or two can relax students and help ease test anxiety and improve performance (Berk, 2000; McMorris, Boothroyd, & Pietrangelo, 1997).

Humor in tests also may help a teacher avoid activating disturbing memories in their students. Though many of us would love a test full of real-life examples, sometimes they are inappropriate. For example, imagine you were writing a multiple-choice question about a person who experiences damage to a particular brain structure involving auto accidents, assault and battery, or military service. Of course, each semester we all probably have students who have known someone injured in one of those ways. Instead, have people experiencing brain damage because of severe paper cuts, unnoticed banana peels, or games of Twister gone awry.

When writing humorous exam items, limit the humor to the question itself and not the possible answers. A humorous answer may be appropriate from time to time, but it will change the item difficulty when a multiple-choice option is clearly invalid.

Humor also can be injected into tests without something zany happening in the question. You can use names associated with familiar television shows and movies. But make sure that the item still is meaningful if a student does not make the humorous connection you are striving for. Students especially seem to enjoy seeing the names of characters from shows from their childhood used in adult settings. I received a number of positive comments about this item:

> Bert enjoys drinking alcohol when he watches football. Oscar will inject himself with heroin to escape the garbage heap he believes his life is. Cookie often gets hungry after smoking marijuana. Elmo enjoys the rush and feelings of confidence he gets when he snorts cocaine. Who has the lowest potential risk of becoming physically dependent on his drug?

> a. Bert
> b. Oscar
> c. Cookie
> d. Elmo

Berk (2000) has more ideas on how to construct humorous exam items.

Use Yourself as an Example

If you have a funny story that can help explain a concept, tell it. Students often seem surprised that their instructor was once young. Such self-disclosure helps create an open atmosphere in the class. For example, when trying to explain visual dominance, I tell my students about a prank a friend and I did when we were 16. We would drive along a one-way street in the city with a lane between us. If we came to a red light with a car between us (and no one behind us), we would put our cars into reverse and let them roll backwards. We would then laugh, as the poor driver between us would slam on the brakes. Yes, I discourage my students from doing the prank. I tell them "road rage" was not a term yet when I was starting to drive, although my prank may have encouraged its development. I also encourage them to experience the visual dominance effect by seeing one of the music shows at our planetarium.

Use Stories and Comments From Students

When a student shares a humorous story or comment, ask if you can use it in future semesters. One example I use came as the semester was winding down and I was covering the last major topic area, social psychology. When I was talking about how changing reference groups can change a person's attitudes, a young man raised his hand and offered himself as an example. He had grown up in Chicago and his parents, his friends, and he were all Democrats. When he began college, his roommate was a young Republican. The student started hanging out with his roommate's friends, also Republicans. My student and his Republican friends remained close, and he was currently sharing an apartment with two of them. That year being an election year, he discussed politics with his parents and siblings when he went home for Thanksgiving, and he found himself arguing with them. His father accused the university of warping his mind. The student concluded by smiling and saying, "Now I can go home and tell my dad that it wasn't school that messed me up — it was my friends."

Using student examples can help open up a class early in the semester. If you can share a story or two from past semesters, it sends the message that it is appropriate and desired that students interact and share in class.

Be Yourself

Just as Robin Williams would not be as funny trying to be like Bob Newhart (or vice versa), you need to find an application of humor that fits who you are. To that point, I would be surprised if anyone reading this column thought, "I agree with everything in here and I'm going to try every suggestion!" Chances are, many of you at some point have thought, "No way – that's not for me." Please pick and choose what might seem appropriate for your teaching style.

Conclusion

One of the greatest sins in teaching is to be boring" (Baughman, 1979, p. 28). I agree with Tauber and Mester (1994), who also cite this quote, that teachers need to go beyond just explaining the information to reach their students. Effective use of humor can help teachers engage students and establish rapport with them, maintain their attention, create an open classroom atmosphere, and even ease distress during exams. You can make yourself less a distant teacher and better connect with students and effectively manage a classroom. Hopefully, students will have a more positive opinion of both the class and the content material. Like any teaching technique, humor should be used in moderation. Not every test item needs to be funny, and not every example should make your class laugh. You want to teach well, not do a standup comic routine.

References and Recommended Readings

Baughman, M.D. (1979). Teaching with humor: A performing art. *Contemporary Education, 51,* 26-30.

Berk, R.A. (2000). Does humor in course tests reduce anxiety and improve performance? *College Teaching, 48,* 151-158.

Bobek, B.L. (2002). Teacher resiliency: A key to career longevity. *Clearing House, 75,* 202-205.

Friedman, H.H., Halpern, N., & Salb, D. (1999). Teaching statistics using humorous anecdotes. *Mathematics Teacher, 92,* 305-308.

McLaughlin, K. (2001). The lighter side of learning. *Training, 38,* 48-52.

McMorris, R.F., Boothroyd, R.A., & Pietrangelo, D .J. (1997). Humor in educational testing: A review and discussion. *Applied Measurement in Education, 10,* 269-297.

Nilsen, A.P. (1994). In defense of humor. *College English, 56,* 928-933.

Pollio, H.R. (2002). Humor and college teaching. In S.F. Davis & W. Buskist (Eds.), *The teaching of psychology: Essays in honor of Wilbert J. McKeachie and Charles L. Brewer* (pp. 60-80). Mahwah, NJ: Erlbaum.

Renner, C.H., & Renner, M. J. (1999). How to create a good exam. In B.Perlman, L.I. McCann, & S.H. McFadden (Eds.), *Lessons learned: Practical advice for the teaching of psychology* (pp. 43-47). Washington, DC: Association for Psychological Science.

Sev'er, A., & Ungar, S. (1997). No laughing matter: Boundaries of gender-based humour in the classroom. *Journal of Higher Education, 68*, 87-105.

Tauber, R.T. & Mester, C.S. (1994). *Acting lessons for teachers.* Westport, CT: Praeger.

Ziv, A. (1988). Teaching and learning with humor: Experiment and replication. *Journal of Experimental Education, 57*, 5-15.

Going for the Gold:
Using Sport Psychology to Improve
Teaching and Learning

TAMI EGGLESTON
McKendree College
GABY SMITH
Elon University

WHO CAN RESIST GETTING caught up in the enthusiasm of the Olympics, Super Bowl, or NBA playoffs? If you ask most of your first-year students to describe Michael Jordan, Jeff Gordon, or Serena Williams, they can do so easily. Ask the same students about B.F. Skinner, Elizabeth Loftus, or Harry Harlow, and you will likely get blank stares. Whereas students will stay up well past midnight watching their favorite sports, they often feel less driven to focus on academics. And yet, there is hope; we can apply lessons from sport psychology to increase motivation and excitement in the classroom. Theoretical approaches used in sport psychology are relevant to any area in which performance is crucial. For example, musicians in an orchestra, actors in a production, or students enrolled in a class all experience the same group dynamics and issues as athletes striving for optimal performance.

The motivational techniques advocated by sport psychologists also help to achieve the "seven principles of good practice" developed by Chickering and Gamson (1987) to enhance classroom instruction (e.g., encourage active learning). We have created three categories of techniques — Bronze, Silver, and Gold — that encourage active learning based on concepts and theories adapted from sport psychology. The level of difficulty and risk in applying these active learning strategies in the classroom increases with each category — from bronze to silver to gold — but so do the rewards.

Bronze: Back to Basics

Many of the basic sport psychology findings relating to athlete-coach dyads can easily extend to student-teacher relationships. Whereas the goal of the athlete-coach partnership is to enhance athletic performance, the goal of the student-teacher partnership is to enhance academic performance.

Time Management

A good coach knows when to call time out, when to implement certain plays, and when to take a player who needs a breather out of the game. In other words, good coaches use effective time management and train their players to do the same. Time management skills can also help create an efficient classroom environment. How many of us require too few assignments at the beginning of the semester, place too much weight on big assignments due right before finals, and thereby overstress students? As instructors, we also feel overwhelmed at the end of the semester as we struggle to complete our grading. For most of us, the end of the semester can feel like a frantic overtime with our team behind by a few touchdowns!

To counter this crunch, we encourage students to think about the semester as split into four quarters like a football game, while emphasizing the importance of staying on top of tasks rather than procrastinating. We advise students to prepare well for exams and assignments during the first three quarters, so that by the fourth quarter (i.e., the final exam) they will be ahead of the game. Of course, students have less course-based knowledge in the first quarter, but small assignments (e.g., quizzes, annotated bibliographies, and labs) due at the beginning of the term encourage practice and time on task.

Goal Setting

If you ask any professional football player what his ultimate goal for the season is, he will most likely say, "Go to the Super Bowl!" If you ask him how he is going to accomplish that goal, he will list specific short-term action plans for himself and the team. On the other hand, ask first-year college students about their goals, and you will probably get vague responses (i.e., do well in school, survive the semester, or get involved on campus).

Moreover, few students will have a specific action plan they can use to help them achieve their goals.

Goal setting is a skill used by sport psychologists working with athletes that can also enhance the individual outcomes for students. In fact, sport psychologists emphasize the importance of having both short- and long-term goals (Burton, 1992). Encourage students to set short- and long-term performance goals for each of their courses early in the semester. These goals should be realistic yet challenging and specific yet flexible. Having the whole class brainstorm effective behaviors (e.g., go to class, study in the library at a certain time, get assistance from the learning center if necessary) can be particularly helpful for first-year students. Faculty members can use these principles to identify goals for each course and to design instructional activities supporting each goal. Although we may believe we have clear-cut goals, often we are too busy in our daily teaching to keep sight of our short- and long-term goals. Just as a coach occasionally tells the team to "get back to basics," a professor might evaluate whether assignments meet the goals of the class. In other words, what does it mean for you to go to the World Series or win the Indy 500 in your class? What are your true goals and how are you attempting to reach them?

Team Building/Group Projects

At the beginning of a soccer game, have you ever noticed how the players all storm on to the field together? At the end of a theater production, have you noticed how the performers all hold hands as they receive applause? In the world of performance enhancement, it truly takes a team to be successful. Yet professors often lament that group projects do not work well in the classroom.

Sport psychologists have long identified team building as essential to effective group work; however, student groups may not be prepared to work together as a team. Groups of students do not become teams without dedicating time to "form, storm, norm, and perform" (Tuckman, 1965). In other words, students first must have time to come together as a group and get to know each other. In this forming stage, they need to learn names and get contact information. They also need to brainstorm ("storm") to assign individual roles, such as leader/organizer of the group and record keeper. Although you may want to encourage students to rotate roles, storming is a natural part of group dynamics. The third stage of group formation requires that members "norm," or figure out, how the group will work (e.g., meet outside of class, e-mail, brainstorm first individually). Finally, in the last stage, the team gets down to business and performs.

Building on the guidelines above, we have learned some successful strategies. We have found it best to avoid cliques by assigning friends to separate groups. We provide time for members of each group to get to know one another and to brainstorm on a specific issue. To function effectively as a team, student groups need tasks that can be delegated to members and individual accountability for those tasks. You should provide guidelines on how groups are expected to work together and step in to resolve conflicts as necessary. If using a course management system like Blackboard, establish a group page and group discussion board to enhance communication among members. Something as simple as having groups create their own name or mascot can help student teams function more effectively. Remember it is much more motivating to yell, "Go Cardinals!" than "Go that one guy who sits over there, and that woman with blonde hair and glasses, and the other guy who never shows up!"

Silver: More Advanced Techniques

To achieve even greater levels of motivation and energy in the classroom and to help students perform at their highest levels, consider the following concepts frequently examined in sports and health psychology.

Stress Management

Unfortunately, discussion of stress management is so commonplace it has almost become cliché. Yet, coaches often spend time with their teams talking about ways to cope with the "big game" or a particularly tough opponent. Top athletes plan their performance and develop back-up plans; they understand that there will be obstacles, but they can refocus to perform at their personal best (Orlick, 1986). Many elite athletes will "walk through" or visualize an important game while focusing on breathing techniques to help maintain attention. These techniques ease stress through problem-based (practice and preparation) and emotional (increasing perceived control and relaxation) coping strategies.

On the other hand, students often cannot or do not mentally prepare themselves for the big exam or presentation. Some may simply be unprepared for college-level work or for balancing academic workload with other areas of college life. You can assist students by providing suggestions for studying for exams (practice), criteria for assignments (game plans), and specific course policies (rules of the game). You can help students mentally prepare for the "big game" or "opening night" by letting them know what to expect (how many questions, what question format, what areas to emphasize, etc.). Even at the hardest competitions such as the Olympics, athletes are aware of the judging criteria and possible penalties prior to the beginning of the games.

Intrinsic and Extrinsic Motivation/Rewards

Intrinsic motivation is the drive to perform to satisfy internal needs, whereas extrinsic motivation is the drive to perform for an external reward. Rewards, such as trophies and money, compel extrinsically motivated athletes, but the best athletes tend to be intrinsically motivated; they want to perform well in order to satisfy themselves (Deci, 1975). In the classroom, external rewards such as grades and points earned motivate many students. And certainly, as professors, we revert to grades to encourage attendance, participation, and completion of assignments. How can we create a more intrinsically rewarding environment in our classroom and meet the needs of intrinsically motivated students? An important way to recognize and increase intrinsic motivation is to design assignments that are personally relevant to students. In addition, we can allow choice on assignment topics and make topics applicable to students' lives. For example, we can use portfolio assignments in which students make choices about what is included in the final portfolio project. Most athletes play "for the love of the game," and perhaps it is our job to help students recognize and appreciate the applicability of psychology to real-life issues.

Team Captains

Athletic team captains are experienced, strong players selected by their team or coach to motivate teammates to perform their best. The concept of team captains is akin to peer-mentoring strategies in the classroom. Specifically, students can be "team captains" by taking the lead on organizing groups, projects, or particular aspects of class (e.g., selecting videos). The use of team captains creates a sense of course ownership and reinforces leadership skills. Students are assigned to teams early in the semester and may not change teams (saving time on forming, storming, and norming). We then allow each team to select its captain by a vote, by nomination, or by someone agreeing to take the responsibility. In our experience, we usually have three group projects (e.g., PowerPoint presentation, debate, paper, Blackboard activity) and require a different team captain for each activity so at least three members of the team will have a leadership opportunity. In classes with 25-40 students, breaking the class into teams with six to eight students and one team captain is optimal. In larger classes, faculty could create co-captains in teams of 10-12 students. We have rewarded team captains with a few bonus points for the best team project in recognition of their extra effort and outstanding coaching ability.

Going for the Gold: Challenging and Risky Maneuvers

There are two types of athletes. Some play it smart and keep it simple. These athletes do not take unnecessary risks and, as a result, are well-rounded. Elite athletes (e.g., Danica Patrick, Lance Armstrong, and Brett Favre), on the other hand, do take risks. These athletes push themselves hard and really go for it! At some point, we each have to ask ourselves: "Do I want to be a safe and well-rounded teacher, or do I want to take risks and go for the gold?"

Psych Your Class Up — Motivation

Part of the reason people love athletics so much is because of the excitement inherent in sports events. Where does this excitement come from? Does it come from the cheerleaders or the competition? Or does the enthusiasm of athletes feed our own excitement? Coaches actively work to psych up their players using motivational techniques. Do we, as instructors, start our classes with the same sense of energy or motivation? If you want to increase enthusiasm and motivation to learn in your course, do not start your class with the predictable and mundane (e.g., "Today we are going to cover the four parts of your brain, any questions from the reading? Anyone? Anyone?").

Who wants to start every game sitting on the bench? An easy, though risky, way to increase motivation is to let students take the lead at the beginning of class. For example, have students begin with a short group activity like listing all of the things that they already know about the topic. Music can also motivate students; simply begin class with a song related to the topic at hand (e.g., "Don't Worry Be Happy" prior to discussing depression, or "I'm Too Sexy for My Shirt" prior to discussing attraction). We have found that using icebreaker activities starts class on the right foot; students become active participants, not benchwarmers.

Team Competitions

We have found that team-based, rather than individual student, presentations enhance the quality of work by allowing students to combine their strengths, be more creative, and reduce performance anxiety. Although we believe that within groups cooperation should be the rule, sport psychologists suggest that competition is not always a bad thing. In fact, competition across groups can enhance motivation and performance. The key to maintaining balance between cooperation and competition is to make competition fun and worth relatively small rewards (e.g., candy, pencils, or a few bonus points). We have used small competitions for group assignments such as presentations, final papers, and community-service projects. When students know there is a small competition between groups, their projects are better.

In our experience, students' natural competitive tendencies kick in, and they want their group to perform better than other teams. For example, we often only award the maximum points (e.g., 20/20) to the winning team. Even if the other groups score within several points of the winners, they will have competed for the title of "best team."

Team Exams

During a typical exam day, students walk in as if they are on a death march, and look at you like you are a monster. During the exam, they roll their eyes and close them tightly in concentration; when they put the exam on your desk, some tell you to be gentle or kind. How can we use principles of sports psychology to enhance exam motivation and performance? One suggestion is to have students work in teams to complete an exam or part of an exam. We have created exams that include individual and team sections. Both kinds of sections allow for assessment of knowledge and comprehension, as well as application of knowledge to original examples. Using team exams encourages students to prepare for the exam together; plus, during the exam itself, students actively evaluate and debate how to best complete the team section. After turning in the team section (usually a case study, applied question, ethical dilemma, research analysis, etc.), students are pumped and ready to work on their individual exam (the more typical multiple-choice, short-answer, matching, essay). For practical and motivational reasons, it works best to have a limited amount of time (e.g., 20 minutes) for the team exam and then to follow this component with the individual exam.

The Reward

Our classes are more dynamic and active, and have a more enthusiastic atmosphere because we use concepts of sport psychology in our teaching. Of course, clichés like "nothing ventured, nothing gained," "no pain, no gain," and "just do it!" all come to mind when considering these techniques, but they can be true. We believe that taking risks in order to teach psychology more effectively is well worth the benefit — let's all go for the gold!

References and Recommended Readings

Burton, D. (1992). The Jekyll/Hyde nature of goals: Reconceptualizing goal setting in sport. In T.S. Horn (Ed.), *Advances in sport psychology* (pp. 267-297). Champaign, IL: Human Kinetics.

Chickering, A. W., & Gamson, Z.F. (1987). Seven principles of good practice in undergraduate education. *AAHE Bulletin, 39*, 3-7.

Deci, E.L. (1975). *Intrinsic motivation.* New York: Plenum.

Orlick, T. (1986). *Psyching for sport: Mental training for athletes.* Champaign, IL: Human Kinetics.

Tuckman, B.W. (1965). Development sequence in small groups. *Psychological Bulletin, 63*, 384-399.

Part II

Enhancing Student Learning, Performance, and Participation

Teaching Students to Work Well in Groups

KRISTA D. FORREST
University of Nebraska at Kearney
EMILY E. BALCETIS
Ohio University

Tips for Creating Effective Groups

Reduce Social Loafing

Creating effective groups is a process. Social loafing and more specifically the "free rider effect" (Kerr, 1983) occur when some group members do less than their share of the work but earn the same rewards as more conscientious individuals. Social loafing can be minimized with careful preparation of group assignments and group members.

Members Do Real Work Together

Real work is more than sharing information. All members must be responsible for working together to create observable outcomes (Johnson & Johnson, 1997). Specifically, "real work" is not dividing a complex task among group members but instead involves each member contributing to each part of the project.

Problem:

Real work in groups rarely happens spontaneously. Rather, one student conducts the literature review, another collects data, and a third enters and analyzes data, etc. Those students consistently responsible for a certain type of task across several projects may never learn the intricacies of all aspects of a research project, making them "specialists" unable to complete an entire project individually.

Solution 1: Educate Students About Normative Group Development

Before assigning projects or members to groups, teach students what to expect during each stage of group development. We describe the forming, storming, norming, performing, and adjourning stages (Tuckman, 1965) and explain that when groups first form, members experience some uncertainty associated with working with new members or a new task. We advise students to expect to spend considerable time addressing procedural issues such as who is responsible for what task or how it should be completed. We also warn students that these discussions often contribute to conflict (storming) when groups can have difficulty integrating members' ideas into a cohesive approach. Once group members combine their individual suggestions into a group plan or approach, they enter the norming stage. These group strategies and techniques lead to the performing stage where the product is presented to the teacher, class, a conference or as a publication.

Solution 2: Prepare Students for Probable Conflicts

Students report the most stress and confusion in the storming stage, especially in long-term groups, because students believe any disagreement indicates future, sustained conflict. We educate students about intragroup conflict to help them differentiate between controversy (beneficial conflict) and conflict of interest (negative conflict). Controversy occurs when members have differing ideas for approaching or solving the problem. It is related to creativity in problem solving and is often a characteristic of effective groups (Johnson & Johnson, 1997). Conflicts of interest, however, can be detrimental. Instead of disagreeing about ideas, members have incompatible goals. Effective groups resolve rather than avoid conflicts of interests. Knowing conflict is normative is usually enough to encourage students to deal with conflicts on their own.

If intragroup conflict still impedes group productivity, there are several things teachers can do. You can monitor the group process. If this is an in-class group activity such as Think, Pair, and Share (Barkley, Cross, & Major, 2005), walk around, listen to group interactions, and comment when students seem off-task or confused. When students see us focused on group process, they conclude it is important. For long-term group projects, meet with students at key decision points such as the choice of topic, method, or data coding scheme. The more interested professors are in the group's process, the more likely students will express their concerns. If conflicts continue some teachers allow groups to "divorce," forming two groups or with single members joining other groups or working alone.

Solution 3: Require Cross-Training

In industry, cross-training requires everyone to be familiar with all aspects of the task, ensuring that group members do real work together. Consider the traditional research project: The individual responsible for the introduction completes the literature review and educates other members on how and why certain articles were chosen. The member responsible for statistics does the same. Other group members can offer ideas on how to improve each part of the project. This involvement is not the same as having all members equally involved in all aspects of the project, but it is more consistent with "real world" group work. In order to encourage cross-training for long-term projects, professors can usually determine who is responsible for what task and generate questions targeted to all areas of the project. In those projects requiring just one class period, we use post-test questionnaires (all students individually answer questions about the main idea, procedure, etc.) to evaluate group members' familiarity with the entire product. A third strategy involves requiring one member, chosen at random, to present the project in class. This process is especially effective for group tasks completed in large lecture classes as long as all members know that they could be the one presenting their group's findings.

Solution 4: Consider Task Type

Many assigned projects are not designed for groups, so task type is important. To encourage group interaction, consider the type of task you are assigning and whether it is complex enough and structured enough for an interactive group outcome. Build assignments so members communicate their findings and complete a collaborative product. Examples of inappropriate tasks include activities that are easier to complete alone than with others (e.g., worksheets) or are too vague for students to follow. Appropriate tasks include well-structured complex activities where members can contribute equally and labor can be divided fairly (Barkley et al., 2005).

Some of the most productive group projects occur within a single class period. Large lecture halls can become group work havens when we stop talking and have students collaboratively complete a task related to the points we have just made. Make the task detailed and relevant to class content to encourage interdependent work.

Social Skills

Teachers assigning group projects often assume the students have worked in groups that have prepared them for their current assignments and have communication skills appropriate for group interactions.

Problem:

There is no guarantee that students' previous group interactions were successful or enjoyable. This becomes particularly important in light of findings suggesting previous group work experiences are predictive of subsequent group satisfaction (Forrest & Miller, 2003). As a result they are often uncomfortable discussing issues and could benefit from more practice in listening, presenting ideas, and learning to accept and give constructive criticism.

Solution: Have Students Practice Communication

Give students an opportunity to talk about past group experiences and current expectations within their groups, ideally after you describe the stages of group development. Social loafing is an excellent place to start. Group members reminded by their peers about the possibility of social loafing are more likely to report the behavior. Reminders from an authority figure, similar to an instructor, did not increase such reporting (Balcetis, Forrest, Preuss, & Benz, 2007).

Emphasize the importance of students' listening to each other in each stage of the group process by operationally defining listening (e.g., paraphrasing or restating comments by others and asking questions to clarify what has been said). Students also should have opportunities to practice expressing feelings and opinions while at the same time recognizing that these do not represent facts. Teaching students rules of good communication such as using personal "I" statements assists them in establishing voice. When each group member's contribution or voice is recognized, rapport and cohesiveness develop.

Members also must be willing to give information and express opinions about how the purpose of the group might best be fulfilled. When students fail to use encouraging words or communicate in ways that may be harmful, instructors can address the problem directly. Teachers can assist by monitoring group interaction, personally or through course management programs such as Blackboard. During the storming or conflict stage, group members must clearly and unemotionally express their opinions and reasons for disagreeing. Because the extensive practice of a newly learned skill is vital to mastery, having groups meet early and often facilitates these cooperative communication skills. By having groups complete several kinds of or increasingly more complex tasks, students gain opportunities to implement these skills.

The Shy or Withdrawn Student

Although shy students appear unwilling to participate in group discussion, in fact they may feel inhibited from doing so (Crozier, 2004). Sharing information about normative group development and providing opportunities to practice social skills reduces such inhibitions. Require each person to speak at least once. Online discussions are easily monitored by instructors and can foster contributions from shy and anxious students. This forum encourages continued debate among peers, develops writing and critical thinking skills, and often allows for decreased feelings of anxiety.

Members Hold Themselves and Others Accountable

Being accountable means students understand their responsibilities toward the group's project (process and performance) as well as their timelines for completing it.

Problem:

Students are not always successful in holding themselves and others accountable.

Solution 1: Evaluate and Grade Both Individual and Group Contributions

Individuals who believe their efforts cannot be evaluated once their work is combined with others are more likely to loaf (Harkins & Jackson, 1985). Consider a split or modified grading system. For example, group members who are rated by others as having made fewer contributions receive a lower score than other members. Those rated as contributing more or being more crucial to the project success can be graded accordingly. Students are comfortable with peers' ratings and take these ratings seriously. Also, when peers rate one another, there is less social loafing and students often do a more accurate job of rating themselves. Peer ratings are never shown to other members. We liken this promise to attorney-client privilege. We also consider all members' ratings when deciding whether to increase or decrease the group average for one individual. There must be general consensus from the group before we consider a grade adjustment.

Tailor individual and group ratings to the assignment (e.g., attended meetings regularly, completed tasks, timeliness, and work quality). Grading rubrics with varying criteria are available in Barkley et al. (2005). Use them in the group orientation process so that students know at the beginning of the semester how group behaviors will be evaluated.

Solution 2: Increase Group Cohesiveness

Group cohesiveness is commonly defined as the degree individuals see themselves tied or belonging to a group (Forsyth, 1999). Students belonging to cohesive groups work together because they want to. Group members are more likely to hold themselves accountable because they are working with individuals they like or respect. If one member's contribution is poorly done or late, it negatively affects the others, similar to letting down a friend. Teachers should let students choose their own groups to relieve the instructor of any responsibility (blame) associated with assigning members to groups. Too much cohesiveness can occur when group members are good friends or significant others, and those who fail to make timely contributions may believe their lapses will be forgiven. However, friends are often the first to report these lapses.

Solution 3: Group Size

Groups should have three to five members to equalize individual effort. Although social loafing can occur in any size group, it is significantly more obvious to the instructor when the group is small.

Provide Clear Project Goals and Rubrics for How Student Performance is Evaluated

A common group work problem is that students do not understand how their performance will be evaluated. This ambiguity contributes to their inability to understand how individual inputs will relate to their group's performance as well as their difficulty in monitoring group progress.

Problem:

In a rush to design or assign group projects, professors often fail to clarify their goals for the project or a typical timeline for completion.

Solution 1: Explain the Purpose of the Assignment

Instructors with firm, clear, and systematic expectations for what constitutes a successful group project will have less difficulty in getting students started and finished. Students need clear connections between what they are doing and how that process is related to the final product.

Solution 2: Be Clear About Expectations

Provide successful and unsuccessful project examples for students to examine to assist them in doing a good job. Write and distribute a grading rubric with points given for specific categories. Instead of saying the group's final project is an in-class presentation; let groups know the criteria (e.g., concise, jargon free literature review, active-learning, and media clips). Grade participation so all students are present and active on demonstration day. To help students do well, provide exemplars of (anonymous) student examples of previous successes and failures.

Solution 3: Set a Realistic Timeline

Provide students a realistic time frame for project completion. These guidelines help in letting students know whether they are completing their individual contributions in a way that is beneficial or harmful to the group.

Solution 4: Develop Contingency Plans

Students are unrealistically optimistic when predicting how quickly they as individuals or as a group will accomplish a task. This bias is even more pronounced when the group discusses the timeline (Buehler, Messervey, & Griffin 2005). To avoid this fallacy, have groups develop contingency plans in case deadlines are not met. Groups might brainstorm a timeline for successful completion, but also predict pitfalls along the way.

Conclusion

While employers are begging for job candidates capable of working with others, instructors continue to struggle with how they can make group work more effective and still teach content. Is there time to do both successfully? Yes. Success in the group-oriented lesson, project, or course is related to effective planning, a willingness to rethink the nature of group work, and an energetic emphasis on group process and outcome.

References and Recommended Readings

Balcetis, E.E., Forrest, K.D., Preuss, G., & Benz, J. (2007). *Combating social loafing in groups: Members must first acknowledge the problem.* Manuscript submitted for publication. Available from forrestk@unk.edu

Barkley, E.F., Cross, K.P, & Major, C.H. (2005). *Collaborative learning techniques.* San Francisco, CA: Wiley.

Buehler, R., Messervey, D., & Griffin, D. (2005). Collaborative planning and prediction: Does group discussion affect optimistic biases in time estimation? *Organizational Behavior and Human Decision Processes, 97,* 47-67.

Crozier, W.R. (2004). Shyness and students' perceptions of seminars. *Psychology Learning and Teaching, 4,* 27-34.

Forrest, K.D., & Miller, R.L. (2003). Not another group project: Why good teachers care about bad group experiences. *Teaching of Psychology, 30,* 244-246.

Forsyth, D.L. (1999). *Group dynamics.* Belmont, CA: Wadsworth.

Halpern, D.F. (2004). Creating cooperative learning environments. In B. Perlman, L.I. McCann, & S.H. McFadden (Eds.), *Lessons learned: Practical advice for the teaching of psychology* (Vol. 2, pp. 165-173). Washington, DC: Association for Psychological Science.

Harkins, S.G. & Jackson, J.M. (1985). The role of evaluation in eliminating social loafing. *Personality and Social Psychology Bulletin, 11,* 457-465.

Johnson, D.W., & Johnson, F.P. (1997). *Joining together: Group theory and group skills* (6th ed.), Boston: Allyn & Bacon.

Kerr, N.L. (1983). Motivation losses in small groups: A social dilemma analysis. *Journal of Personality and Social Psychology, 45,* 819-828.

Ryan, M.M. & Olgilvie, M. (2005). The preference for group work-not always the case: A case study. In E. Manalo & G. Wong-Yoi (Eds.), *Communication skills in university education: The international dimension* (pp. 150-158). Auckland, New Zealand: Pearson Education Limited.

Tuckman, B.W. (1965). Developmental sequences in small groups. *Psychological Bulletin, 63,* 384-399.

Helping Students Do Well in Class: GAMES

Marilla D. Svinicki
University of Texas at Austin

I STUDIED SO HARD FOR this test, and I still did badly! What can I do? I know that a few students are going to appear at my door with this lament after I return exams each semester. I am usually as distressed by their performance as they are and often at a loss to offer sage advice on what they can do differently. Over the years, I've tried to help students apply what they are learning in my psychology of learning class to their own behavior, and I've found a fairly successful mnemonic for studying — GAMES — that conveys much of what we know about learning. I share it with my students at the beginning of every course so they will apply it and also as an example of what they will be studying. For some reason, however, until recently I never thought to apply it to myself as a way of helping the students I teach and advise. This column reviews GAMES and its relevance for both students and instructors.

GAMES

The letters of this mnemonic stand for my best advice to students as they study. Each letter is supported in the theory and literature.

G Goal-oriented study
A Active study
M Meaningful and memorable study
E Explaining to someone as a study strategy
S Self-monitoring during study

Teachers can increase students' performance by applying what we know about effective learning to their own behavior and using these findings to support student studying. A sample handout that you can give to your students is shown in Appendix A.

Goal-Oriented Studying

Having a goal when you study is much more efficient and effective than just sitting down and reading. When I ask about students' study goals, they usually mention time spent or pages reviewed ("I'm going to study for two hours." "I'm going to finish chapter two."). Although such goals are better than nothing, they don't match what we know about learning. Spending time or simply completing assignments is not the real course goal, students need to understand the concepts. Do students actually mean the same thing that we mean when we say "understanding?" I don't think so; I would speculate that even we instructors don't always mean the same thing by "understanding." That was one of the reasons behaviorists were originally loathe to phrase instructional objectives in terms of understanding; they pushed for a clearer specification of actual behavior.

Here is where instructors can be most helpful to students. We want them to set "understanding" goals for their studying, so we should help them recognize what that means in this context. For example, when I say I want students to understand how theory informs practice in psychology, I mean that I want them to be able to explain a theory in everyday language, recognize examples of its application, suggest examples of its application to their own actions as practitioners, and possibly even provide arguments for and against using a theory as a basis for practice in alternative application settings. Those goals serve as clear checkpoints that students can use to measure their understanding of the theories. When they study, I would expect them to keep working at it until they can do those things with a given theory. They will not be able to do that just by reading. Good goals require that students make connections between what they are learning and what they already know, a key concept in learning, and between what they are learning and how they intend to use that learning in the future, an important foundation for transfer. So now when students come to me for advice, I can suggest that they make similar concrete goals, and I can model what that might mean in behavioral terms.

The G of GAMES reminds me that setting clear goals for a unit or an activity helps students. Why are we practicing this stuff in this way? Helping them understand the answer will both make what we do more productive from a learning standpoint and serve as a good model of strategic learning for them. In class, I should share my goals for each activity. In addition, I should verbally and openly model the process of goal setting so that in a type of cognitive apprenticeship, students can see how a skilled learner approaches setting goals.

Active Study

In office consultations about study strategies, students often proudly tell me that they spend a lot of time retyping their lecture notes, and then read them over until they know them by heart. That kind of activity may be all right if the goal of studying is to memorize information or to form simple stimulus response bonds, but unless exam items consist of the exact same words and examples as their notes, memorizing is not good preparation.

A big difference exists between "being active" and "active learning." Copying notes and reviewing text are not activities directed toward learning. The productive activities suggested by the research on learning and memory (Alexander & Murphy, 1998; Bransford, Brown, & Cocking, 1999) involve the "deep processing" of ideas. Activities that encourage surface processing, such as memorizing lists, recopying notes, practicing with flash cards, and other repetitious activities will not result in flexible use of information. Students have to engage in activities that transform the information into something that emphasizes structure and connections, key features, and paradigmatic examples.

Annotated Notes

It is hard to convince students to abandon old strategies for totally new, untried ones, so suggest slight modifications to their study habits; rather than simply recopying notes, recommend that students annotate their notes as they recopy them. For example, they can create two columns, one with the recopied notes and one that highlights main ideas, turns statements into questions, lists key vocabulary, and maybe even identifies ways that the instructor might ask a question about that material. Figure 1 shows an example of "transformed notes."

Granted, this type of studying activity is more complex and time-consuming initially, but it results in a deeper understanding. A less intense strategy is to reorganize notes rather than just recopy them. The goal is not simply for students to have well-organized notes (which they could get by borrowing someone else's), but for them to create their own organization and cues.

The lecture said	What I should know

I. Strategies for eliminating conditioned responses
  A. Extinction — stop giving the reinforcement.
      Ex. Don't pay attention when kid misbehaves.
  B. Punishment — two types- present aversive
     stimulus or remove positive stimulus
     Ex. Spanking or loss of privileges
  C. Counterconditioning – reinforce incompatible
     behavior
     Ex. Praise kids for sitting quietly to eliminate running around
	Three ways to eliminate conditioned response (create a mnemonic – **PEC** away at behavior)
	punishment (paraphrase definition)
	(give two different examples)
	extinction (paraphrase definition)
	(give own example)
	counterconditioning (paraphrase)
	(give own example)
	
	Possible test questions:
	(Describes behavior) Apply different strategies to get rid of this unwanted behavior in a classroom.
	(Describes situation) What type of strategy for eliminating conditioned responses is being used here?

II. Sources of reinforcement in education, etc.	Four types of reinforcers used in education, etc.

Figure 1: Sample Student Annotated Study Notes

Reading the Text

Active learning also can be applied to reading the text. A good strategy for students is to pause periodically and summarize what they just read. These paraphrases can form the bases for flashcards. The key is that students do more than read quickly through an assignment; they need to take some time to work with the ideas. Sometimes it is sufficient to take notes or write questions in the margins of the text; many students feel that highlighting the text is an effective strategy. But if these things are done mindlessly, they are no better than straight reading. If, however, students highlight a sentence and then ask themselves why they chose that sentence to highlight, they will take highlighting to a deeper, more active level.

Flashcards

Similarly, students will get a lot out of creating flashcards if they do more than simply copy what is in their book or notes. The act of selecting information to put on a card is a form of deeper processing. Teachers can encourage students to think about why some ideas deserve a separate card and some do not. Mindfully selecting discriminating features to include on flashcards is a form of deeper processing.

Meaningful and Memorable Study

Research (Alexander, 2000; American Psychological Association, 1995) shows that during learning students make connections between new and existing information, major and minor points in a concept, abstractions and concrete examples, and especially between general and personally specific references. Learners create a unique, structural understanding of what they are learning, in which the relationships among components and to the learners themselves are clarified. This happens naturally as we try to think of examples from our own experiences to understand a new idea.

We can model the process of making connections as we present the course material. Students often learn the examples we give first, and then use them to recall the principles they represent. We also can point out examples in the textbook so they will not be skipped in favor of the main idea. We can help students understand how important examples are for turning abstract ideas into concrete representations, which are generally much easier to understand and remember. Most of all, we can encourage and even require students to create their own examples by asking for them during class and basing homework assignments on them.

Structural Understanding

We model structural understanding when we provide outlines for lectures or charts and diagrams for ideas. In my classes, I use a lot of comparative organizers (Figure 2).

What is the procedure?	After the response, the stimulus is presented.	After the response, the stimulus is removed.
Stimulus is positive	Positive reinforcement	Punishment
Stimulus is negative	Punishment	Positive reinforcement

Figure 2: Sample Comparative Organizer

This type of chart is designed to emphasize the analytical process I am using to compare ideas or organize information. The analytical process involves determining what the contingencies are and what procedure is being described by each set of contingencies. As we learn about a given topic, we place it in the chart in relationship to the other most common contingencies. I sometimes give the students partially completed charts and have them attempt to fill in the empty cells based on their readings. We use them so often that students have reported beginning to think in terms of comparative organizers and to use them during studying, which is precisely what I want them to do.

Explaining to Someone as a Study Strategy

The old saying "to teach is to learn twice" reflects the idea that it is not until you try to explain something to someone else that you really understand it yourself. No matter how prepared you thought you were, it requires a whole other order of magnitude of understanding to clearly communicate an idea to another person. A good study strategy is to find a partner and then explain ideas to one another. Better yet, students should try to find a willing listener who is not in the class and try to explain the main ideas to that person. I would settle for trying to explain the ideas to a dog. The act of saying the words out loud is what makes a difference here. I cannot provide any research data for my hypothesis, however.

It is a rare friend who is willing to sit through explanation after explanation, so students will probably have to save the live practice until test time. However, as a temporary substitute students can write summaries and paraphrases of ideas as if they were writing a letter home and trying to justify paying all that tuition by showing how much they learned.

The Principle of Understanding.

As instructors, the principle of explaining to understand is embodied in our use of group work in class. It takes a while to overcome student reluctance to engage in group work, but if it is a regular part of class, they eventually find that comparing their ideas helps them follow what is going on. In my classes, a major part of each class period is spent applying concepts to real scenarios in groups of three that remain the same throughout the semester. I create groups of students who have majors in common so they can apply the concepts to their fields of interest. I don't have to think up examples from widely divergent fields; the students do it themselves. I check over written documentation of their discussions, but in reality we have already checked their work since we discuss their ideas after each exercise. The discussion is the important thing.

Self-Monitoring During Study

Our students really struggle with self-monitoring. Students often suffer from the "illusion of understanding"— that feeling that it was all so clear when someone explained it, but when you try to do it yourself, you can't (Bransford, Brown, & Cocking, 1999). When students watch us solve problems or describe concepts in class or read the text, they think they understand. But when they attempt to use information or solve problems, they realize they do not. That is why it is important for students to attempt to apply the concepts while studying.

Of course, students are not experts at monitoring themselves. They can easily get into the habit of only asking themselves questions to which they think they know the answers. Our task as instructors is to model what it means to monitor understanding. In fact, all the foregoing letters of GAMES provide strategies that students can use to improve their self-monitoring. As we incorporate these activities, we can help students see how taking the kinds of actions we do in class and making them a part of the way they study will make them better learners. If they set good goals, they will have a better basis for self-monitoring. If they are active in their studying, the results of that activity will be good feedback on understanding. As they try to make connections between the content and their prior knowledge or future uses, they will be checking whether or not they have interpreted the content correctly. Finally, when they try to explain what they know, they see where they need to shore up their understanding. Unless they recognize the need for acting on all this feedback, they will not reap the full benefits of the GAMES system. Self-monitoring is the final brushstroke that completes the picture.

Conclusion

This is the system that works with my students. I try to incorporate as many of these components into my day-to-day class planning as I can in the hope that seeing me use them will convince students of their value. I certainly use the GAMES structure to help students whose test performance did not meet their expectations. Whether they carry through with the suggestions or not is up to them, but as I frequently say, to the groans of the students, "Let the GAMES begin."

References and Recommended Readings

Alexander, P. (2000). Toward a model of academic development: Schooling and the acquisition of knowledge: The sequel. *Educational Researcher, 29*(2), 28-33, 44.

Alexander, P. & Murphy, P. K. (1998). The research base for APA's learner-centered principles. In N.M. Lambert and B.L. McCombs (Eds.), *Issues in school reform: A sampler of psychological perspectives on learner-centered school* (pp. 25-60). Washington, DC: American Psychological Association.

American Psychological Association. (1995). *Learner-centered psychological principles: A framework for school redesign and reform.* Washington, DC: Author.

Branford, J., Brown, A.L., & Cocking, R.R. (1999). *How people learn: Brain, mind, experience, and school.* Washington, DC: National Academy Press.

Svinicki, M.D. (2005). *Learning and motivation in postsecondary classrooms.* San Francisco: Jossey-Bass.

Each letter in GAMES represents a characteristic of good studying. If you transform your own study habits to incorporate a little of each, you'll be applying what psychologists know about learning to your efforts and you'll get much better results.

G Goal-Oriented Study

Before you study, set some goals about what you want to know or be able to do with the information you're about to learn. For example, instead of saying "I'm going to study economics for one hour." Or "I'm going to read the chapter on the GNP." Say:
> "I'm going to be able to describe all the different bases that are used to calculate the Gross National Product and why each basis is used. I'm also going to be able to explain what the GNP is and why it is important in this course and in general."

Having a goal will focus your attention, help you monitor whether you are learning, and help you direct your study at those things that will give you the most bang for the buck.

A Active Study

When you study, go deeper than simple memorization tricks. Try to understand the content in terms of how it all fits together and what causes and effects underlie the content. Don't just read; read actively.

♦   For example, instead of just recopying your notes, annotate them (comment on them, summarize or paraphrase them, question them, etc.)

♦   Instead of just creating flash cards by copying items directly out of the book, pick out key ideas and their key features and put those on cards. Ask yourself: Is this concept important enough to be a main category?

♦   Instead of just reading or highlighting your textbook, make notes in the margin about key ideas, ask yourself why you chose to highlight something, ask yourself questions about the material.

M Meaningful and Memorable Study

When you study, try to make connections between what you are learning and what you already know or what you have experienced personally. For example, in addition to taking note of any concrete examples that the instructor or the textbook give you, make your own examples. As many as you can. Think about where in your present or future you've seen a concept or will use a concept that you're learning about.

E Explaining to Someone as a Study Strategy

After studying alone, it is helpful to work with another person. Explaining an idea to someone else is probably the best way to be sure you understand it.

For example, find another person in the class who wants to study together and spend time trying to explain the course concepts to one another.

Think about how you would explain an idea to someone unfamiliar with the content of the course.

S Self-Monitoring During Study

While you're studying, constantly check to see if you are understanding or just going through the motions. For example, when you start studying, write down a set of questions that your instructor might ask you about the material, and then keep checking to see if you can answer those questions. Periodically stop and ask yourself if you are still studying mindfully. If not, you need to redirect your efforts back to your initial goals.

Appendix A: The keys to effective studying may lie in the simple word GAMES.

On Taking Attendance

RAYMOND J. GREEN
Texas A&M University-Commerce

Setting: *Coffee room of the Psychology Department at the University of Everywhere.*

Dr. Bob: *I can't believe it! I am so frustrated lecturing to a half-empty room. What's wrong with students today? Why don't they show up for class? Why don't they want to learn?*

Dr. Mary: *Hmm, my class is usually full. What percentage of the student's grade is based on attendance in your class?*

Dr. Bob: *None, I don't believe in taking attendance. It's up to the students to decide whether they will attend class or not. I don't believe I do any good by forcing students to come to class.*

Dr. Mary: *Well, that's one way to look at it. My way is to offer that little extra motivation to get to class and then to make them see that it's worth their time. Maybe shift that extrinsic motivation to intrinsic...*

UNDOUBTEDLY, THIS type of conversation has occurred on numerous college campuses over the last 100 years. I do not purport to resolve this debate, as much of it is based on personal and organizational philosophy. However, there is a wide range of literature on attendance in the college classroom that I will use to continue the dialogue. I will begin by discussing the arguments in support of attendance policies and then move to those against taking attendance in psychology courses. In my concluding section, I will share my personal thoughts on attendance policies and discuss some suggestions on implementing an attendance policy if you choose to do so.

Arguments For Taking Attendance
Increased Attendance and Learning

Perhaps the question most germane to this debate is whether taking attendance impacts student learning. At an intuitive level it seems almost self-evident that increased attendance would positively impact learning, but perhaps we professors give ourselves too much credit! Luckily, the research literature indicates a significant relationship between attendance and student grades (e.g., Hancock, 1994; van Blerkom, 1992). Of course, one may wonder if there is a link between attendance and grades given that some instructors award points for attendance. However, Shimoff and Catania (2001) report that merely taking attendance (without awarding points) increased attendance and improved grades, even on material covered in the text but not in class. Overall, it appears that students are more likely to attend — and to succeed — in courses where attendance records are maintained. Despite the importance of these findings, this may not be the only reason why it is worth taking attendance in your classes.

May Reveal Academically Challenged Students

The research above suggests that attendance may have a causal impact on grades. However, Jones (1984) suggested that lower grades may also lead to an increase in class absences. In essence, he reported a downward spiral where absences led to poorer grades, which led to more absences, which led to even poorer grades. Thus, attendance patterns might be a useful diagnostic tool for identifying at-risk students. Even in the absence of test grades, students may perceive that they are doing poorly in the class (e.g., they feel that they just don't "get" the material). Thus, they may become frustrated and begin missing class more frequently. Noticing this change in attendance may provide the instructor with the opportunity to intervene and help students before too much time has passed.

Reduces Academically Dishonest Behavior

People like to be recognized and to feel important. Yet, in some larger introductory undergraduate courses it is fairly easy to feel like nothing more than a student ID number. By taking attendance — and, perhaps more importantly, contacting those who are not attending — you are indicating that you recognize and care about students as individuals. If this notion sounds too touchy-feely for you, there may be more pragmatic reasons for reaching out to students and affirming their uniqueness. The social psychological literature is rife with examples of deindividuation leading to generally negative social behaviors. Thus, it would not be surprising to see an increase in negative behaviors like cheating and plagiarism in classes where students felt deindividuated (Houston, 1976; McCabe, Trevino, & Butterfield, 2001). Recognizing and highlighting your students' individuality could reduce the temptation to be academically dishonest.

Provides a Model of the "Real World"

As I prepared to write this article, I asked my colleagues whether they had an attendance policy and if so, why? One compelling argument was that professors have the responsibility to prepare students for the world of work. My colleague continued, "If you don't show up for work, you don't get paid and you may very well get fired." Thus, his argument revolved around the idea that good attendance is a skill that we can help develop along with the other skills we work on with students. This argument can be viewed as a facet of Goal 10 (Career Planning and Development) of the APA's Undergraduate Psychology Learning Goals and Outcomes (Halonen, Appleby, & Brewer, 2002).

Arguments Against Taking Attendance

Although the arguments for using an attendance policy are compelling, there are many instructors who provide equally compelling arguments against attendance policies. I turn to this viewpoint next. Arguments against attendance policies range from the philosophical to the pragmatic.

Motivation, Attributions, and Responsibility

The prevailing philosophical argument made by those who disagree with attendance policies is the belief that it is ultimately the students' responsibility to attend class and learn the material. This basic argument has a number of variants. Pintrich (1994) ties motivation to a sense of control. He argues that compulsory attendance may reduce students' perceptions of control over the environment, in turn leading to reduced motivation to attend class. This argument is in line with the cognitive dissonance research on education. This body of research indicates that strong rewards are likely to diminish the internalization of the desire to learn (e.g., Lepper, Greene, & Nisbett, 1973). Thus, by taking attendance and rewarding those who would normally attend of their own volition, we may mislead them to attribute their attendance to the policy and not their own internal motivation.

Another variant of this argument uses the same "real world" logic mentioned above, while coming to the opposite conclusion. The argument is that we are providing a model for the real world, where there are no attendance policies and no benevolent souls calling you to remind you to attend work. Instead, there are expectations that you will show up at your workplace and that you will produce quality work. If you do not fulfill these expectations, there are serious consequences (i.e., you will be fired). Thus, if we truly want to prepare our students for the real world, we may be better off asking them to be responsible for their own behavior.

Consumer Model

One model of higher education is that students are consumers. They have paid for the right to attend an institution of higher learning and may do with that as they please. For instance, if I buy a new CD and realize I do not enjoy it, I am not compelled to keep listening to it. It may be that students do not feel that they are receiving sufficient value from attending class, thus they choose to spend their time doing something more valuable (St. Clair, 1999). For example, perhaps students have discovered that the class is designed so that they can do just as well on exams by reading the textbook as they could by attending class. Thus, they may choose to spend that class time studying for another class. Further, viewing attendance from the perspective of the consumer allows professors to receive feedback on how they are doing. If students consistently skip a certain part of your course (or the whole course!), it may be time to rethink what you are doing (Sperber, 2005). One offshoot of this theory is that the onus is on professors to make class worthwhile if they expect students to attend class.

Organizational and Instructional Headaches

Taking attendance each class day can be extremely time consuming (Forsyth, 2003). If the professor calls roll (which undoubtedly is a good way to learn the names of the students in the class), this could easily take anywhere from 2-15 minutes depending on class size. Most faculty members would argue that they cannot afford to consistently lose this much time each class. However, if professors pass around a list that students are expected to sign, they run the risk of students signing in absent friends. Occasionally calling the role after passing around and collecting the sheet could limit such behavior.

Further, if professors take attendance each day and include it in the calculation of students' grades that means they will also need to sift through the mountain of excuses that are offered for absences. These excuses will range from the mundane to the inane, and it may at times be difficult to tell which is which! Many faculty do not want the added responsibility of acting as judge and jury concerning the legitimacy of a student's excuse (Royse, 2001).

A strict attendance policy can lead to classrooms filled with disinterested and unprepared students (Forsyth, 2003) who may become a distraction to those interested in the lecture or in contributing to the discussion. Extending this logic, these students may change the normative environment of the classroom from one of excitement about learning to one of apathy. Although it may seem silly to us, many of our students are still concerned with appearing "cool." If there are students in the class who appear disdainful and resentful, better students may participate less to avoid appearing as if they are "brownnosers" or "uncool." Referring to this change of ambiance, Sperber (2005) reflects that he would prefer to teach a smaller number of volunteers than a large army of conscripts.

Conclusions and Advice on Attendance Policies

Before I delve into my personal philosophy, let me emphasize that the most important rule to consider is whether your university has an attendance policy. Many universities have attendance policies influenced by state funding guidelines and financial aid considerations. If there is a policy, you need to adhere to it to protect yourself and to be fair to the students who do not have an option to "revise" the policy as they see fit.

However, if you do have latitude in instituting an attendance policy in your classes, I suggest a flexible policy based on the maturity level of your classes. That is, I believe a middle ground can exist between the attendance-policy and the no-attendance-policy camps. I teach a range of courses — from Introduction to Psychology to upper-level graduate seminars — and use an attendance policy in my introductory class but have no official policy for upper-level undergraduate and graduate courses. Many entry-level college students are generally experiencing freedom for the first time and have numerous temptations that probably seem more compelling than coming to class. Thus, I believe that providing some extrinsic motivation to attend class is appropriate. Even so, I do not take roll every day. Instead, I have students complete 13 in-class assignments (e.g., practice quizzes, group assignments, surveys) during the semester (approximately one per week). If they are in class and complete the assignment, they receive 1 percent toward their final grade. Thus, one absence does not significantly impact their grade (everyone misses class now and then), but receiving 13 percent of their grade by merely showing up provides a substantial "carrot." Davis (1993) argues that grades should be based on a student's mastery of course material and not on nonacademic factors such as attendance. However, I believe this option, again, provides a middle ground allowing one to account for attendance while assessing the quality of the students work.

Practical Issues

Encouraging Attendance

Although I believe my system works at encouraging attendance, it certainly is not the only teaching practice that can be used to reach this goal. Some faculty deduct points for each missed class, whereas others do not begin to deduct points until a fixed number of classes is missed (Weimer, 1993). An alternative approach is to reward students by providing bonus points for a high percentage of classes attended or attendance on randomly selected days (Weimer, 1993). Nilson (1998) offers the following suggestions: 1) base part of the course grade on class discussion; 2) cover different material in class than that in the readings; 3) do not allow commercial production of your lecture notes; and 4) conduct cooperative learning group activities that include a peer evaluation of performance.

Even in the absence of an attendance policy, there may be some days where you feel attendance is particularly important (e.g., returning exams, guest speakers). One way to increase attendance is to design your syllabus so that there are required in-class writing assignments on those particular days. Another possibility, although somewhat less effective in insuring attendance, is to have homework assignments due that day. This strategy is likely to increase attendance over that of a typical class, but some students may just send their assignment along with a friend.

Taking Attendance

As discussed earlier, both taking attendance by calling roll or passing around sign-up sheets have their potential shortcomings. What are some alternatives for those not blessed with a teaching assistant? One possibility is to design a seating chart with required seating for students. Of course, those troubled by the restriction of freedom inherent in mandatory attendance will find this solution equally disturbing! Another possibility for those who can consistently arrive at class a few minutes early is to take attendance as you greet students at the door of the classroom. An additional benefit of this strategy is that you will increase interpersonal contact with students. However, one potential downside is accounting for students who arrive late to class. Finally, one can extend my strategy of random in-class assignments to daily in-class assignments that can be completed in a very short time.

Closing Thought

The question of whether to take attendance is truly a complex issue. There are many logical and compelling arguments both for and against attendance policies. Further, the issue of needing to take attendance is ultimately tied back to the larger issue of whether we are doing our job well. As Forsyth (2003) argues, if we make our classes so educationally rewarding that students want to attend, then the issue of attendance policies is moot.

References and Recommended Readings

Conard, M.A. (2004). Conscientiousness is key: Incentives for attendance make little difference. *Teaching of Psychology, 31,* 269-272.

Davis, B.G. (1993). *Tools for teaching.* San Francisco: Jossey Bass.

Forsyth, D.R. (2003). *The professor's guide to teaching: Psychological principles and practices.* Washington, DC: American Psychological Association.

Halonen, J.S., Appleby, D.C., & Brewer, C.L. (2002). *Undergraduate psychology major learning goals and outcomes: A report.* Retrieved September 6, 2005, from http://www.apa.org/ed/pcue/ taskforcereport2.pdf

Hancock, T.M. (1994). Effects of mandatory attendance on student performance. *College Student Journal, 28,* 326-329.

Houston, J.P. (1976). The assessment and prevention of answer copying on undergraduate multiple-choice exams. *Research in Higher Education, 5,* 301-311.

Jones, C.H. (1984). Interaction of absences and grades in a college course. *Journal of Psychology, 116,* 133-136.

Lepper, M.R., Greene, K.D., & Nisbett, R.E. (1973). Undermining children's intrinsic interest with extrinsic reward: A test of the 'overjustification' hypothesis. *Journal of Personality & Social Psychology, 28,* 129-137.

Lucas, S.G., & Bernstein, D.A. (2005). *Teaching psychology: A step by step guide.* Mahwah, NJ: Erlbaum.

McCabe, D.L., Treviño, L.K., & Butterfield, K.D. (2001). Cheating in academic institutions: A decade of research. *Ethics & Behavior, 11,* 219-233.

Nilson, L.B. (1998). *Teaching at its best: A research-based resource for college instructors.* Bolton, MA: Anker.

Pintrich, P.R. (1994). Student motivation in the college classroom.In K.W. Prichard & R. McLaran Sawyer (Eds.), H*andbook of college teaching: Theory and application* (pp. 23-43). Westport, CT: Greenwood Press.

Royse, D. (2001). *Teaching tips for college and university instructors: A practical guide.* Needham Heights, MA: Allyn & Bacon.

Shimoff, E., & Catania, C.A. (2001). Effects of recording attendance on grades in introductory psychology. *Teaching of Psychology, 28,* 192-195.

Sperber, M. (2005). Notes from a teaching career. *Chronicle of Higher Education, 52*(3), B20-B21.

St. Clair, K.L. (1999). A case against compulsory class attendance policies in higher education. *Innovative Higher Education, 23,* 171-180.

van Blerkom, M.L. (1992). Class attendance in undergraduate courses. *Journal of Psychology: Interdisciplinary and Applied, 126,* 487-494.

Weimer, M. (1993). *Improving your classroom teaching* (Vol. 1). Newbury Park, CA: Sage.

Teaching Students With Disabilities: A Proactive Approach

DENISE R. BOYD
Houston Community College

PERHAPS YOU HAVE found yourself in the midst of a conflict like one I faced in my introductory psychology class. A student with a documented disability e-mailed me on the day the required, five-page research paper was due. She said that, because her accommodations letter required that I provide her with extra time to complete written assignments, she would be submitting her paper late. How could I reconcile her request for extra time with my policies regarding late work? The conflict was ultimately resolved with the help of the head of my college's office for students with disabilities, but it left me regretting that I had not addressed the issue at the beginning of the semester. Such situations underscore the need for making preparations for serving students with disabilities.

Learn More About Students With Disabilities

The process of developing a general set of strategies for accommodating students with disabilities should begin with becoming better informed. First, it is helpful to know how the law distinguishes among instructor, institutional, and student responsibilities. Further, it is important to understand that the catch-all term "disabilities" can include conditions ranging from physical limitations such as confinement to a wheelchair, to cognitive impairments like ADHD, to psychiatric disabilities such as bipolar disorder, or to students with chronic medical conditions (e.g., diabetes) as well as those who are recovering from substance abuse. Obviously, the kinds of accommodations faculty must provide to a given student depend to some degree on that student's disability. Thus, it is difficult to anticipate every accommodation that may arise. The reference list at the end of this column includes several Internet sources that can help you become more familiar with both the legal and the practical issues associated with teaching students with disabilities.

Just as general student characteristics vary across colleges, one school's population of students with disabilities may be quite different from another's. The location of a given college, the availability of accessible housing, or a particular degree program may cause a school to attract more students of one disability group than another. Your institution's office for students with disabilities can acquaint you with the characteristics of your college's population of students with disabilities as well as the kinds of accommodations you will be expected to provide for them. Colleagues can probably also provide a wealth of information that is specific to your institution regarding student characteristics and the logistics involved in working with your institution's disabilities services staff.

Familiarize Yourself With the Services and Policies of Your College

Like student characteristics, the strategies colleges use to implement the disability law requirements vary across institutions. For instance, the most common accommodation for students with disabilities across all colleges in the United States is extended testing time (Ofiesh, Mather, & Russell, 2005). However, some schools require professors to provide both a setting and a proctor for students who need extended testing time; at others, disability offices provide these services. Thus, it is a good idea to meet with the director of services for students with disabilities on your campus to address this and other issues:

- ♦ *Extended testing time.* If the disabilities staff are responsible for administering extended-time exams, find out how and by whom the exams will be handled. If you have any doubts about the security of the process, you may decide that you will be better off proctoring the exam yourself.
- ♦ *Distraction-free locations and proctoring.* If your college requires you to provide these, identify an appropriate place in advance and find a time when you or someone in your department can serve as a proctor. Ideally,

the student should take the exam at the same time as others in his or her class. If you do the proctoring yourself, one solution is to administer the test to the student immediately before or after class.

- *Accessibility of campus resources and services.* Ask whether the school has a dedicated computer lab for students with disabilities. If not, find out whether it has taken steps to ensure that there are accessible computers in all or some of the institution's labs. You also should find out whether the office for students with disabilities provides tutoring for specific classes or tasks such as writing research papers.
- *Academic advising.* Find out whether the staff provides students with academic advising. If so, tell staff your thoughts about enrolling such students in psychology classes. For instance, you might suggest that students enroll in small rather than large sections of introductory psychology. You might also provide guidance as to how the reading demands of introductory psychology might be balanced with the demands of other courses.
- *Personal attendants.* What are your institution's policies regarding personal attendants? In most cases, attendants support students' physical needs and should not be present in the classroom unless absolutely necessary. Some colleges specifically forbid attendants from being present during testing, but others decide on a case-by-case basis. The primary goal of an attendant policy is to ensure that the student's work is his or her own, and to respect the rights of other students in the class. Thus, if an attendant attends class, it needs to be clear that he or she must remain in the classroom for the entire class session and abide by policies regarding the use of cell phones and other behaviors that may disturb students.

Examine and Improve the Accessibility of Your Course

Armed with a body of relevant knowledge, you are ready to examine and, if needed, improve the accessibility of your course.

- *Develop your own policies for students with disabilities and incorporate them into your syllabus.* Most colleges require that professors incorporate a brief "ADA" paragraph stating that students must be registered with the school's office for students with disabilities in order to receive accommodations. Build your own policies on your college's generic disability statement. For example, state that students must notify you of their accommodation needs as early in the semester as possible.

+ *Examine your testing and assignment procedures.* If you give online exams, for example, you may have to provide an alternative testing format for students with disabilities. Similarly, machine-scored answer sheets may present problems for some students. As noted earlier, many students with disabilities require extra time for testing. Consider how you might adjust your normal testing procedures. For instance, you might give more frequent, but shorter, exams and allot twice as much time as you know most students will require to accommodate students whose only testing modification is extended time.

+ Extra time also is an issue for written assignments. Choose due dates that allow you to extend deadlines for students with disabilities and still get their work in by the end of the semester. I shifted the research paper due date in my introductory psychology course from the 14th to the 10th week of the semester for this reason. (I also shortened the required length from 10 pages to five in light of the reduced amount of time available for students without disabilities.)

+ *Give some thought to transportation issue.* This is particularly true if you teach at a commuter school. Many students with disabilities, especially those with motor and visual impairments, rely on transportation arrangements that are less flexible than those of students who have their own cars. Course requirements may need to be modified accordingly. For instance, it might be extremely difficult for students with disabilities to participate in a study group or a group research project. Similarly, an extra credit opportunity involving volunteer work might be impossible for one of these students to accomplish.

+ *Examine any online course components and other kinds of instructional media from the perspective of a student who has a visual or hearing impairment.* IT departments are generally responsible for ensuring that the platforms they use (e.g., Blackboard, WebCT) are accessible. In addition, they often provide information about how to incorporate the accessibility features of these platforms into online course content. To a great extent, though, the needs of students with disabilities can be met by providing online information in alternative formats such as printed syllabi. However, some kinds of information cannot be adequately represented in an alternative form. For instance, an animation of the action potential can be described in text, but certain aspects of the animation probably cannot be well represented in words. In such cases, the professor's responsibility is to ensure that the student with a disability has an equal opportunity to learn the required information, not to come up with an equivalent presentation (Johnson & Brown, 2003).

Meet With Students at the Beginning of the Semester

Consider requiring students with accommodations letters to meet with you to work out how their needs will be met in your class. It is a good idea to create a set of standard procedures for these meetings. Write down the points you want to make about student responsibilities and the questions you need answered. (Remember, the nature of the disabling condition is confidential, so do not ask about that.) You might begin the meeting by chatting a bit to develop rapport. Make it a point to explore the transportation issues alluded to earlier. Move on to the accommodations letter, and seek clarification of any items that are unclear. For instance, if the student has a visual impairment that requires sitting near the front of the room, find out how close the student needs to be. Accommodations letters often say "as needed," so you should clarify practical issues surrounding the student's responsibility to let you know when accommodation is needed. It also is a good idea to find out the name, telephone number, and e-mail address for the student's contact person in the office for students with disabilities.

Alternative Materials

Many students with visual impairments and learning disabilities use alternative texts. To speed up the process of getting these materials to your future students with disabilities, contact your publisher's sales representative to find out whether such materials have been prepared and how students can get them.

Many publishers have plain text files of textbooks on CD-ROM disks that can be converted to speech by special computer software (often provided to students by state agencies). Similarly, many textbooks have been recorded by Recording for the Blind and Dyslexic (www.rfbd.org). At their website, you can search for your textbook and find out how your students can order it, if it is available. Pass along the information you get to the students, then advise them that obtaining the required course materials is their responsibility. You should probably also point out that there may be a delay in getting the alternative text and that the student will be responsible for keeping up with assignments.

If alternative materials are not available, the disabilities office may arrange for the text to be tape recorded by their staff, especially for students who have visual impairments or are completely dyslexic. For students with other kinds of learning disabilities, the disabilities office may advise you to allow extra time to complete reading assignments. This advice naturally raises the issue of the reasonableness of expecting the student to complete the course in a single semester. In my view, spending a little time investigating the availability of alternative materials is preferable to negotiating an extension of course length. In fact, when choosing textbooks and other materials, it is a good idea to consider availability of alternative materials.

The Student's Ability to Benefit From Class Lectures

If the student is hearing impaired, you need to find out whether she reads lips or will be accompanied by an interpreter. Advise the student that she may need to remind you to talk in her direction if she reads lips. If the college is providing an interpreter, talk to this person about how issues such as signing difficult terms will be handled.

Tape Recording Lectures

Many professors give permission to students with disabilities to tape record their lectures in order to address a "needs help with note taking" accommodation. If you do so, include a tape recording policy in your syllabus that applies to all students, stating that students who tape must respect others' privacy and not disrupt class to change batteries or tapes. It also is a good idea to obtain permission from all students in the class before you or anyone else tapes a class session. Students' comments and questions might be considered part of their confidential educational record. Further, it may be illegal in your state to record people's statements without permission.

Typed Lecture Notes and Pre-Recorded Lectures

If you do not want class sessions recorded, consider preparing typed lecture notes for students with disabilities. Save these files in plain text format so they can be converted to speech by the computer software mentioned above. You also might consider making your own recordings. One of my colleagues has created MP3 files of his lectures that all students can download from the course homepage. He provides the files on CDs if students do not have an MP3 player or the hardware to burn their own CDs. Although this approach is quite time consuming, the hassle-reduction advantages become clear when a student presents you with an accommodation letter that requires help with note taking and you simply hand him or her a few CDs or pages of printed notes. There may be media services personnel at your college who can help with this task. If you are concerned about commercial misuse of such aids, tag the notes or audio files with copyright notices stating that they cannot be reproduced without your permission and are provided solely for the purpose of personal study. (See http://ethics.csc.ncsu.edu/intellectual/classnotes/ for links to articles about intellectual property issues associated with professors' lecture notes.)

When Prepared Notes and Taped Lectures Are Insufficient

When I teach statistics, I work problems on the chalkboard that I have prepared in advance and could include in typed notes. However, I often work problems in response to students' questions. Students whose disability prevents them from following what I am doing on the chalkboard will miss a substantial proportion of the instruction even if they record the session. Last semester, after each class, I met with a statistics student who had limited vision. I guided her in copying critical problems from the board and, essentially, retaught each one as she copied it.

A surrogate note taker for the student with a disability also works. You might ask another student in the class to volunteer, but what happens if the note taker is absent? Moreover, how do you know at the beginning of the semester which students will be good note takers? Logistical issues surround the necessity of copying the note taker's notes. The best solution is to solicit help from the office for students with disabilities. It may have funds to hire a note taker. This is how my own daughter, who is legally blind, managed undergraduate math classes. The state agency that serves the visually impaired paid a note taker to accompany her to every class. She was required to find the note taker and to complete all necessary documentation for the agency. Her professors' only responsibility was to grant permission for the note taker to attend classes.

Testing Issues

Try to establish the testing procedure for students with disabilities in the most concrete terms possible. Even if students take their exams in the disabilities office, most instructors and disability services professionals insist that students take exams at the same time as their classmates; tell the student so in unequivocal terms. This is especially important if you have a "no make-up exam" policy. If you do not establish a specific time when students are supposed to take an exam, you risk sending students the implicit message that they can take the exam at a time of their choosing, giving them a distinct advantage over their classmates, which is not consistent with either the letter or the spirit of disability law.

Extended Deadlines for Written Assignments

Accommodations letters often operationally define "extra time." They may say students should get 50 percent more time, or twice as much, or something of this kind. However, such accommodations are typically developed with testing in mind, not written work for which all students have an extended period of time. Consequently, deadlines for such assignments have to be negotiated on a case-by-case basis. If you cannot come to an agreement, consult with the director of the disabilities office regarding a reasonable deadline.

Falling Behind and Concerns About Course Performance and Grades

Tell students about any available tutoring services for your course and any services to help with essays or research papers. However, keep in mind the "barriers" principle. As long as standard tutoring services are accessible to students with disabilities, there is no need to provide tutoring or help beyond that you would provide for any student. Still, you should emphasize your belief that, given sufficient effort, most students can do well in your course. Of course, you may want to operationally define "doing well." I do this for all students at the beginning of each semester by talking about the factors that predict their grades. If a student faces a specific obstacle that is somewhat beyond her control, then she must compensate by manipulating another factor that is in her control. For instance, one uncontrollable factor for many of my students is that English is not their primary language. By contrast, the decision to take introductory psychology either before or after they have completed their required ESL courses is within their control. Likewise, the amount of time they devote to studying and the degree to which they access tutoring services is up to them. Thus, a non-native English speaking student who has not completed the ESL sequence and who has little time for studying or tutoring should adjust her grade expectations downward. In this way, I communicate to students that, although I enthusiastically support their achievement goals, I also advocate realistic expectations. In conversations with students who have disabilities, I emphasize my willingness to do everything possible to ensure that the outcome they experience in my course will be a product of their own ability and effort.

Require Students to Sign a Contract

You might be wise to require students with disabilities to sign a "learning contract" that specifies both instructor and student responsibilities. Many college offices for students with disabilities require these students to sign contracts in their office that outline the responsibilities of the student and staff in the disability office. They also state procedures students must follow when they have a complaint or need to have an accommodation modified. A similar contract involving a student and a professor would specify how any testing accommodations would be implemented and specify due dates for written assignments. If I had entered into such a contract with the student I described in my opening paragraph, it would have included a date on which the research paper was due. After that date, the no-late-work policy in my syllabus would have applied.

Benefits of a Proactive Approach

There is little doubt that providing accommodations for students with disabilities can add frustration and stress to teaching.

When I received the "extra time" e-mail I described at the opening of this column, I felt that I was being taken advantage of. I had only myself to blame, though, because I should have addressed the paper deadline at the beginning of the semester.

Anyone teaching in today's higher-education environment will face making such accommodations. A relatively small investment of time can greatly reduce stress when accommodation needs arise. That is, if we professors have acquired relevant information and consid-ered the process of adapting our courses for students with various kinds of disabilities, then we will be less likely to feel exploited or ineffectual. Instead, we can focus our energies on helping students with and without disabilities achieve an understanding of their own and others' behavior.

References and Recommended Readings

Chaffey College Disability Programs and Services. (2005). *Professional development*. Retrieved December 11, 2005, from http://www.chaffey.edu/dps/fac_staff.html

College of the Desert. (2005). *Disabled students programs & services*. Retrieved December 11, 2005, from http://www.collegeofthedesert.edu/students/programs/dsps/index.asp

Ethics in Computing. (2005). *Online course notes*. Retrieved December 12, 2005, from http://ethics.csc.ncsu.edu/intellectual/classnotes

Johnson, D. (2003). Teaching students with disabilities. In W. Buskist, V. Hevern, & G. Hill IV (Eds.), *Essays from excellence in teaching, 2002* (Chapter 4). Retrieved May 30, 2005, from http://teachpsych.lemoyne.edu/teachpsych/eit/eit2002/eit02-04.html

Johnson, K., & Brown, S. (2003). *Why make your websites accessible in post-secondary education?* [Webcast transcript]. Retrieved May 30, 2005, from http://www.ilru.org/html/training/webcasts/handouts/2003/09-24-SB/transcript.txt

LaGuardia Community College Office for Students With Disabilities. (2001). *Reasonable accommodations: A faculty guide to teaching college students with disabilities*. Retrieved December 11, 2005, from www.lagcc.cuny.edu/osd/faculty/guide_intro.htm

Lincoln College. (2005). *Applying for accommodations*. Retrieved December 11, 2005, from http://www.lincolncollege.edu/normal/ods/applying.htm

Ofiesh, N., Mather, N., & Russell, A. (2005). Using speeded cognitive, reading, and academic measures to determine the need for extended test time among university students with learning disabilities. *Journal of Psychoeducational Assessment, 23*, 35-52.

U.S. Department of Education, Office for Civil Rights. (2002). *Students with disabilities preparing for postsecondary education: Know your rights and responsibilities*. Retrieved December 12, 2005, from www.ed.gov/about/offices/list/ocr/transition.html

Brave New World...Wide Web: Blending Old Teaching Methods With a Cutting-Edge Virtual Learning Environment

MICHAEL SCHULTE-MECKLENBECK
University of Bergen

HAVE YOU EVER thought students in your course were listening to what you say, and yet they barely communicate with you? Have you ever wanted to provide a large number of documents and information to your students without using the copy machine? Have you ever had the intention to guide students to certain topics, but found that there were too many in your class to be able to do this? If your answer to any of these questions is "yes," a Virtual Learning Environment(VLE) may be a solution. VLEs provide many possibilities to use online tools in and of themselves, or even better, as an addition to a face-to-face class. In a VLE, course and content management are incorporated and easily coordinated through Web-based software. Alternative teaching and discussion methods like online quizzes, forums, chats, or Wikis (comparable to a white board on which anyone can write anything) are built in. Best of all, working on the teacher's (as well as the student's) side of a VLE is simply a lot of fun.

What Exactly Is a VLE?

A VLE is a set of teaching and learning tools designed to enhance a student's learning experience by including computers and the Internet in the learning process. A common scenario is that the VLE software runs on a server so that it can be accessed from a convenient place (e.g., a university, home, or Internet café) with an Internet connection.

A Web page for your courses is a good starting point and literally the simplest form of a VLE. It offers fast and easy access to publishing schedules, papers, or Internet links (Ansburg, Caruso ,& Kuhlenschmidt, 2003). A more sophisticated approach to online teaching and learning is the usage of a VLE package that includes tools such as electronic communication (e-mail, forums, chat), syllabus, reading lists, and timetables. All of these are manageable without HTML knowledge. It can further provide quizzes, Internet links, assignments (that can be fulfilled by uploading a file to the server or solving a task online), electronic delivery of teaching materials (presentations, documents or sound files), and finally the tracking of students' work (a convenient feature for instructors that automatically checks for deadlines, shows participation rates and plots quiz results).

What VLE Packages Can I Choose From?

The freely available Moodle (www.moodle.org) is a prominent VLE used by scholars all over the world. Currently there are more than 1,200 installations in over 80 countries. Handling is easy and intuitive, community support is great, and there is the possibility of suggesting new features and working on them in the spirit of open source software.

On the commercial side, Blackboard (www.blackboard.com) or WebCT (www.webct.com) are commonly used packages. In most universities, there are ready-to-use installations available. Ask your tech people for access to them.

Advantages and Disadvantages of VLEs

O'Leary (2002) and Perrie (2003) discuss advantages and disadvantages of VLEs. The following issues are a selection of their extensive listings.

Disadvantages

Both instructors and students need training in order to be able to use the VLE. As with every new tool, it takes some time to learn usage and gain confidence. A VLE can become a "dumping ground" for material not designed for online delivery. Filling up a VLE with hundreds of journal articles, long lists of links, or high-resolution pictures/videos hinders accessibility and lowers satisfaction. Often, the advice faculty give to students about how to sign on a VLE or use it is ignored, and the students do not take advantage of the VLE in a course. A VLE does mean additional work in students' spare time, so make the added value transparent to your students and propose reachable goals.

Advantages

Learning materials can be updated with some mouse clicks and take a variety of forms (e.g., text, graphics, audio, or video). Changes in electronic documents are simple; the upload onto the server is done in seconds. This flexibility and speed enables the instructor to quickly react to new demands or changes in the nature of assignments and the rhythm of the course. For example, if a course module must be skipped or greatly condensed because of time constraints, summaries or study guide material can be distributed to students in the course quickly and easily.

Student-student and student-instructor communication can be stimulated. Because of the promotion of contact between peers, students start communicating on a regular basis with each other and personal communication is possible even in larger classes. This is also true for communication with the instructor.

A VLE demands thinking about the structure and aims of a course before providing materials and therefore helps course organization. Each lesson gets its own area in the VLE, and all necessary information for students (a quiz before the lesson, literature to read, or assignments to complete) is together in one place. Preparation for classes becomes more convenient because the teacher has an overview on completed assignments or possible questions raised before the actual lesson. Of course, this assumption of convenience assumes there is a sure way to ensure that students read and think about the material before class.

Clarifying Misconceptions About VLES
The Tech-Myth: An Enormous Amount of Technical Knowledge Is Needed to Work With a VLE.

The truth is that technical knowledge is not necessary to work with a VLE, but of course a little always helps. Many universities offer access to pre-installed VLEs and provide detailed documentation and usage support. The learning curve for administering a VLE is not steep and comparable to learning your word processor.

The Timesaving-Myth: Using a VLE Requires No Additional Time for Class Preparation

The truth is that with a VLE, class preparation may stay the same or even increase (especially at the beginning of usage). Nevertheless with the scope for new teaching possibilities, a favorable forum for communication and transfer between the two, classes become more interesting.

The Uniqueness Myth: Once You Turned to a VLE, There Is No Way Back and Everything Has To Be Done Within This Framework

There is absolutely no need to change an idea or a method that works well. Use the advantages of a VLE and combine them with the advantages of a face-to-face class. The term "blended learning" summarizes this approach. The idea is to combine lectures with case studies, audio, or video recordings is not a new one. Delivering content online is just an ingredient that cannot function well without all the other parts.

The First Time

Experience a VLE for a topic that interests you. Try what you want your students to do and modify your ideas with the insights you get.

Because you are interested in VLEs, why not start at www.moodle.org and learn something about virtual learning environments? Register to the site (it's free!), or login as a "Guest" to the Community Discussion. Take a look at "Using Moodle." You will find tons of messages discussing teaching with VLEs, providing solutions, giving hints on methods, or offering links to interesting Web pages. With these experiences in mind, start your work with small steps. Take a look at your local university's VLE; set up a test course and play around with the features. In most of the common learning environments, templates for courses are already available.

Give students small tasks and talk to them about what they liked or disliked about the VLE. Through this evaluation, you will get valuable insight into their learning process and needs that should be incorporated into your VLE.

Before the Course Begins

There are some things you should do *before* your course starts:

- Set up a forum for general announcements and discussions with a welcome message for your students. State why you think your VLE is a good idea, what students can expect, and what you expect from them (e.g., frequency of access, netiquette for communicating)
- Provide an overview of your course for download. This information could be a simple text file, a table, or a small presentation.
- Refer to your course schedule and update it as soon as there are changes.
- Differentiate online activities from face-to-face meetings.
- Write a quiz for the first two or three lectures. General questions are as good as specific ones with some searching or reading necessary to be able to answer them. This is a nice feature to get students into using your VLE. Ask students to complete the quiz between two lectures and talk to them about their experiences and answers. Pay close attention to students who are silent, and query if they did the assignment. Emphasize the importance of using the VLE.

With these steps completed before your lecture starts, you are well prepared for the "first contact." In your first lecture, give students the URL address of your VLE, and tell them to register and download the schedule for the following weeks. Make slides or a short online demonstration of the registration process and the starting page, and consider also distributing this information on paper. After this first step is done, tell them to try a quiz each week (for the first two or three weeks).

Encourage students to discuss possible answers in the forum. Minimize your comments in these discussions (unless you are addressed directly). Postings from you as an expert virtually "kill" any other communication in the forum.

Give your students time to get used to the new medium, and let them find answers to questions on their own first. You may find that some students are already used to the format from other courses. If there is the need for clarification or comments, you should, of course, respond, but still try to formulate a new question with your answer in order to continue the discussion.

When the VLE is up and running, refer to topics from it in your lecture and vice versa. Provide additional information on what you are dealing with in your lecture in the VLE (e.g. links, papers, and room for discussion).

Even with this slow introduction of the VLE, some students might not participate and may need some selective attention and hints from you. Look at the usage statistics of your VLE from time to time to identify such students. Ask these students in your face-to-face class whether there are technical problems with their Internet access or troubles with the VLE in general.

Following these simple steps makes it easier for students to get used to the medium and more willing to come back to it.

Teaching Scenarios Using VLEs

Lectures

Lectures are a widely used form for teaching large amounts of knowledge in a one-to-many communication style. Because student numbers are often large, three types of VLEs are especially applicable: forum, chat, and Wiki Pages.

Forums and Chats

Forums are asynchronous (writing and reading of messages do not occur at the same time), whereas chats are synchronous (writing and reading takes place at the same time). Three types of communication are possible: one-to-one, one-to-many, and many-to-many. All of these offer a convenient possibility for instructor announcements, discussions, or questions and answers. One can expect more discussion of questions because students are not forced to answer immediately as in class. They can think about an answer, perhaps check with their books, and then respond. In chats, however, urgent problems can be discussed in real time (synchronous).

Wiki Pages

A Wiki Page (a hybrid between synchronous and asynchronous tools) is comparable to a whiteboard on which anybody can write, change, or delete something. All of your students can access the page through a browser without any additional software. They can add news, correct words and structure, or delete unnecessary parts. For the instructor, a detailed list of changes and modifications is available. In a cognitive psychology course, a possible Wiki task could be the collaborative writing of a taxonomy of decisions in everyday life. Such a process normally begins with some brainstorming until a participant starts categorizing. The unique dynamic of collaborative writing opens completely new learning possibilities; I do promise that you will love it! To see what is possible through collaborative writing/ working, look at the largest free online encyclopedia — www. wikipedia.org — completely done within the Wiki system.

Seminar

In a seminar, a small group of students typically read journal articles, prepare group projects or work on presentations.

Shared Work Groups

A shared group work is useful with groups of four to six participants. Groups not only work together in real life but also have an assigned space in the VLE. Students are allowed to share group files and communicate with each other through a forum and to edit the same files and post comments on work of the other group members. Different perspectives on a task can be assigned to different groups. For example, in a personality course, group one tries to identify the advantages of a theory, whereas group two collects critical discussion points. Each group prepares a short summary that is put into the VLE. In an online discussion with the two groups and the instructor, the value of the theory is discussed.

Give a quiz for each new topic in a seminar. A short quiz gives feedback to the students about their level of understanding and reactivates knowledge connected to the new topic. The generation of such quizzes is easy, and with the statistical analysis that is included in most VLEs, a picture of student performance can be drawn.

Scavenger Hunt

This assignment is a good method to teach online information search and search engine usage. The instructor asks a question and gives a hint on a starting point for the students (e.g., a link posted in the VLE or a list of keywords for triggering the search process). Students perform the search online and post answers into the VLE. These answers can be assessed or graded by the other students or discussed later. The advantage of this method is that it is flexible in inducing reading depth; questions about easy-to-find facts elicit only scanning through a text or a Web page, whereas questions with answers hidden in the text force students to read through it more precisely.

Try it on your own! Start your favorite search engine and find answers to the following two questions:

1. What is Brooke Broadbent facing in her paper on the Learning Circuits platform?
2. What is the largest Moodle course Martin (the inventor of Moodle) is aware of?

It should be possible to answer Question 1 with a short search, whereas Question 2 is a little trickier (hint: go to the source of Moodle).

Two things happen while you search. You learn that there is a Web page called Learning Circuits that has a lot of information on teaching methods (on and offline), and you see and use Moodle (welcome to the world of VLEs!).

Lectures and Seminars

The final two methods do not necessarily depend on the number of participants and can therefore be applied to lectures as well as to seminar formats.

Team Building Exercises Combined With Group Critiques

Such exercises enhance communication and help build up team spirit as well as exposure to criticism. Each team works on a part of the whole task and posts results into the team forum (internal use for discussion) or on the course forum (for presenting results). A list that can be accessed by all participants shows the progress of all teams. Each team is then assigned to critique another team. Establish rules beforehand that emphasize the importance of critiquing the method or discussion but not the other group members.

After completion of this process, it can be altered so that all participants discuss the integration of single parts into the big picture. In this phase, feedback from the instructor is particularly useful.

Virtual Laboratories

If an experiment is difficult to conduct at your local university because of limited resources or a lack in laboratory space, a virtual laboratory can give students comparable insights. The discovery of a principle by students increases its validity to them and makes it more knowable.

At the PsychExp Web page (run by Ken McGraw, Mark D. Tew, and John E. Williams and found at http://psychexps. olemiss.edu), various experiments from the areas of perception, reasoning or learning are offered. Each of the experiments can be done online, and data are available for download. Students can try the experiments, analyze data they generated themselves, and get better insight into a method or research idea. Ulf D. Reips offers WEXTOR (http://psych-wextor.unizh.ch/wextor/en/index.php), a "Web-based tool that lets you quickly design and visualize laboratory experiments and Web experiments in a guided step-by-step process." The complete generation of a between- or within-subject design is possible. Data can be collected afterwards on a local server and analyzed with additionally offered tools. As a third example, WebDip (developed by Schulte-Mecklenbeck & Neun, 2005, http://webdip.sourceforge.net) is especially useful for decision-making researchers with an interest in information search.

Conclusion

All of the methods described here should be used interchangeably to meet course objectives. The tools/didactical methods presented and their combination are only one possible solution. Try to find your own blend of traditional and online methods that fit your teaching style best.

What the "Master Blender" of Chivas Regal says about the whisky also is true for teaching psychology: "A master blender's job is creative, artistic, and technical all at the same time. He must be able, using nose and palate, experience and memory, to assess and identify whiskies every day and to understand how they will interact with each other" (Colin Scott, 2004, www.chivas.com/).

Update to Original 2004 Text

In this short update section, I would like to take a look at the development of Moodle during the last four years and introduce two new methods suitable for a VLE: podcasts and videos.

Time flies when one is talking about the Internet. When I wrote this article back in 2003/2004, Moodle was an infant. 1,200 installations in 80 countries were impressive for such a young project but still small compared with the commercial alternatives. These numbers are now the long tale on the current "Moodle Sites" chart at http://moodle.org/stats/. The project has grown dramatically. As of July 2007, 28,407 sites are registered in 175 different countries. The power of Open Source software becomes even more obvious when you consider that the package is available in 75 different languages and the community of registered users moves towards 265,000. Several books are available about course development in Moodle — a good introduction into the usage can be found in Rice (2006).

Not only Moodle has changed; new technologies that are suitable as construction parts in a VLE have been developed during the last years. I would like to mention podcasts and videos as two promising examples. We learn from Wikipedia that the word "podcast" is composed from iPod and broadcast. This technique adds audio to the learning experience. Although the production of a podcast involves quite some investment in software and hardware, the possibility for your students to listen to what you have to say, basically anywhere, holds rather great potential.

Embedding videos into VLEs is another rather new possibility mainly enabled through the much larger bandwidth today. You could explain what "Bounded Rationality" is to your students, but you can also let Nobel laureate Daniel Kahneman do it for you: http://nobelprize.org/nobel_prizes/economics/laureates/2002/kahneman-lecture.html.

The number of ideas for Moodle, podcasts, or videos with content suitable for teaching is growing day by day — the matter of picking from the large selection and adding to the blend becomes the central task today.

References and Recommended Readings

Ansburg, P.I., Caruso, M., & Kuhlenschmidt, S. (2003). Getting started on the Web. In B. Perlman, L.I. McCann, & S.H. McFadden (Eds.), *Lessons learned: Practical advice for the teaching of psychology* (Vol. 2, pp. 81-89). Washington, DC: Association for Psychological Science.

Horton, W. (2000). *Designing web-based training.* New York: Wiley.

O'Leary, R. (2002). Virtual learning environments. Retrieved June 13th, 2007, from http://www.alt.ac.uk/docs/eln002.pdf

Perrie, Y. (2003). Virtual learning environment. *Pharmaceutical Journal, 270,* 794-795.

Rice, W. (2006). *Moodle E-Learning course development.* Birmingham, AL: Packt Publishing.

Schulte-Mecklenbeck, M., & Neun, M. (2005). WebDiP - a tool for information search experiments on the World-Wide-Web. *Behavior Research Methods, 37*(2), 293-300.

Tucker, S. (2001). Distance education: Better, worse or as good as traditional education? *Online Journal of Distance Learning Administration, 4*(4), 1-12.

Part III

Tests and Grading

For the "Grader" Good: Considering What You Grade and Why

BRIAN L. BURKE
Fort Lewis College

COLLEGE GRADING FIRST appeared at Yale University in 1783, primarily for ranking students (Milton, Pollio, & Eison, 1986), and around the turn of the 20th century, Max Meyer's (1908) five-letter (A through F) grading scheme began to gain widespread acceptance. Despite minor modifications such as plus/minus grading, Meyer's system has remained intact, yielding the all-important, enigmatic 400-point scale known as the grade point average or GPA (Milton et al., 1986). Although this grading scheme has received much criticism (e.g., Milton et al., 1986), it is deeply interwoven into the fabric of higher education. Therfore, rather than exploring grading alternatives, educators' efforts are more productively spent reflecting on what we grade and why and particularly on the myriad of seemingly minor grading decisions we face each semester.

How Can We Use Grades to Motivate Students?

For better or worse, grading is a powerful part of the motivational structure of the college course. Instead of fighting this, educators can use it to their advantage by employing grades as "academic carrots." Here are some examples.

Grades as Incentives

If you have students do work, grade it. Grading student assignments increases both the quantity and quality of assignment completion. I created a "textbook detective" weekly reading assignment for my lower-level classes, each worth 1-3 percent (for a total of 20 percent) of the final course grade. As evidence that even minor grade amounts are potent motivators toward assignment completion, the proportion of students who said they read before class increased from 21 percent (before the weekly assignments) to over 50 percent. In similar research, students who were told they would be tested on an assigned article were more likely to read it and scored 20 percent higher on a related quiz than did students who were told the article would be beneficial to class discussion (Marchant, 2002).

Traditional Versus Pass-Fail Grading

Students achieve more academically when they are graded under a traditional system rather than a pass-fail system (Merva, 2003). To maximize student achievement, it is best to grade their assignments with percentage or letter grades. It appears to make little difference in the long run whether you use Meyer's (1908) straight (A-F) letter grades or newer plus-minus grading schemes. Cumulative GPA does not change significantly, although students and faculty generally prefer straight letter grades to plus-minus alternatives (Baker & Bates, 1999).

Grade Inflation

Grade inflation has become a fact rather than a myth, with GPAs increasing on average by 0.6 points from 1967 to 2001, and private schools experiencing grade inflation at a rate that is about 25-30 percent higher than public schools (Rojstaczer, 2003). Despite these trends, many educational experts recommend grading within our current sociocultural context, offering the following analogy as an illustration: Just as you would never pay employees in outdated currency (e.g., colonial coins), you should not grade students using past standards of achievement (Walvoord & Anderson, 1998). In other words, because grade inflation has become the norm, we need to grade our students according to these new (albeit inflated) standards. Whether you choose to do so is, of course, up to you and makes for lively faculty debate.

Increase Students' Control

Increasing perceived control helps students achieve more in school, procrastinate less, and have lower test anxiety (Carden, Bryant, & Moss, 2004). How can you do this using grades?

◆ *Provide frequent, specific grade feedback that helps students make progress.* For example, I routinely allow students to "redo" certain aspects of their exams or papers. I encourage students to hand in their papers early and then allow them to make changes based on my feedback and to resubmit their papers as many times as they want up until the due date. I also inform students in my introductory classes that 10 (out of 40) questions from the midterm will appear on the final so they will get a second chance to answer those questions correctly.

◆ *Use grading arguments as a teaching opportunity.* Motivation can be undermined by students arguing about their grades, but you can turn this into a "teachable moment" and bolster students' sense of responsibility and control. A colleague who teaches in Canada allows students to choose their own grading scheme: He offers "Plan A," wherein students' exams count for two-thirds of their final grade with the remaining third based on broad contributions to the class (including participation, attendance, and effort); or "Plan B," where the entire final grade is based solely on exam performance. Another colleague listens patiently to the student's complaints before calmly outlining the student's current choices (e.g., study hard for the final or drop the class and take it next semester).

What Can We Grade?

To enhance the effectiveness of your grading practices, you should consider what you want your students to learn and then select tests/assignments that assess the learning you value most (Walvoord & Anderson, 1998). Here is a shopping list of gradable items.

Tests, Exams, and Quizzes

According to my survey of Project Syllabus, an online collection of more than 80 refereed syllabi in a variety of psychology courses (http://www.lemoyne.edu/OTRP/projectsyllabus.html), this component counts for about 75 percent of the final grade in introductory psychology classes. It is imperative to think carefully about what levels of knowledge and comprehension we want tests to measure, because 91 percent of college exam questions assess lower-level comprehension rather than more complex thinking skills (Walvoord & Anderson, 1998).

Oral Presentations

Although these assignments compete with other uses of class time, they assess highly valued real-world skills such as organization, preparation, and public speaking. In my upper-division classes, students give an oral presentation each semester. During the presentations, each nonpresenting student completes the same grading rubric that I do (see Walvoord & Anderson, 1998, p. 69, for more on rubrics), including qualitative comments and quantitative evaluations, which are later given to the presenters as part of their feedback. Although I do not "count" these student-graded rubrics as part of the presentation grade, you certainly could. When students judge other students' presentations, they become more critical consumers — and producers — of academic work.

Written Homework

According to my survey, written homework generally comprises 20 percent of final course grades in lower-level psychology classes. Teachers can grade short homework assignments on readings, class questions, practical activities (e.g., students trying out a course concept outside of class and reporting on their experience), lab reports, or even term papers (see below). I regularly give brief homework assignments to entice students to process the course material outside of class. These assignments can provide teachers with valuable feedback regarding what students know and which concepts they may be struggling with.

Term Papers

For term papers to be a meaningful learning experience, teachers should keep in mind two key points. First, when students see the phrase "term paper," their eyes often glaze over, they feel overwhelmed, and they want to minimize their effort and anticipated pain. You can call the assignment something else depending on what you want students to learn: persuasive essay, literature review, thesis paper, etc. Second, as most students enter college lacking the skills to prepare a quality paper, we must teach (and grade) smaller components of these larger assignments, such as a thesis statement, outline, literature review, and/or first draft.

Attendance

Recording attendance, not necessarily grading it, has been shown to increase both attendance and academic achievement in large classes (Shimoff & Catania, 2001). If teachers want to "grade" attendance, what are the alternatives?

+ *Levels of attendance.* Different levels of attendance count for "x" percent of a final grade. For instance, perfect attendance can earn a perfect score (or even extra credit, discussed below), whereas missing 10 percent of classes earns 90 percent of that "x" percent of the final course grade.

+ *Deducting points.* Instead of giving points for attendance as a component of the final grade, you can deduct points for missing class. For example, state in your syllabus that students missing a certain number of classes will have their final grade lowered by "x" points.

+ *Passing requirement.* In many freshman-level courses at Fort Lewis College, students must attend over 80 percent of the classes or receive a course grade of F. This strict policy encourages good study habits (i.e., regular attendance, which is positively correlated with grades) in many foundational college classes.

+ *Other attendance-based incentives.* In my Personality class, I tried an intriguing tactic: Students who missed five or fewer classes all semester would not have to take the comprehensive final exam (there was a noncumulative in-class exam the preceeding week). Students who missed more than five classes would have to take the comprehensive final — and pass it — to pass the course. Attendance rose from 70 percent the previous semester to well over 90 percent.

Class Participation

As grading attendance is a passive assessment (all students must do is "show up"), you may prefer to grade class participation instead, which encompasses attendance but is much more active and dynamic. To foster student engagement, objectively-graded participation — written, oral, and group — comprises one-fourth of a student's grade in my classes. After each class, students hand in a sheet of paper with their name on it and on which they have done one (or more) of the following: answered a series of questions about a film clip shown that day; completed a "freewrite" (i.e., an open-ended, broad question such as the meaning of life or how others have influenced them); taken notes on a cooperative learning activity (group work); or reflected on their score on a questionnaire handed out in class. These are leniently graded Pass/Fail, so students who made a reasonable attempt receive credit for that day's class participation. The student's final course grade reflects how many participation points they "passed" (i.e., 24 out of 30 "participation opportunities" yields 80 percent on the participation component of the final grade). The participation point is forfeited if the student arrives late to class or leaves early for any reason. Since I have put this "lateness policy" into effect, the number of students arriving late in my large classes has decreased dramatically, from 10-20 percent to less than 3 percent per day.

Extra Credit

Eighty-two percent of psychology teachers provide opportunities for "extra credit," mainly in the form of research participation (Palladino, Hill, & Norcross, 1999). For ethical reasons, offering extra credit for participating in research requires that you also offer alternative assignments that students can choose to complete instead (Ethical Standard 8.06 in APA Ethics Code, 2002). Furthermore, allowing students to "make up" grade points by participating in research may send mixed messages: While conveying the importance of a scientific approach to psychology, teachers may be concomitantly undermining the perceived importance of true academic work. Think about whether your own use of "extra credit" matches what you want to communicate to students and modify your grading scheme accordingly.

How Should We Compute The Final Grade?

For a detailed discussion of the strengths and weaknesses of various grading schemes such as weighted letter grades, median grading, and criterion- versus norm-referenced grading, see Zlokovich (2004) or Walvoord & Anderson (1998, pp. 93-104). I focus on several decisions relevant to computing final grades below.

The Decimal Dilemma

In some cases, students' final grades may be decided by a decimal point. My colleague at a midwestern university believes that painting with a wide brush can circumvent the decimal dilemma and advises that exams and papers should count for large amounts of the final grade. His experience is that a teacher who designs a course with many small assignments — each counting for a small portion of the final grade — invites the decimal dilemma. My own approach to avoiding the decimal dilemma uses a "fudge" factor (see below).

"Take-the-Test" and "Do-the-Assignment" Passing Criteria

Although students tend to find the "loopholes" in our grading schemes, we can plug many holes with advanced planning. To encourage my lower-level students to take their comprehensive final seriously, I state that they must pass the final exam in order to pass the course. On average, roughly 5-10 percent of my students fail the final, and, with rare exceptions, most would have failed the class anyway. Thus, my pass-the-final-or-fail-the-course policy has not significantly increased my failure rate, but it has sent the message that the final exam is important.

In some cases, students may not do assignments or take exams depending on how the final course grade is computed. For instance, students may skip the last exam because they have already earned enough points to obtain the grade they want, or they may skip assignments that count for a small proportion of the final grade. To plug these potential loopholes, you can state in the syllabus that if any exam or assignment is not done, the student will fail the course.

Grading on the Infamous "Curve"

My preference is to avoid norm-referenced ("curved") grading systems, as it is fairer to compare students with a predefined standard (such as a rubric) than to the other students who happen to be in their class that semester (Milton et al., 1986). As an example, only the top students are given permission to register for my upper-division Counseling Skills class due to limited space and the advanced nature of the curriculum. Grading on a "curve" would force me to give many A students considerably lower grades than they deserve. In many lower-level classes, however, grading on a "curve" may not be as problematic because students may be normally distributed in abilities and effort.

Make Your Grading Scheme As Clear As Possible

State your grade breakdown explicitly in your course syllabus by using a box or table outlining the specific allotment of points. For whatever reason, many faculty fail to do this. Further, it is often confusing to present the grade breakdown to students solely by "points" that do not sum to 100. Students will have a better understanding of their grade makeup if you use percentage points rather than (or in addition to) a non-percentage-based point system.

How Can We Protect Ourselves From Grade Disagreements?

As my Canadian colleague likes to say, "You need to build self-protection into your grading scheme to avoid burnout, because you are the one who will be doing this for 30 years."

Use "Fudge" Factors

Building a "fudge" factor into your grading scheme will help you avoid arguments regarding "border grades" (i.e., performance on the cusp of two letter grades). A departmental colleague states clearly in her syllabus: "Plus and minus grades are at the discretion of the instructor." I routinely change final grades of 89 percent to either 90 percent or 88 percent without the students' realization by raising or lowering their participation grade (which is 5 percent subjective) by one point, so the posted grade reads 90 percent or 88 percent. In other words, no student ever gets a "border grade" in my classes, because I can always bump them up or down based on their effort and improvement during the semester. In my experience, students are far less likely to complain that their 88 percent was only two points away from an A- grade than they are to complain that they missed the elusive cut-off by a single point.

Teach Students How to Calculate Their Grades

My wife teaches her students (in a math class) to compute their grades by themselves, using a detailed gradesheet handed out on the first day of class. Students are encouraged to use the gradesheet to record (and compute) their own grades throughout the semester. Final grades are posted by letter only, so students do not know whether they received a "border grade" unless they calculate their percentage grade themselves (interestingly, few do). This approach also has the beneficial effect of enhancing student responsibility.

Minimize Unpleasant Confrontations

To avoid unnecessary arguments, do not discuss students' grades by email, telephone or in class. Instead, tell them you will be glad to discuss their grades in the privacy of your office (you can cite The Family Education Rights and Privacy Act of 1974, FERPA). My wife has used this stragegy and finds that many argument-ready students never come to her office hours. Additionally, you can refuse to discuss college grades with a student's parents; I cite FERPA and apologize for not being able to discuss their student's records with them unless the student is present.

Conclusion

Although many educators have criticized college grading as the quintessence of uncertainty and arbitrariness, it is clear that students stand to benefit immensely from a thoughtful and well-constructed grading scheme. It is my hope that you will use this article as you make the detailed decisions that drive much of what our students do, so that you can arrive at an optimal grading system to serve "the grader good."

References and Recommended Readings

American Psychological Association. (2002). *Ethical principles of psychologists and code of conduct.* Washington, DC: Author.

Baker, H.E., III, & Bates, H.L. (1999). Student and faculty perceptions of the impact of plus-minus grading: A management department perspective. *Journal on Excellence in College Teaching, 10*(1), 23-33.

Carden, R., Bryant, C., & Moss, R. (2004). Locus of control, test anxiety, academic procrastination, and achievement among college students. *Psychological Reports, 95*, 581-582.

Marchant, G.J. (2002). Student reading of assigned articles: Will this be on the test? *Teaching of Psychology, 29*, 49-51.

McKeachie, W.J. (2002). *McKeachie's teaching tips: Strategies, research, and theory for college and university teachers* (11th ed.). Boston: Houghton Mifflin.

Merva, M. (2003). Grades as incentives: A quantitative assessment with implications for study abroad programs. *Journal of Studies in International Education, 7*, 149-156.

Meyer, M. (1908). The grading of students. *Science, 28*, 243-250.

Milton, O., Pollio, H.R., & Eison, J.A. (1986). *Making sense of college grades: Why the grading system does not work and what can be done about it.* San Francisco: Jossey-Bass.

Palladino, J.J., Hill. G.W., IV, & Norcross, J.C. (1999). Using extra credit. In B. Perlman, L.I. McCann, & S.H. McFadden (Eds.). *Lessons learned: Practical advice for the teaching of psychology* (Vol. 1, pp. 57-60). Washington, DC: Association for Psychological Science.

Rojstaczer, S. (2003, January 28). Where all grades are above average. *The Washington Post*, A21.

Shimoff, E., & Catania, A.C. (2001). Effort of recording attendance on grades in introductory psychology. *Teaching of Psychology, 28,* 192-195.

Walvoord, B.E., & Anderson, V.J. (1998). *Effective grading: A tool for learning and assessment.* San Francisco: Jossey-Bass.

Zlokovich, M.S. (2004). Grading for optimal student learning. In B. Perlman, L.I. McCann, & S.H. McFadden (Eds.), *Lessons learned: Practical advice for the teaching of psychology,* (Vol. 2, pp. 255-264). Washington, DC: Association for Psychological Science.

Enhancing Learning and Exam Preparation: The Review Session

REGAN A.R. GURUNG
DENISE BORD
University of Wisconsin-Green Bay

EXAMS OFTEN ARE anxiety provoking; the first exam of a course is even more so, as students do not know exactly how the professor tests. For many students, an exam review session is the magic balm that can alleviate exam woes and stress. Many courses favor breadth over depth, and students may be left with only a quick introduction to terms, topics, and theories, without the time to properly digest the material, let alone analyze, evaluate, synthesize, or apply it. Worse, students are pressured to study to do well on the exam versus studying to gain a thorough understanding of the material. This problem is particularly evident in introductory psychology, where voluminous material is covered and assessment is primarily in the form of multiple-choice exams. It is no wonder that many students clamor for review sessions.

Arguments Against Review Sessions

Many instructors avoid holding review sessions because they take time away from valuable lecture or discussion if held during regular class time and are a time consuming additional burden if held outside class time. In addition, publisher-provided study guides, extensive study aids (quizzes, glossaries) available online at textbook sites, and other textbook pedagogical aids may seem to lessen or eliminate the need for them. After all, if a teacher keeps tabs on student learning during class sessions, why have a review? Other instructors fear that students will attend but not participate, thereby not justifying the time spent in the preparation of the session. Furthermore, students may study only what is discussed in review sessions and not everything that could be important. It also is difficult to conduct a review session to satisfy everyone. Students may arrive expecting only to be told what is on the exam (a poor review session strategy for faculty), complain about missing them, and so forth. These arguments notwithstanding, there are many reasons to hold review sessions (and ways to compensate for them taking class time or proving burdensome to hold outside class).

A Case For Holding Review Sessions
Focusing Students on What They Know and Do Not Know

Regardless of how much time is given during class to ensure students are comprehending material, students are often unaware of what they do not know or do not understand until closer to the exam, often a day before it occurs (Gurung, 2005). Review sessions can thus serve to help clarify questions about the materials/notes, make students feel more confident about possible exam material, and provide a valuable metacognitive opportunity to examine what they know and do not know.

Assist in Organizing Course Material

Well-designed review sessions help students organize the material to be studied. Studies show that perhaps emphasis should not be on total study time but on the way students study (Gurung, 2005). A much stronger relationship has been found between test scores and time spent organizing the course content than with total study time (Dickinson & O'Connell, 2005). One way to reach more students in a review session would be to present the material in a different form than it was presented in class. If PowerPoint was the main form of presentation, for example, distribute or use overhead transparencies or handouts of other graphic representations. Conversely, if transparencies of charts and graphs were used, then a PowerPoint presentation could be used to restructure the material and allow students to visualize the material in another way. Students could be encouraged to create their own concept maps or outlines that group and organize the material in a way that best organizes the material in their minds (cooperative and active learning). Even if not done specifically in the review session, if the behavior is modeled for them, perhaps students can leave class and try it themselves while studying.

Support for this suggestion comes from an experiment comparing exam performance between two groups of students who had attended different types of review sessions. One group was provided with a basic question and answer review session, the other, in addition to time allotted for questions, received exam content only in an outline form. All the major concepts were discussed and then time was allowed for questions. Results showed that the students who attended the second type of review session outperformed those in the former (Aamodt, 1982).

Foster Cooperative Learning

Motivation is generally a key factor in the amount students learn. Therefore, it is imperative to discuss ways in which students can be motivated to learn or participate in review sessions. One study showed that student athletes in their freshman year favored a mandatory, weekly afterschool program because it emphasized cooperative learning where they had to collaborate in order to maximize their own and each other's learning. Due to these combined learning efforts, more on-task behavior and higher academic self-esteem, and lower levels of extrinsic motivation ensued (Dudley, Johnson, & Johnson, 2001). Suggestions for review sessions include encouraging more group work and discussion as opposed to the same straight lecture that so many students already receive in class. All of these efforts will have the students working together and getting immediate feedback from one another.

- ♦ Instead of lecturing on what material students should review, give that responsibility to the students. Have them work in groups to create an outline of the highlights from the material that could potentially be on the exam.
- ♦ Encourage students to quiz each other and question each other's thinking and reasoning of the material.

Increasing Student Engagement — Playing Games

Another key factor in the amount of learning students take away from a review session is the level of student engagement. Once again, if a review session is all lecture and the students are not engaged, then the chances of them leaving feeling prepared for the exam are not good. Games can be a good means of engaging all students. The use of one game, *Jeopardy*, was found to be quite useful in facilitating studying before the review session as well as engaging students during it (Gibson, 1991). It is important to keep in mind that this procedure may not work with all classes or even all students. Ideally, students would study at least a little bit beforehand and come to the review session ready to play and learn. However, not all students will find this intrinsic motivation or the extrinsic motivator of winning the game enough to study before the session or to participate upon attending.

- Dividing students into different groups for each review increases competitiveness and engagement with the task.
- Presentation of the material assists students' mastery and flexibility of thinking. Giving students the answer and requiring them to provide the question restructures how they learn.
- *Jeopardy* organizes course content into categories. The five or six categories the faculty chooses for each chapter or module, or themes from the entire course, help students visualize how to organize the material in order to better help them study (Aamodt, 1982).
- Finally, *Jeopardy* helps students think about how questions could be phrased on the upcoming exam and what areas of the material they need to spend more time studying.

Active Learning and Practice — Study Guides and Practice Exams

Study guides provide a means for students to not just memorize the material but to critically think about the main terms and concepts. They can provide practice at multiple choice questions and with retrieval cues that can help with recall on an exam (Dickson, Miller, & Devoley, 2005). In fact, Dickson et al. (2005) compared two introductory psychology courses. One class was required to complete a study guide (e.g., fill-in-blanks, true and false) whereas the other was not. The class that was required to complete the study guide performed significantly better, supporting the notion that study guides do benefit students in classes with multiple choice exams.

- Have students in a review session complete or discuss study guides in groups and then present or teach that section to the rest of the class.

◆ Use the study guide as an outline for creating a *Jeopardy* game as discussed previously or for creating a practice exam from which the students can test themselves.

Practice exams are another review option. Studies show benefits to providing a practice exam if given in the same manner as the actual exam, that is, students should study beforehand and take the practice exam without using notes. Students who participate in such an activity have a better idea of how well they would do on the exam without any further practice or studying, allowing them to adjust their studying accordingly or to focus on areas that need more of their attention (Balch, 1998). Koriat and Bjork support this concept of self assessment, reporting that judgments of learning following study are generally more accurate than retrospective assessments made following an exam (Koriat & Bjork, 2005). Holding a review session in this format also allows students to be engaged in the session because they have the opportunity to answer the questions themselves, either out loud or mentally, before receiving the answers.

Aid in Metacognition

The final and perhaps most important component for review sessions is metacognition, defined as the knowledge of one's knowledge, processes, and cognitive and affective states, and the ability to consciously and deliberately monitor and regulate these (Hacker, Dunlosky & Graesser, 1998). With the ability to assess their knowledge in this way, students can study accordingly. So whichever method of study or presentation is modeled in the review session should include the aspect of metacognition. Faculty could ask students to rate on a 1 to 7 scale how much of the material they know well, what material they need to study more, to predict their exam score if it was taken today, and so forth. A practice exam obviously contains metacognition. Students can see their score on the practice exam, evaluate their confidence with the material, and assess what they know and what they need to study further. Answers to these questions can be encouraged in other forms of review sessions. Through the presentation of the organized subject matter, for instance, students can reflect on which sections of the content they know and which are more elusive. During the *Jeopardy* game, the instructor can encourage metacognition through questions that cause students to think about how they arrived at an answer and why they drew the conclusions they did. Anything to promote critical thinking and self assessment will likely help students when it comes to test day.

Some Pragmatics

How Many Review Sessions?

If an instructor cannot give up class time for a review session it is best to offer at least three to four different times for review sessions spread out over the morning, afternoon, and evening. This scheduling offers students with heavy work schedules (and those taking a full load of classes) sufficient opportunities to attend. If an instructor's class has Supplementary Instruction (SI), or other programs where students are offered tutoring by peers or other campus organizations, it is prudent to dovetail the instructor review with these and to be aware of the nature of these other reviews for students.

When To Offer Review Sessions?

It is optimal to hold a session the day or class period before an exam as it helps students to plan their studying, giving them an idea of what areas they do not understand well. Holding sessions prior to two days before an exam will likely not have a high turnout as most students have not studied yet, and those who attend may be more likely to do so for answers (and possible exam material) rather than questions for clarification.

How Long Should Review Sessions Be?

The best answer is as much time as an instructor can afford. Without a set time period, students can leave early if their questions are answered and the faculty has gone through the agenda (see agenda below). Some students expect a "complete review," a minimum of a 50 minute or 1 hour class session and often are disappointed with less.

What Should the Format and Content Be?

Three rules prevail:
- It is not advisable to use review session time for a simple rehashing.
- A teacher should never introduce new material during this time.
- It is important to remember that active student learning typically is better than passive.

Some faculty think of a review session as a time when they ask what questions students have, and if those attending do not have any, everyone leaves. Often having students ask questions leads to quiet sessions in which students either have not adequately studied or are too shy to talk. On the other hand, having prepared questions can cause students to sit back and passively take notes (with the hope that the review questions are on the exam). A blend of formats is optimal, especially if the leader prepares questions using an engaging, entertaining format as discussed previously (e.g., quiz shows). Some faculty use reviews to clarify and emphasize difficult course material.

Do Students Who Attend Review Sessions Get Better Grades?

In a recent study of student behavior, Gurung and Bord (2007) found that students who attended review sessions scored significantly higher on exams (80 versus 76 points) than did students who did not attend, even after controlling for student GPA. We asked 216 students in an Introductory Psychology class to rate which of six different formats they preferred (lecture, group work, trivia/game show, mock exam, questions/answer format, PowerPoints of main points) for review sessions. Using a 1-5 scale (1 = not at all, 5 = very much so), students preferred mock exam (Mean = 4.06), and PowerPoint (Mean = 3.87) formats the most and group discussion and additional lecturing (2.85 and 2.74) the least. Given that enhancing self-testing and other metacognitive strategies are optimal for learning (Koriat & Bjork, 2005), it is promising to see the mock exam format rated best for review sessions. For students who may just want more material, briefly discussing the research findings (e.g., during classroom discussion of cognitive psychology or memory research or even before the first exam) and providing a rationale for why that format is used will decrease student resistance and increase motivation for it.

Conclusion

Many factors contribute to the success of a review session. However, the fundamental elements that remain the same in any review session are the engagement of all students, the motivation of the students, and the presence of metacognition. If the students are motivated by the instructor to learn the material, they will be engaged in whatever format is used: the *Jeopardy* game, class discussion, or a practice exam. Then with a little prompting the students can assess what they know and that insight will assist them in productive studying, content mastery, and exam performance.

References and Recommended Readings

Aamodt, M. (1982). A closer look at the study session. *Teaching of Psychology, 9*, 234-235.

Balch, W.R. (1998). Practice versus review exams and final exam performance. *Teaching of Psychology, 25*, 181-185.

Dickinson, D.J., & O'Connell, D.Q. (1990). Effect of quality and quantity of study on student grades. *Journal of Educational Research, 83*, 227-231.

Dickson, L.K., Miller, M.D., & Devoley, M.S. (2005). Effect of textbook study guides on student performance in Introductory Psychology. *Teaching of Psychology, 32*, 34-39.

Dudley, B.S., Johnson, D.W., & Johnson, R.T. (2001). Using cooperative learning to enhance the academic and social experiences of freshman student athletes. *Journal of Social Psychology, 134*, 449-459.

Gibson, B. (1991). Research methods jeopardy: a tool for involving students and organizing the study session. *Teaching of Psychology, 18*, 176-177.

Gurung, R.A.R. (2004). Pedagogical aids: Learning enhancers or dangerous detours? *Teaching of Psychology, 31*, 164-166.

Gurung, R.A.R. (2005). How do students really study (and does it matter)? *Teaching of Psychology, 32*, 39-41.

Gurung, R.A.R., & Bord, D. (2007). *What makes review sessions optimal?* Unpublished Manuscript. For a copy, email gurungr@ uwgb.edu.

Hacker, D.J., & Dunlosky, J., & Graesser, A.C. (1998). *Metacognition in educational theory and practice.* Mahwah, NJ: Erlbaum.

Koriat, A., & Bjork, R.A. (2005). Illusions of competence in monitoring ones knowledge during study. *Journal of Experimental Psychology, 31*, 187-193.

A Self-Correcting Approach to Multiple Choice Tests

JOANN M. MONTEPARE
Emerson College

WHEN YOU WERE A student, did you have any of the following experiences?

♦ You dreaded taking multiple-choice tests.
♦ You thought of the right answer after you had handed in the test.
♦ You never went over the exam questions in much detail when it was returned.

As an instructor, have you had any of these experiences?

♦ Students complained they were not good at taking multiple-choice tests.
♦ The average class grade on an exam was much lower than anticipated.
♦ Students did not understand fully material they just studied and it was relevant to upcoming class work.

You are not alone. The bright, engaging, and committed students I teach repeatedly declare that they hate multiple-choice tests and suspect that instructors design them just to trick students. I had the same attitudes as a student. Nevertheless, during my 15 years of teaching, I have used multiple-choice tests extensively despite their "dubious" reputation. However, by appreciating students' concerns, considering the goals of my tests, and thinking more broadly about the test-taking experience, I believe I have learned some valuable lessons about how to enhance the learning potential of my multiple-choice tests. Certainly, designing good questions is an important first step.

Equally, if not more importantly, it is vital to consider what you wish to accomplish with your tests and how your testing format can help achieve your goals. I view tests as an opportunity for learning. Thus, I have developed a multiple-choice testing format fueled by observations that learning is facilitated when students are given opportunities to practice for exams (Balch, 1998), when they are encouraged to thoroughly consider alternative answer options (McClain, 1983), and when they are given immediate feedback about their performance (Friedman, 2002).

I use standard multiple-choice tests in my classes. However, instead of coming to class, taking the exam, and waiting until it is graded to see how they did, students engage in what I call self-correcting. Students come to class prepared as they would be for any other multiple-choice exam, take the exam, and then they take it home and review each question to assess whether their answer was indeed the best one. Students can use class notes, readings, and even discuss the questions with their class-mates (indeed such collaboration is encouraged). As they do so, they can change their answers. Students return exams during the next class period, and the self-corrected version determines their final grade, as follows. For each correct answer (no change) students receive full credit. For each corrected answer (wrong to right), students receive half-credit. Incorrect answers — originally wrong and unchanged, or changed to wrong — receive no credit.

I have observed that students do not just perform better than with a more traditional testing format, but they also learn better. Why? Students no longer see tests as teaching weapons but as learning tools. Certainly students are still concerned about their performance but they feel more in control of the experience and its outcome. As well, they have the opportunity to reflect on the material and correct misunderstandings, making learning subsequent material more efficient. Students also learn how to take multiple-choice tests more effectively and, because tests now require using a variety of skills, they appeal to students with diverse learning styles.

Frequently Asked Questions and Answers

Surely this self-correcting approach invites questions. Here are some frequently asked questions along with my responses.

Can't Students Just Change Their Answers to All the Right Ones and Not Show Any Corrections?

No. Students know that I have a copy of their original answers so I can track any changes they make.

Couldn't Students Simply Take Answers From Other Students Without Participating in Any Constructive Discussion? Doesn't This Set the Stage For More Extreme Cheating Schemes?

Sure. Although students are forewarned that their minds and grades will benefit the most by approaching the test as advised, some will attempt a bit of "social loafing". Some may even contemplate ways to "beat the system". However, I am open with students about the advantages and disadvantages of their test-taking attitudes and strategies, and I hope our discussions provide an opportunity for another level of learning. It is my opinion that cheating behaviors reflect situational and interpersonal demands of the classroom context and are not simply the mark of corrupt or lazy students. Thus, if students are resorting to serious and systematic cheating, then there likely is a bigger issue of concern in the classroom that warrants attention. Moreover, invariably a case arises when a student took a friend's word about an answer that turned out to be wrong, which in turn gave the student pause about taking advice blindly in the future. This is a good lesson to learn.

Don't Students Study Less?

I often have students take a second class with me and ask them to describe their experience with my exams and give advice to new students. Consistently, their advice is to study as best they can for the exams because they are challenging and they need to be prepared. Some students report studying less than usual for the first exam but then realize that the boost that comes from self-correcting is built on starting off on solid ground. Thus, they report putting in more effort for subsequent tests.

Aren't Your Grades Inflated?

No. The means of my exams are a bit higher than in previous classes but not so much that they would be considered inflated. Moreover, there is always a good range of scores. Also, exams generally count for no more than 60 percent of the final grade and so grades become refined and distributed through other class requirements. In comparison to other courses, I often award a lower percentage of As (yet I have very high course evaluations with approving comments about the testing format). Thus, the format does not appear to inflate grades. It does seem to improve morale and attitudes toward tests.

Why Not Just Give Practice Tests?

I think the reflective experience and the opportunity to personally correct errors that this format affords is an important element of the learning process.

Are All of the Exams Self-Correcting?

I typically give three exams. The first two are self-correcting. The final exam is not and it is cumulative.

Why Not Have the Final Be Self-Correcting?

This testing format is directed toward helping students refine their working knowledge and learn how to approach a test to assess that knowledge. I think the cumulative final helps to further these goals by giving students an opportunity to "walk on their own." Besides, getting a corrected version back before final grades must be assigned would be a problem. In addition, the final cumulative exam can serve as an evaluation tool.

What Are the Downsides of the Format?

There are two time-related challenges. I give students back their exams after they have been officially corrected. They are encouraged to use them to study for their cumulative final. This means that prior exams are in circulation and new students may use them. Although I have not seen direct evidence of this, I initially needed to spend extra time generating new questions. However, I now have a large pool of questions from which I can generate exams with ease.

I have teaching assistants who correct exams in classes that average about 60 students, and it takes about two hours to complete the scoring. Instructors with larger classes without assistants may find a manual correcting process difficult, especially if it is used in multiple classes. Perhaps an innovative instructor will discover a technological solution.

Does This Format Work Better for Some Students Than Others?

This is an interesting question about which I wish I had empirical data. Research suggests that "A" students work through question options more than "C" and "F" students (McClain, 1983), and so I would predict that students who may otherwise perform poorly would benefit the most. However, I often find "A" students are very anxious and report that this format relieves some tension, so they have more of an opportunity to "digest" rather than to "regurgitate" information. Thus, I would like to believe this format offers something of benefit to all students.

If you have read to this point, you are hopefully now interested in seeing how the process operates in more detail. Described below are a few suggestions for writing multiple-choice questions, how to implement this format, and some advice about how to approach this testing experience.

Writing Good Questions

There are a number of excellent resources for more detailed information about how to construct good multiple-choices tests (e.g., Clegg & Cashin, 1986; Renner & Renner, 1999; Sechrest, Kihlstrom, & Bootzin, 1999). I have found the following suggestions especially useful.

- ◆ Write questions that make use of a variety of thinking skills. The taxonomy suggested by Bloom (1956) and presented in Table 1 is a useful guide.
- ◆ Write questions that reach for more complex thought processes as often as possible. Include words that point to the kind of thinking you expect the question to utilize.
- ◆ Present the problem in the simplest form with precision and clarity, and the options in the simplest form possible. Do not repeat material unnecessarily.
- ◆ Do not include unnecessary descriptive material in questions and answers. It does not contribute to interest or complexity, and it just adds confusion and reading time.
- ◆ Use options such as all of the above or none of the above with caution. Avoid implausible or absurd distracters in the options. They make questions easier to answer simply because the option can be easily rejected. However, an amusing or entertaining option used

sparingly can break tension and remind students about the constructive goal of the test.

♦ Avoid giving irrelevant clues to the answers such as length of clue (longest is often the correct option) or inconsistencies in grammar. Avoid the use of specific determiners (all, never, and always suggest incorrect options whereas usually, sometimes, typically, and maybe suggest correct options).

♦ If a question contains controversial material, cite the author whose opinion is stated. For example, "according to class lecture..." or "as stated by Rosenthal..." This citation helps reduce subjective interpretations.

Thought Process (Simple to Complex)	Learning Activity	Words to Use in Questions
Knowledge	Remembering facts, terms, concepts, definititions, principles	Define, list, state, identify, label, name, who? when? where? what?
Comprehensions	Explaining or interpreting the meaning of material	Explain, predict, interpret, infer, summarize, is an example of, can account for
Application	Using a concept of principle to solve a problem	Apply, solve, show, make use of, modify, demonstrate
Analysis	Breaking material down into its component parts to see interrelationships and hierarchy of ideas	Differentiate, compare and contrast, distinguish __ from __, how does __ relate to __, why does __ act this way?
Synthesis	Producing something new or original from component parts	Design, construct, develop, formulate, imagine, create, change
Evaluation	Making a judgment based on established set of criteria	Appraise, evaluate, justify, judge, which would be better?

Table 1

Implementing the Self-Correcting Format

Students should be given an exam with instructions and questions similar to those below with a separate numbered answer sheet. Be sure names are recorded on all materials.

Sample Instructions

Welcome. Keep in mind that exams in our class are treated as opportunities for learning. To this end, complete this exam by circling the best answer to each question on your exam. Do not skip any questions. Also, record your answers on the separate sheet that has been provided and hand it in before you leave. When you are done, take your exam home and review each question using your notes, text, and discussions with classmates (be sure to consider each answer option thoroughly). If you wish to change an answer, indicate it in the space provided on the exam. Use this space only for changed responses. Return your corrected exam at the next class meeting. Late exams lose the self-correcting option.

Sample Question Format

A researcher interested in the impact of story telling on the development of social norms asks a fifth grade teacher to read stories to his class involving cooperation. Another teacher reads stories involving competition. The researcher then codes the amount of sharing children from each class displayed during their lunch periods. In order to avoid experimenter bias in the coding of behaviors, what should be done?

    a. The children from each class should wear different colored tee shirts.
    b. The children should be observed over the course of several lunch periods.
    c. A researcher unfamiliar with the manipulation should record the behaviors.
    d. The researcher should read the stories to the children in each class.

Corrected answer: _____

Advice for the Instructors

Listed below are points to keep in mind when using this format in your class.

Take a Few Trial Runs

At the same time, take seriously the need to think the format out fully to avoid confusion and frustration. It might be useful to pilot test the format on a quiz rather than a lengthy exam.

Expect Students to Be More Willing to Voice Their Reactions to the Test

When I enter the classroom on the day exams are due, students are always chattering about the test. I purposefully acknowledge the energy – even tension – in the room to remind students that the test was designed to promote this activity. Some will ask to discuss certain questions. I ask them to make note of the questions, and after exams are handed in, I address ones about which several students have concerns. Each instructor will need to decide how to gauge these discussions, bearing in mind the importance of modeling constructive dialogue. I keep discussions short and focused. Time for additional discussion is offered after class or via e-mail. Students also sometimes include written comments on their exams. These comments have been invaluable in helping me craft better questions.

Describe Your Exam Philosophy in Your Syllabus

Explain your testing philosophy to students on the first day of class and how it is reflected in your exam format. The notion that tests can be opportunities for learning will be a novel perspective, and you can use it to generate discussion and interaction. You might begin by asking who does and does not like multiple-choice exams, and why they do or do not. Drawing on their responses, explain why you selected this new format. Students do not need to know all of the procedural details at this point, a preview should be sufficient. A short time before the first test, go over the testing procedures and how students should prepare for the exam.

Do Not Make Tests and Questions More Difficult Than Usual

Keep in mind the goal of your test as a learning tool as you decide what material to include.

Learn to Write Good Multiple-Choice Tests

If your tests are learning tools, they should represent the material to be learned and ask questions that encourage students to use a range of thinking skills.

Sometimes Students Will Change an Answer From Correct to Incorrect and They Will Want to Know What Happens if They Do This

This is typically treated as a wrong answer, and no credit is given. It has been my experience that this happens for one of three reasons:

♦ The question was "bad," and several students got it wrong in this manner. If this appears to be the case, you can drop the question or accept the answers that make sense with hindsight.

♦ Students simply listened to their friends and changed their answers without further scrutiny. In this case, students need to be reminded how to approach reviewing their answers and relying on more reliable sources.

♦ A student reads too much into the question. Sometimes students get questions wrong for the right reasons because the instructor failed to realize how a question might be perceived or interpreted by someone with a different level of knowledge. These instances can be dealt with on a case-by-case basis and by the instructor's assessment of the student's knowledge of the topic and question at hand. This is a benefit because you get to know your students better as learners.

Students Should be Told in Advance How These Details Will Be Handled

Given the opportunity, this format provides for students to obtain a better grade through self-reflection and revision, typical complaints about the wording of questions, trick questions, lack of information, and the like are often significantly reduced. Moreover, when I do encounter debates about questions (which will happen), I remind students that this type of involvement was something the test intended to inspire. Having students more actively in charge of their learning experience is uplifting for them as well as the instructor.

Look at Students' Exams and Answer Sheets Before They Leave Class

A few students will fail to record their answers on both the exam and the answer sheet. It is important that all materials are completed.

Return Exams So Students Can Go Over Corrections

It is important that students have the opportunity to review their exams after they have been formally corrected. I give exams back with incorrect and partial credit answers marked as well as an answer sheet with correct answers to the entire exam. If you give a cumulative final, it will be helpful for students to use previous exams as a study tool. Suggest to students that they mentally rewrite questions so that they point to different answers as a way to test themselves. Also point out that it is not sufficient for students to merely learn what the right answer was. They need to know why they were wrong so that when they see a different question on the same topic they will be able to answer it correctly.

Advice for Students

For optimum effectiveness, it is important to inform students about how to approach and manage the testing format. Emphasize these points.

Tests Are Another Opportunity for Learning. Take Full Advantage of Them

Tests can help you identify your strengths and weaknesses in the learning context. Try to reframe your perspective on taking tests by approaching this new format with a serious and open attitude. Use this opportunity to take a closer look at how you handle tests — what you study, how you organize time, how you answer questions — and what skills you can polish for future use.

Study as You Would for Any Multiple-Choice Test

Do not put too little effort into preparing for the test because you have an opportunity to review and revise your answers.

Do Not Answer a Question Hastily With the Expectation That You Can Change It Later

If you want a good grade, you need to get full credit for as many questions as you can. This means trying your best to work through the question accurately the first time.

Consensus Does Not Insure Accuracy

If you are working with classmates and they say a particular answer is correct, but it is different from your answer, be sure they have satisfactorily justified their choice and that you understand and accept fully the reason.

Conclusion

You may think of issues or concerns I have overlooked in designing the testing format I have described. If so, I hope you will share your thoughts with me. I also hope you will share with me the experience of developing other new and novel ways to enhance the potential for learning in your classes.

References and Recommended Readings

Balch, W.R. (1998). Practice versus review exams and final exam performance. *Teaching of Psychology, 25,* 181-185.

Bloom, B.S. (Ed.). (1956). *Taxonomy of educational objectives: The classification of educational goals: Handbook I, cognitive domain.* New York: Longmans, Green.

Clegg, V.L., & Cashin, W. E. (1986). *Idea paper no. 16: Improving multiple-choice tests.* Kansas State University: Center for Faculty Evaluation and Development.

Friedman, H. (2002). Immediate feedback, No return test procedure for introductory courses. In R. Griggs (Ed.). *Handbook for teaching introductory psychology* (p. 132). New York: Erlbaum.

McClain, L. (1983). Behavior during examinations: A comparison of A, C, and F students. *Teaching of Psychology, 10,* 69-71.

Renner, C.H., & Renner, M.J. (1999). How to create a good exam. In B. Perlman, L.I. McCann, & S.H. McFadden (Eds.), *Lessons learned: Practical advice for the teaching of psychology* (Vol. 1, pp. 43-47). Washington, DC: Association for Psychological Science.

Sechrest, L., Kihlstrom, J.F., & Bootzin, R.R. (1999). How to develop multiple-choice exams. In B. Perlman, L.I. McCann, & S.H. McFadden (Eds.), *Lessons learned: Practical advice for the teaching of psychology* (Vol. 1, pp. 49-56). Washington, DC: Association for Psychological Science.

Dealing With Students Missing Exams and In-Class Graded Assignments

Baron Perlman
Lee I. McCann
University of Wisconsin-Oshkosh

TEACHERS OFTEN BECOME more aware of students' out-of-class activities than they might wish. Announcements and memos from the dean of students inform about sporting teams and their games and tournaments, forensics, service learning conferences, community-based work, and the like. And teachers quickly become familiar with student lifestyles and illnesses: mono, strep throat, hangovers, the opening of deer and fishing seasons, quilting bees, family vacations, and their family mortality statistics. The relationship between exams and mandatory in-class work and the death of students' cousins and grandparents is so high it should be a concern of the National Center for Disease Control. Given all this, it is a certainty that students will miss exams and other required activities. What is a teacher to do?

If you want to hear colleagues express frustration, ask them about make-up exams and assignments. Despite knowing intellectually that such absences will occur, teachers hope and pray, even in public institutions, that all of their students will take exams as scheduled. Alas, such prayers are rarely answered, and teachers are faced with the practical issues of keeping track of students who miss exams and assignments, as well as managing make-ups.

All of our advice, except that related to ethics, should be read through the filter of the type of institution where you teach and the types of courses you teach and how large they are. For example, at a small liberal arts school, where teaching is a faculty member's primary responsibility, more time may be spent with students who miss exams or assignments, and more creative (time consuming) alternatives may be practical as compared with someone teaching classes of 300 or 500 or more in a Research I institution.

Ethics

Teachers are not to cause students harm; we must treat them fairly and equitably, and they must be allowed to maintain their dignity (Keith-Spiegel, Whitley, Balogh, Perkins, & Wittig, 2002). Whatever your procedures are for students who miss exams and required in-class work, they must be equitable, providing students equal chances to earn a good grade by demonstrating equal knowledge. The hard part may be balancing academic rigor and accountability for what students are to learn with a fair and manageable process for those who miss required exams and assignments.

Make-Up Exams

These should not be more difficult than the original test but must be, as best as you can design, alternate forms of the same exam. Exam banks that accompany texts make designing such alternate forms of multiple-choice tests relatively easy, and colleagues teaching two or more sections of the same course in a semester, who give alternate forms of exams, are often a good source of advice on this matter. Be thoughtful about the following:

- ◆ An essay make-up exam may be unethical if regular exams are multiple choice or short answer (or vice versa), as students must study differently and they may be more difficult.
- ◆ An oral exam may "punish" students who do not think well on their feet or are more socially anxious.
- ◆ Scheduling make-up exams at inconvenient or undesirable times may express your frustration, but you or someone else will have to be there at the "inconvenient" time also, and such arrangements raise issues of foul play.
- ◆ It may be inequitable to students who meet all course requirements to allow their peers to do extra credit or drop their lowest grade instead of making up a missed exam.

In-Class Assignments

The same considerations exist for students who miss in-class required presentations, or other graded work. If possible, students who were to present should be given opportunities to make up the assignment using the same grading criteria.

Planning Ahead

Spell Out Missed Exam Procedure in Course Policies

No matter how well you teach or what inducements or penalties you impose, some students will miss exams and required class activities. Good educational practice argues that you plan for this reality as you design your course, not two days before (or after) your first exam. You want as few surprises as possible once the course begins.

Put Your Policies in Your Syllabus

Have a section in your syllabus on exams and other graded work. Specify your policies and procedures if students know in advance they will be absent, or how to notify you if, for whatever reason, they were absent, and any effect, if any, absences will have on their grade.

Keep Your Policy Clear and Simple

Before finalizing your syllabus, ask a few students to read your make-up policy to determine if it can be easily understood. If your explanation of what students are to do in the case of missing an exam, and how their grade is affected, is not easily understood, revise it. In developing your policy, do you want students to:

- ◆ Notify you if they know they will miss, preferably at least 24 hours in advance, and give you the reason? Talking with you before or after class offers the best opportunity to provide feedback if the reason is questionable, to work out alternatives, and so forth. E-mail also can be useful.
- ◆ Notify you as soon as possible after missing an exam or required assignment and give the reason? Again, in person or e-mail work best.
- ◆ Present a letter from an authority (e.g., physician) documenting the reason? Keep in mind any student can "forge" such documentation or manipulate it in other ways, (e.g., "Fred came to see me complaining of

a severe headache").

♦ Have their grades lowered if their absence is not "acceptable" (e.g., overslept vs. seriously ill)? How will you decide what is acceptable? Our experience suggests that "legitimate" reasons for absence include, but are not limited to illness of the student or a close relative, accident, court appearance, military duty, broken auto, hazardous weather, and university activities (e.g., athletics, forensics).

Policies Should Reflect the Nature of the Exam or Graded Assignment

If you are teaching an introductory course and each module largely stands alone, it may be appropriate for students to make up a missed exam late in the semester. But if you want students to demonstrate knowledge or competency on an exam or assignment because future course material builds on that which comes earlier, you want to give the students much less time to make up the missed work.

Common Policies

A common procedure is for the teacher, teaching assistant, or departmental secretary to distribute and proctor make-up exams during prearranged times (Perlman & McCann, in press). You might also consider allowing students to take make-up exams during exam periods in other courses you are teaching.

Make Your Policies Easy to Implement

To maintain your sanity and keep your stress level manageable, you must be able to easily implement your policies. For example, even if you, a secretary, or a graduate student distribute and proctor make-up exams, problems can arise. For example:

♦ The secretary is ill or on vacation, or you are ill or have a conference to attend. You never want to change the time make-ups are available to students once these are listed in the course syllabus. Have backups available who know where make-up exams are stored, can access them, and can administer and proctor them.

♦ Too many students for the make-up space. Investigate room sizes and number of rooms available. You may need more than one room if some students have readers because of learning disabilities.

- Students often forget there is a common make-up the last week of the semester. Remind them often, and announce this policy on class days when students are taking an exam, as this may be the only time some students who have missed a previous exam come to class.

Encourage appropriate, responsible, mature behaviors. Take the high road and let students know how they "should" behave. For example, one colleague includes this statement in the syllabus:

I expect students to make every effort to take required exams and make course presentations as scheduled. If you know in advance you will miss such a requirement, please notify me. If you are ill or other circumstances cause you to miss a required graded activity, notify me as soon as possible.

One of our colleagues states in her syllabus for a psychology of aging class, "It is very bad form to invent illnesses suffered by grandparents!" By giving students exemplars on how to behave appropriately, you can then thank them for their courtesy and maturity if they follow through, positively reinforcing such behaviors.

God Lives in the Details

Always err on the side of being "concrete." If a make-up exam is at the university testing center, tell students where the testing center is. If you or a secretary hold make-up exams in an office, you may want to draw a map on how to get there. It is not uncommon for students to fail to find the office at the time of the exam and wander around a large university building.

Students Who Miss Exams

You have a variety of alternatives available on how to treat students who miss a scheduled exam. Select those that fit your course and the requirements of learning students must demonstrate.

Requiring Make-Up Exams

If you collect all copies of your multiple choice or short answer exams, you may be able to use the same exam for make-ups. Our experience is that it is extremely rare that students deliberately miss an exam to have more time to study, whereas asking peers about specific exam questions more commonly occurs. Your experiences may be different. However, if you put exams on file at the university testing center, and students can take them weeks apart, you may want different forms. If you have concerns, you will need to prepare an equivalent, alternative form of the regular exam, as is often the case for essay tests.

Using Procedures Other Than a Make-Up Exam

Some faculty have students outline all text chapters required for an exam, use daily quiz scores to substitute for a missed exam, use the average of students' exams to substitute for the one missed, score relevant questions on the comprehensive final to substitute for the missed test, or use a weighted score from the entire comprehensive final substituted for missed exam. Some teachers just drop one test grade without penalty (Buchanan & Rogers, 1990; Sleigh & Ritzer, 2001). Consider whether students will learn what you want from various alternatives and whether this work is equal to what students must demonstrate on exams before adopting such procedures. If your course contains numerous graded assignments of equal difficulty, and if it is equitable for students to choose to ignore a course module by not studying or taking the exam, you should consider this process.

Other teachers build extra credit into the course. They allow all students opportunities to raise their grades, offering a safety net of sorts for those who need to "make-up" a missed exam by doing "additional" assignments such as outlining unassigned chapters in the text.

Scheduling Make-Ups

Pick one or two times a week that are convenient for you, a department secretary, or teaching assistant, and schedule your make-ups then. Some faculty use a common time midway through the semester and at the end of the semester as an alternative.

Students Who Miss Other In-Class Assignments

Allowing students to demonstrate learning on nonexam graded assignments can be tricky. Such assignments often measure different kinds of learning than exams: the ability to work in groups, critical thinking as demonstrated in a poster, or an oral presentation graded in part on professional use of language. But you do have some alternatives.

Keeping the Required Assignment the Same

If the assignment is a large one and due near the end of the semester, consider using an "incomplete" grade for students who miss it. Alternatively, students can present their oral work or poster in another course you are teaching, if the content is relevant and time allows it. The oral required assignment also can be delivered just to the teacher or videotaped or turned in on audiotape.

Alternative Assignments

As with missed exams, you can weigh other assignments disproportionately to substitute for in-class graded work — by doubling a similar assignment if you have more than one during the semester, for example. The dilemma, of course, is not allowing students easy avenues to avoid a required module or assignment without penalty. For example, oral assignments can be turned in as written work, although this may negate some of the reasons for the assignment.

When we asked colleagues about alternatives for missed in-class graded assignments (as compared with exams), almost everyone cautioned against listing them in the course syllabus. They felt that students could then weigh the make-up assignment versus the original and choose the one that gave them the greatest chance of doing well and the least amount of anxiety (in-class presentations often make students nervous). They recommended simply telling students that arrangements would be made for those missing in-class required graded work on a case-by-case basis.

Students Who Miss the "Make-Up"

On occasion, students will miss a scheduled make-up. Say something about this event in your syllabus, emphasizing the student's responsibility to notify the instructor. We recommend that instructors reserve the right to lower a student's grade by "x" number of points, or "x" letter grades. If you place exams at a university testing center, you may not find out the work has not been made up until the course is over, leaving you little choice but to give the student an "F" on that exam or assignment.

When the Whole Class Misses a Required Exam or Assignment

On rare, but very memorable, occasions the entire class may miss an exam or assignment. For example, both authors have had the fire alarm go off during an exam. After a bomb threat cleared the building during his exam, the campus police actually contacted one author to identify whether a person caught on camera at a service station was a student calling in the bomb scare. (It was not.) The other author experienced the bomb squad closing a classroom building during finals week due to the discovery of old, potentially explosive, laboratory chemicals. Of course, the blizzard of the century or a flood might occur the night before your exam. What is a teacher to do?

The Exam or Graded Assignment Must Be Delayed

Prepare beforehand. Always build a make-up policy into your syllabus for the last exam or student presentation in a course. Talk with your department chair or dean about college or university policy. State that if weather or other circumstances force a make-up, it will occur at a certain time and place. This forethought is especially important if you teach at a northern institution where bad winter weather is not unusual. For exams and assignments during the semester, the policy that works best is to reschedule them (again, stating this in your syllabus) for the next regular class period. Call attention to this policy early in the semester, and post it on your course website. The last thing you want to do is call or e-mail everyone in the class to tell them an exam has been cancelled.

An Exam or Graded Assignment Is Interrupted

Graded assignments such as oral presentations are easily handled. If time allows, continue after the interruption; if not, continue the next class period or during your designated "make-up" time.

If something interrupts an exam, ask students to leave their exams and answers on their desks or hand them in to you, take all personal materials, and leave immediately. A teacher can easily collect everything left in most classes in a few moments. Leave materials on desks if the class is large, or be the first person back to the room after the interruption. Fire alarms, bomb scares, and the like usually cause a lot of hubbub. Only if you have a lengthy two- or three-hour class, with time to allow students to collect themselves and refocus and no concern about their comparing answers to questions during the delay, should the exam be continued that same day or evening.

If the interruption occurs late in the class period, you might tell students to turn in their work as they leave. You can then determine how you want to grade exams or the assignment, using pro-rated points or percentages, and assign grades accordingly.

If the interruption is earlier in the hour, the exam will have to be delayed, usually until the next class period. With a multiple-choice exam, we advise giving students the full (next) class period to finish their exams. If you are concerned about students comparing questions they have already answered, you will have to quickly develop an alternate exam.

A teacher's decisions are more complicated if the exam is short answer or essay. Students may have skimmed all essay or short answer questions before an interruption. Will they prepare for those questions before the next class period? What if some students only read the first essay question but do not know the others they must answer? Preparing an alternate exam may be feasible, but students need to know you will do so, so they do not concentrate their studying on specific topics you will not ask about.

We know that such class interruptions are rare, but they can wreak havoc with students and teachers, be stressful, and raise issues of fairness that echo throughout the rest of the course. We advise teachers to talk with colleagues, and we have found a department brown bag on the topic fascinating. Your colleagues may have some creative and sound advice.

Summary

A teacher needs to plan ahead. Take some time to think about what it means for you and students who miss required in-class work. A little preparation can save a lot of time and hassle later in the semester. Students deserve and will appreciate policies that are equitable and manageable.

Author's Note: The authors are interested in how teachers deal with missed or interrupted graded in-class work (and their horror stories). Contact us with your ideas and experiences at perlman@uwosh.edu.

References and Recommended Readings

Buchanan, R.W., & Rogers, M. (1990). Innovative assessment in large classes. *College Teaching, 38,* 69-74.

Carper, S.W. (1995). Make-up exams: What's a professor to do? *Journal of Chemical Education, 72,* 883.

Davis, B.G. (1993). *Tools for teaching.* San Francisco: Jossey-Bass.

Keith-Spiegel, P., Whitley, B.G.E., Jr., Balogh, D.W., Perkins, D. V., & Wittig, A.F. (2002). *The ethics of teaching: A casebook* (2nd ed.). Mahwah, NJ: Erlbaum.

McKeachie, W.J. (2001). *Teaching tips: Strategies, research, and theory for college and university teachers* (11th ed.) Boston: Houghton Mifflin.

Nilson, L.B. (2003). *Teaching at its best: A research-based resource for college instructors* (2nd ed). Bolton, MA: Anker.

Perlman, B., McCann, L.I., Dettlaff, D.M., & Palladino, J.J. (2003). Teacher evaluations of make-up exam procedures. *Psychology Learning and Teaching, 3*(1), 36-39.

Sleigh, M.J., & Ritzer, D.R. (2001). Encouraging student attendance. *Observer, 14*(9), 19-20, 32.

Part IV

Teaching Challenges

Evaluating and Improving Your Teaching

WILLIAM BUSKIST
JARED KEELEY
JESSICA IRONS
Auburn University

FACULTY WHO TAKE teaching seriously will inevitably ask themselves one especially important question: "How can I become a more effective teacher?" The question implies that an individual's teaching, no matter how good it may be, can become better. Its answers can lead to improved teaching practices and student learning. Faculty may have been "perfect" in the classroom yesterday, but it is almost impossible to string together a week of such days, let alone an entire semester's worth.

Pondering this question is the first step on the road to helping one's students learn more effectively. The second step is to seek answers, which often leads faculty to explore two effective teaching strategies: reading the teaching literature and seriously evaluating their teaching. A review of this literature is beyond the scope of this article, although good starting points include McKeachie (2002), Perlman, McCann, and McFadden (1999, 2004), and the journal *Teaching of Psychology*. Instead, we focus on different strategies for evaluating teaching.

Why Evaluate Teaching?

The evaluation of teaching has two purposes. The first, called formative evaluation, is aimed squarely at improving teaching. It centers on two questions:

- ♦ "Am I an effective teacher?"
- ♦ "How can I become a more effective teacher?"

Formative evaluation emphasizes personal reflection and growth and finding new and better ways to convey information to students, helping them to appreciate the subject matter, and empowering them to become self-learners.

The second purpose emphasizes accountability and addresses two questions:

- Am I a good teacher relative to my peers?
- Is my teaching an aid or hindrance to tenure, promotion, and merit salary?

This type of evaluation, called summative evaluation, entails processes that often make faculty uncomfortable — after all, professional status and money are on the line.

Interestingly, both types of evaluation entail many of the same assessment processes. Indeed, if teachers focused primarily on becoming better teachers through formative evaluation, they would have little concern about the outcome of summative evaluation. For this reason, we emphasize formative evaluation.

What Is To Be Evaluated?

When teachers consider teaching and its evaluation, they generally think about what they do in the classroom: the clarity of lectures, the extent to which they engage students in discussion, and so on, but teaching involves more than classroom performance. Faculty prepare for hours in advance of class, create and grade tests, and meet students during office hours, to name but a few teaching activities. Students should learn something about our subject matter because of what faculty do outside of class, and the outcome of this process also is relevant for evaluation. Thus, a broader perspective on teaching encompasses four dimensions: course organization and preparation, classroom performance, approachability and availability, and assessment of student learning.

Course Organization and Preparation

In evaluating teaching, faculty often overlook course organization and preparation in deference to classroom performance. How they prepare and organize their courses should drive what they actually do in the classroom and thus what students learn. Ideally, courses are organized around what faculty wish their students to learn. Once this issue has been addressed, teachers must entertain three other important questions to evaluate course preparation and organization:

- Are these outcomes appropriate to the level and content of the course?
- How do I connect these outcomes with specific course activities?
- Will these outcomes stimulate intellectual growth and enjoyment of learning?

Answers to these questions should appear in the class syllabus and unambiguously convey student-learning outcomes, the nature of the subject matter, the teacher's orientation to learning (e.g., lecture versus a greater emphasis on student involvement), the kinds of classroom learning activities practiced, how students will be engaged, the approach to assessing student learning, and classroom management practices.

Classroom Performance

Being able to communicate psychological knowledge clearly and enthusiastically is one key to effective student learning, and therein rests a secret to becoming a truly great teacher. Becoming a successful teacher hinges on teachers' abilities to establish rapport, an interpersonal dynamic that increases the likelihood that students will pay attention to and understand the teacher's message. Essential aspects of building rapport include, among other things, learning students' names, using relevant examples, treating students respectfully, using appropriate humor, and starting and ending class on time (Buskist & Saville, 2004). Clearly, the quality of faculty teaching transcends their disciplinary knowledge — it includes their personal characteristics as well.

Approachability and Availability

Faculty demeanor in the classroom influences their students' willingness to initiate one-on-one contact with them outside of class. If students perceive faculty to be supportive and caring, they are likely to perceive them as being approachable outside the classroom. Questions to ask to assess approachability and availability include:

- What is my interactive style with students?
- Do I encourage students to meet with me?
- Am I in my office during my office hours?
- Do I pay attention to my students when they are talking to me?
- Do I respond promptly and courteously to student phone calls and e-mail?

Assessment of Student Learning

Perhaps the most overlooked factor in the evaluation of teaching is how faculty assess students' learning. This oversight is perplexing because the ultimate goal of teaching is, of course, to facilitate student learning. Teachers need a logical rationale for assessing how well they are accomplishing this goal, and contemplating possible answers to several questions helpful in their teaching:

- What is the relation of my assessment protocol to my student learning outcomes?
- How frequently do I assess student learning and why?
- What formats do I use to assess student learning and why?
- How promptly do I return graded materials?
- How much feedback do I provide students regarding their learning?
- What procedures do I use for remediation of poor student performance?
- Are my assessment and grading procedures fair?

Teachers' approaches to assessment of student learning ideally should reflect their commitment to helping students become more effective learners. Sometimes, however, the nature of exams and other graded assignments reflect teachers' needs. The less time faculty spend grading and providing feedback, the more time they have for other responsibilities and interests. In the latter case, however, students might learn less than they might otherwise. Moreover, this approach may impede student learning by offering only limited feedback on their performance.

Choices in Assessment of Teaching

A teacher's preparation and organization, classroom performance, approachability and availability, and assessment of students' learning are all fair game for evaluation. The question, of course, is how to go about the assessment process.

Who Provides Evaluative Data?

Students are the most common source of evaluative information. When most faculty think "teaching evaluation," they imagine their students completing a survey at the end of the semester. Although the validity of data from student evaluations has been questioned (e.g., Greimel-Fuhrmann & Geyer, 2003), they remain a primary source assessment tool. Nonetheless, additional forms of assessment, such as self-assessment and peer review, provide useful supplemental information that is not available from student evaluations such as feedback regarding developing appropriate student-learning outcomes, developing and revising syllabi, understanding the relationship of student-learning outcomes to student learning, and creating effective formats for assessing student learning.

When Should the Evaluation Be Conducted?

Evaluations are most commonly given at the end of the semester, providing a snapshot of teaching over the entire course. The disadvantage to this approach is that it provides no opportunity for a teacher to address problems that may exist in the class, and so students' learning and enjoyment of the course may suffer.

The alternative is to evaluate one's teaching earlier in the semester. That way, the end-of-the-semester evaluation can be used, in part, to gauge how successfully a teacher has resolved previously identified problems. Students frequently voice their appreciation of a teacher's willingness to incorporate their suggestions into improving their classroom learning experience.

Some faculty may wish to evaluate their teaching more than once or twice a semester, even weekly, but students may find such frequent assessment obsessive and annoying. Instead, faculty may wish to solicit feedback from students when trying a new technique or demonstration for the first time or when making other modifications to teaching. Two or three evaluations per semester will likely provide ample data for assessing your teaching effectiveness.

Although most institutions typically have a required instrument for end-of-the-semester evaluations, developing one's own questions for an earlier evaluation allows a faculty to tap student perceptions that the required instrument might overlook. Such "home grown" evaluations also allow questions that faculty deem especially critical to understanding their approach to teaching. For example, if teachers incorporate specific types of learning activities not reflected on the institutional instrument, they may wish to develop a few questions to address their effectiveness.

What Assessment Techniques Might Be Used?

Student feedback, self-assessment, and peer evaluation may be used alone or in combination. Data can be collected several ways ranging from the typical paper and pencil course evaluations containing forced-choice and open-ended items to in-class learning assessment techniques (e.g., the muddiest point, in which students express to their teacher, in writing, the point or points that they had the most difficulty understanding during lecture — see Angelo & Cross, 1993) and student focus groups.

Paper and pencil evaluations provide global information regarding overall teaching effectiveness and typically center on teacher qualities. In-class learning assessment focuses on what students learn during any given class period. Lastly, randomly selected students may be brought together outside of class to meet in focus groups to provide feedback on specific aspects of a course — clarity of lectures, testing and grading procedures, and so on. Focus groups also are useful in providing feedback regarding a teacher's rapport with students and building stronger rapport.

Self-assessment techniques provide valuable data regarding all aspects of one's teaching and, like student evaluations, exist in several formats including informal reflection after class, course portfolios, videotape analysis, teaching journals, review and revision of a teaching philosophy statement, and comparisons of student learning outcomes to actual student achievement. Informal reflection involves assessing how well faculty perform on any given day. One useful metric for these judgments is the extent to which students appear attentive and engaged in class discussion. "Great" days, of course, are those in which students generate many questions, comments, and insightful remarks.

Daunting as it may seem, watching oneself on videotape captures how one's teaching personality, mannerisms, and communication skills appear to students. This process is extremely beneficial in identifying problems and strengths in classroom delivery.

Writing about one's approach to teaching as well as actual teaching experiences creates opportunities for reflection — the chance to lead an "examined life" as a teacher. Contemplating both what one does well and poorly as a teacher may provide insights into strategies and actions to undertake to become better.

Finally, determining how well students achieve course objectives permits a teacher to identify ways to help students achieve these goals in the future. It also provides a means of assessing how well course preparation and organization help students achieve these outcomes.

Peer evaluations most often take the form of a departmental colleague visiting a class and providing feedback. However, peers may also analyze video of colleagues' teaching, review syllabi (e.g., learning outcomes, content, and grading procedures), and review their philosophy of teaching statement and teaching portfolio.

Most faculty members' departmental peers have not been trained in formal analysis of teaching strategies and style, so they may not provide concrete suggestions for teaching improvement. However, departmental peers do know psychology and often provide helpful suggestions regarding course content, demonstrations and examples of specific topics and issues, and the relationship between student learning objectives and content. Peers also know the student population and can offer insights on how best "to reach" specific segments of that population.

Keep in mind that because faculty have ongoing social relationships with their colleagues, they may be reticent to share their true feelings. In other words, it may difficult to find a peer willing to provide completely honest feedback on one's teaching.

Using Evaluative Data to Improve Teaching

Some general guidelines provide a comprehensive approach to evaluating and improving teaching. Global feedback such as "You're a really good teacher" or "You need to be more approachable" is not helpful in identifying ways to improve teaching. Seek feedback that emphasizes specific behaviors to change or to be adopted. For example, "You did a great job getting our term papers back to us two days after we turned them in" or "I sent you an e-mail three days ago and you still haven't answered it" identify precise behavior a teacher may need to change or maintain.

More Feedback Is Better Than Less

The more feedback teachers gather, the more information they will have with which to assess their teaching effectiveness. Although the numerical information from objective portions of student evaluations may provide the overall impression that students have of one's teaching, faculty should gather as much specific written commentary from students and peers as they can. This information is useful in interpreting the numerical data and is more likely to pinpoint specific aspects of teaching that are meritorious or need improvement.

Take Context Into Consideration

As faculty examine their teaching strengths and weaknesses, they should consider context as a potential factor influencing their teaching and students' motivation to learn. Sometimes students' willingness to study for classes succumbs to their extracurricular interests. If so, a teacher's task is to inspire students to adopt more effective study habits. At other times, teaching may not be appropriate for the course level, especially for new faculty who, coming right from graduate school or a postdoctoral experience, demand that undergraduates read nearly as much as they did.

In addition, some courses faculty teach may be prerequisites for other courses in the curriculum. Colleagues who teach these other courses expect students to have particular knowledge and skills when the prerequisite course is completed.

Seek Consistent Themes Within and Across Evaluative Measures

Examine evaluative information as a gestalt and look for patterns. Skillful teachers reflect on both critical and positive themes, and link valid criticisms — those comments that identify teaching deficits — to specific teaching behaviors they can adjust to improve teaching effectiveness. They do not focus on criticism to the extent that they overlook what is positive about their teaching. Experienced teachers know that the key to teaching enhancement is to refine what they do well while simultaneously improving what they do less than well.

Ignore the Lone Voice of Gloom

No matter how good student teaching evaluations may be, they are rarely perfect. Most faculty have at least one student with whom they do not connect despite their best efforts. Sometimes they do not know that this student exists until they receive their teaching evaluations and read a comment such as: "You are the single worst teacher I have ever had. I should get my tuition back for this class." For most faculty, this comment is the one that they will remember best, even when the bulk of the other commentary is glowing. Ignore student commentary that is mean spirited, or harshly critical, or offered without any evidence to substantiate it, especially when it is provided by a single student. This advice also applies to extremely positive commentary.

Use Multiple Measures

Do not limit evaluation to a single source (e.g., students) or a specific teaching dimension (e.g., classroom performance). Faculty have the best chances of learning about their teaching and improving it if they gather evaluative information from both students and peers on all aspects of their teaching.

Develop an Individualized Assessment Plan for Each of Your Courses

Adopt a reflective approach to the evaluation of teaching. As teachers prepare syllabi for next semester, they need to consider how they will assess their teaching in each of their classes. Faculty may wish to incorporate evaluative plans involving their students into their syllabi. Those who do so often contact colleagues, prior to each semester, whom they wish to visit their classes or review their syllabi and presentation materials. Such advance planning allows teachers to design assessment strategies tailored to providing specific information about their teaching strengths and weaknesses.

Conclusion

Teaching is a dynamic blend of performance art and science that is influenced in no small measure by the teacher's personality, the students' motivation, and institutional vagaries. Becoming a better teacher requires understanding how these factors interact and change over time—and such comprehension seems most likely to be prompted by intentional and reflective evaluation and analysis.

References and Recommended Readings

Angelo, T.A., & Cross, K.P. (1993). *Classroom assessment techniques: A handbook for college teachers* (2nd ed.). San Francisco: Jossey-Bass.

Benassi, V.A., & Seidel, L.F. (2006). Using student evaluations to improve teaching. In W. Buskist & S.F. Davis (Eds.), *Handbook of the teaching of psychology* (pp. 279-284). Malden, MA: Blackwell.

Buskist, W., & Saville, B.K. (2004). Rapport-building: Creating positive emotional contexts for enhancing teaching and learning. In B. Perlman, L.I. McCann, & S.H. McFadden (Eds.) *Lessons* learned: Practical advice for the teaching of psychology (Vol. 2, pp. 149-155). Washington, DC: Association for Psychological Science.

Greimel-Fuhrmann, B., & Geyer, A. (2003). Students' evaluation of teachers and instructional quality: Analysis of relevant factors based on empirical evaluation research. *Assessment & Evaluation in Higher Education, 283,* 229-238.

Knapper, C., & Cranton, P. (Eds.). (2001). *New directions for teaching and learning: No. 88. Fresh approaches to the evaluation of teaching.* San Francisco: Jossey-Bass.

Lewis, K.G. (Ed.) (2001). *New directions for teaching and learning: No. 87. Techniques and strategies for interpreting student evaluations.* San Francisco: Jossey-Bass.

McKeachie, W.J. (2002). *McKeachie's teaching tips: Strategies, research, and theory for college and university teachers* (11th ed.). Boston: Houghton Mifflin.

Perlman, B., McCann, L.I., & McFadden, S.H. (1999). *Lessons learned: Practical advice for the teaching of psychology* (Vol. 1). Washington, DC: Association for Psychological Science.

Perlman, B., McCann, L.I., & McFadden, S.H. (2004). *Lessons learned: Practical advice for the teaching of psychology* (Vol. 2). Washington, DC: Association for Psychological Science.

Acknowledgments

We thank the following individuals for their thoughtful comments on an earlier draft of this article: Barney Beins, Brian Burke, Drew Christopher, Amy Hackney, Katherine Kipp, and Loreto Prieto.

Getting the Most Out of Your Student Ratings of Instruction

JOHN C. ORY
CHRISTOPHER P. MIGOTSKY
University of Illinois at Urbana-Champaign

"After reading them I usually go home and very aggressively mow my lawn."

"I'll stay up a few nights wondering who could have said that about my teaching."

"I start revising some class presentations right after seeing them."

How do you react after reading your student ratings of instruction? How is it that professionals with advanced degrees who have taught for decades can be devastated or elated based on a comment or two from an 18-year-old student? But we are. We are because it is difficult to discover, or to be reminded, that what we do in the classroom is not always working or appreciated by ALL of our students. Well, get over it. Rather than fret, stew, deny, blame, curse, or whine, we can accept student ratings as valuable feedback and consider how we can use them to improve our teaching. We offer the following suggestions for getting the most out of your student ratings.

Choosing Rating Content

We begin by reminding you that what is put into ratings at the start influences what you can get out of them. We are referring to both the content of the rating forms and their administration. Of the 90 percent of the nation's colleges and universities using student ratings (Seldin, 1999), many of them allow faculty to select some, or all, of their rating items. So what content should be included on your rating forms? First, we believe the only "content" inappropriate for student comment is "course content." Students seldom know if course content reflects dated or current thinking in the discipline. We believe it is appropriate to ask for student opinion about other topics. Although their responses may not reflect state-of-the-art thinking on teaching styles, methods, or assessment techniques, students have legitimate opinions of what affected their behavior, attitudes, and learning in a course.

We recommend assessing areas of both perceived strength and weakness. Obviously, if you only ask questions about your strengths you learn nothing of your weaknesses. However, if you place too much emphasis on your weaknesses you may negatively bias the students' overall impression of you and your course. If your results are for your eyes only, it may be more useful to concentrate on your weaknesses; however, when they are shared with departmental administrators, you certainly do not want a total review of your mistakes. If you can, choose items that make the results useful for personal improvement while keeping in mind the ratings may be used by others to judge the overall quality of your teaching.

Administering Rating Forms

To get honest and useful feedback from your classes, your students must take the evaluation process seriously. This will not happen when you hand out the rating forms saying, "OK class, it is time again to fill out those insipid university forms." In addition to following the standard directions provided by your institution, we recommend taking a few minutes to inform students how you use their responses to improve your teaching and how the institution uses them for personnel decisions, such as promotion and tenure. Hopefully, you also follow the first part of this recommendation each time you begin a new course. We cannot stress enough how much instructors can bolster the credibility and validity of student ratings by beginning each semester with a brief statement explaining how the course was changed based on student ratings from previous semesters. By doing so, a favorite English professor of ours would say you are showing, not telling, the students how much you value their responses.

Interpreting Results

After your ratings have been collected and you have submitted student grades, the campus testing office returns your ratings results to you. We cannot keep you from quickly scanning your numbers and making that first emotional impression somewhere around "they loved me" or "they hated me." But we can ask you to take a deep breath, pause a second, and begin to carefully inspect and interpret the results as you would data collected in your research.

First, inspect the data. Make sure you understand how the results are reported. This sounds obvious, but our office is consistently dismayed by questions asked by some of our more experienced professors. Some faculty go years without understanding the norm group to whom their ratings are compared or continually confuse item frequencies with percentages. Be certain your results are accurate. Both professors and testing offices make mistakes. Check to see if a large number of students skipped any of the items, that an appropriate number of forms were completed, and if you were compared with the appropriate norm group. We remember once having the most confusing conversation with an agitated professor only to find out he mistakenly switched the forms in his two courses.

Second, interpret the data. Begin by thinking holistically and attempt to see the "big picture." What did the majority of students say about your teaching? Do not ignore the outliers, but do not allow a few isolated opinions color the consensus. If class averages are reported as means rather than medians, remember the impact of extremely high or low ratings, especially if the N is small. Look to the standard deviation as a measure of consensus to spot areas of disagreement among students.

Many institutions provide a relative comparison of your results with those of other faculty teaching across the campus or within your department. No doubt by now you have learned two things involving student ratings. First, students are rather generous with their ratings; second, your colleagues are a tough comparison group. At our university, a mean course rating of 4.0 (on a five point scale) places you around the 50th percentile for the campus! These results are typical for most colleges and universities.

Think absolutely as well as relatively. Be challenged by how your ratings stack up with other faculty, but do not lose sight of their absolute interpretation. The average class rating of 4.0 mentioned above can be relatively viewed as near the bottom half of faculty ratings, but it can also be "absolutely" interpreted as one scale point below excellent. Try not to be so discouraged by a less-than-desired normative comparison that you lose sight of the good aspects of your teaching. Try to identify these good (and bad) aspects of your teaching by looking for trends or patterns of responses across rating items within a course.

You can also use within-course comparison to interpret your open- and closed-ended item responses. Use responses to a few global or general closed-ended rating items to understand the impact or importance placed on the complaints or praises offered in the students' open-ended comments. For example, assuming a five-point scale was used for a global item such as, "Rate the overall teaching effectiveness of the instructor," place the completed forms into two stacks with ones, twos, and threes in one stack, and the fours and fives in the other. Read the open-ended item responses for the two stacks to identify the common complaints about your teaching coming from students who rated you low and from those who gave you high ratings. Most likely, the complaints made by low-rating students reflect areas of your teaching with the greatest impact on student perceptions and thus, require the most attention for your teaching improvement. You can follow the same procedure to analyze your teaching strengths.

Comparing Results Over Time

In addition to comparing your ratings results within a course, you can look for trends and themes across courses and time. Start with the "global" items that measure "overall" teaching quality. Have your general ratings gone up? Down? Stayed the

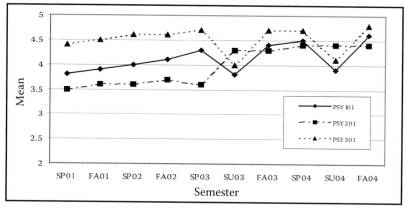

Figure 1 : Student Rating of Instructor Effectiveness

Association for Psychological Science

same? It helps to graph the results of these overall items. In just a few minutes, faculty can create a basic Excel spreadsheet that will display the results of their student ratings over time. As they say, a "picture is worth a thousand words." Figure 1 shows results over time for three example courses.

You can see in the figure that each course improves over time, but the weakest course in the beginning (PSY201) improves the most especially starting in summer 2003. This dramatic increase may be connected to your intense reworking of the course or to curricular changes in prerequisite courses. There seems to be a drop in the two other courses each summer. Is that due to a different summer cohort of students or your preparation for those summer courses? Graphing allows you to easily spot trends that might have been missed when looking at individual course ratings.

Likewise, you can chart specific items of interest to you. If you are working on your course assessments, you might want to select and chart the results of items related to "fairness of grading," "difficulty of exams," or "exams matched course content." By looking at specific items over time you can see whether your changes have made a difference in how students perceive your course.

Comparing Pieces of Evidence

Although it is vital to reflect on your ratings over time, you also need to think about how your ratings compare to other pieces of evidence, such as peer observations or classroom videotapes. If peers visit your classroom and discuss their observations, check to see if their comments fit with past student ratings. If you are videotaped, look at the tape in context of past student evaluations. Are you teaching at a very abstract level without examples? Are you asking for, but not answering, student questions? Peer or teaching center staff observations or classroom tapings are excellent ways to get extra feedback about your teaching. We sometimes think of student ratings as an "x-ray of your teaching." They show the bones but can sometimes miss the meat seen through other methods of teaching evaluation.

Do you ever utilize classroom assessment techniques like "minute papers" or "muddiest points" discussed by Angelo and Cross (1993)? The idea is to have students reflect and briefly write about what the most important points were in the day's class session or what the most confusing/muddiest point was that day. These classroom tasks not only help students think about course content, but they offer glimpses into what is working or not working in your teaching. This information can be used to validate student ratings from the past and anticipate ratings at the end of the current term. Likewise, we encourage faculty to administer an early informal feedback form to students in the middle of the semester. It does not need to be a formal survey, but rather a small set of rated and open-ended questions about how the course is going and what the students think could be changed to improve the course. This collection of early feedback reinforces your interest in student input and desire to use it to improve the quality of your teaching and your students' learning this semester.

Seeking Help From Others

Now that we have you fully engaged with interpreting your current student rating results, we strongly encourage you to look to others for help in diagnosing what students are saying about you and the course. Do not rely only on your interpretation of the results. This bears repeating ... do not go it alone! Doctors often seek second opinions and so should professors. Connect with a trusted colleague who is considered to be a good teacher to review your student ratings. Just like you, your colleagues are wondering how to best interpret their student ratings. By seeking them out, you will open the door to a dialogue about teaching that can support and motivate both of you to improve. People are curious about what ratings and comments their peers receive; so seeking a second opinion from a peer can capitalize on this curiosity to determine what is "normal." Most likely, they will find something you missed. If not, they will at least confirm that you are on the right track in how you interpreted your own ratings. It is a win-win situation.

Another second opinion can come from teaching center staff who are *paid* to assist you — take advantage of their service. These individuals can provide both a campus and research perspective to your ratings and student comments. They have seen hundreds of teaching evaluations at your institution and know the current research on teaching and learning. Not only can they say, "Like others in your college, your students are concerned the classroom assessments do not match what is being taught," but they can also offer practical suggestions for addressing the concern. It is one-stop shopping that offers help interpreting results, a campus and research literature perspective, and suggestions for improvement. Cohen (1980) has shown that consultation is a critical element in utilizing student feedback for instructional improvement. Without consultation, feedback can easily be misinterpreted or ignored. If needed, teaching center staff can also help in collecting more feedback to supplement your existing student rating data.

Making Changes to Your Teaching

So now you have scrutinized your most recent student evaluations, compared them with past evaluations and supplemental feedback, and even spoken with others about your teaching evaluations. What is left to do? Student ratings, and other assessments, are virtually worthless unless they lead to improved teaching. The next step is to utilize the results to build on strengths and remediate weaknesses. Avoid saying, "The students are probably right about needing more course structure and organization." Say it and *then* use it to develop a plan of attack. *Start slowly.* It is daunting to tackle all the areas that might need attention all at once so begin by taking some small steps. Pick one or two spots you would like to improve and then return to your teaching center staff or colleague to discuss possible improvements. Possible changes include your syllabi, lesson plans, tests, papers, group assignments, grading feedback, office hours, etc. Once those changes are implemented, tell your current students about the changes you have made and the rationale behind them. From what we hear from students, they will appreciate your thoughtfulness and willingness to use their ratings to make course changes.

Interpreting and using student feedback is a cyclical process. Once you have completed one cycle (selected good items, reviewed your results, talked to a colleague, compared results with other data, planned and implemented instructional changes) it is time to start again by selecting new items for your next course evaluation. Do not forget to tell your current students how you have used student advice to improve the course over time. This continual improvement sequence engages students in an important feedback loop and increases the validity of the student ratings themselves.

We have given you a lot of advice on how to effectively and efficiently use your student ratings of instruction. In the end, it is up to you to change. We believe students can provide truthful and honest information that allows faculty to improve their teaching. Please do not dismiss student feedback. Mow your lawn aggressively if needed, but return to those student rating forms, find an area that needs attention, and plan a change. In most cases you do not need to make a major overhaul, only a few steps in the right direction. Over time, these small steps will add up to huge improvements. Of course, those improvements will show up in higher future student ratings!

References and Recommended Readings

Angelo, T.A., & Cross, K.P. (1993). *Classroom assessment techniques: A handbook for college teachers.* (2nd ed.). San Francisco: Jossey-Bass.

Braskamp, L.A., & Ory, J.C. (1994). *Assessing faculty work: Enhancing individual and institutional performance.* San Francisco: Jossey-Bass.

Centra, J.A. (1993). *Reflective faculty evaluation.* San Francisco: Jossey-Bass.

Cohen, P.A. (1980). Effectiveness of student-rating feedback for improving college instruction: A meta-analysis of findings. *Research in Higher Education, 13,* 321-341.

Seldin, P. (1999). *Changing practices in evaluating teaching: A practical guide to improved faculty performance and promotion/ tenure decisions.* Bolton, MA: Anker.

In Pursuit of the "Perfect" Lecture

JEFFREY S. NEVID
St. John's University

THOUGH I HAVE BEEN
lecturing in the college classroom for more than a quarter
century, I leave each lecture thinking how I can improve my
presentation the next time around. After all, perfection is more
a Platonic ideal than a realized state. Yet, on the other hand,
there is something to be said for the "relentless pursuit of perfection," to borrow a phrase from an advertising copywriter. So
let me offer some modest suggestions to guide the relentless
pursuit of perfection, based upon both personal experience in
the classroom and research on effective learning.

Many college instructors spend more time lecturing in the
classroom than in any other professional activity. Yet few instructors have had formal training in the skills of lecturing, and
few researchers have directed attention to studying skills and
processes that make lecturing an effective form of instruction.
Still, every Tuesday and Thursday or every Monday, Wednesday,
and Friday when college is in session, legions of instructors organize their notes, march into their classrooms, stand in front
of a class, and engage in a practice as old as the institution of
college itself.

The traditional lecture form of instruction has taken its
knocks in recent years. Critics contend that the traditional lecture encourages passive learning that is limited to absorbing
information — mostly facts and figures — or regurgitating material recycled from the accompanying textbook. Other commonly
heard complaints include the charge that the traditional lecture
fails to encourage students to engage in personal reflection, critical analysis, or hypothesis testing. This article does not call for
replacing lectures, but rather offers some modest proposals to

help improve them.

Lecturers seem to "get it" from both ends. Students complain when a lecture sticks too closely to the textbook, and they complain even louder when it departs too far from the assigned readings. Effective lecturers expand upon textbook material rather than merely regurgitating it. I recall a professor who taught child psychology exactly the same way for more than 20 years, until one day a student excitedly entered the professor's office.

"Professor, professor," the student shouted. "You'll never guess what I found in the library." The professor looked up to see a familiar book that was ragged-edged from age. The student continued, "I found this in the back of the stacks. I can't believe it. It's word for word from your lectures. Someone stole your lecture notes and put them in a book!"

I do not know whether the professor ever corrected the student about who had stolen what from whom, but the point is that the effective instructor does not lecture from a book.

Effective Learning in the Classroom

The metaphor of the brain as a sponge that absorbs information passively does not square with modern research on the learning process. Though some forms of implicit learning may occur without conscious effort, the kind of explicit learning required in college courses depends upon active engagement of processes of attention, encoding, and elaboration of newly acquired information.

We can conceptualize effective learning in terms of four key steps I call the "Four Es":

- ♦ Engaging Interest
- ♦ Encoding Information
- ♦ Elaborating Meaning
- ♦ Evaluating Progress

These four principles of effective learning apply to learning in many forms, including textbook learning, classroom learning, and distance learning. Let me offer some suggestions for applying these principles to the classroom.

Engaging Interest

Experimental studies provide strong support for the importance of focused attention in the encoding process (e.g., Iidaka, Anderson, Kapur, Cabeza, & Craik, 2000). Divided attention impairs learning, possibly because it interferes with the deeper, elaborative processing needed for effective learning. Experimental findings support the common-sense belief that students are unlikely to encode and retain key points from lecture material if they are not paying full attention.

In a youth culture in which attention spans may be limited to MTV-length videos — or even shorter screen changes in video games — a lecturer who reads prepared notes for a 45- or 50-minute period will likely be lecturing to an ever-shrinking audience of attentive listeners. The flow of the lecture, not just the content, needs to be thought through in advance to both capture and hold student attention. To maintain attention, we can divide the lecture into briefer segments, with each lasting no longer than perhaps 15 minutes. As student attention spans tend to become shorter over the course of a lecture (Beard & Hartley, 1984), the length of the segments should follow suit, with longer segments at the outset followed by shorter segments as the lecture progresses. We should also change pace every few minutes, such as by moving from the desk to the podium, using overhead transparencies, and so on (Murray & Murray, 1992).

Encoding Information

Attention may be a prerequisite for effective learning, but attention alone does not ensure that encoding will occur. Students must have the knowledge structures to enable them to incorporate and integrate new knowledge. They also must be able to identify material that is important to encode and retain. However, students may mistake the chaff for the wheat when they take notes in class and come away learning facts and figures but miss important concepts.

Signaling is a pedagogical device for identifying material that is important to learn (Nevid & Lampmann, 2003). Textbooks include a variety of signals, such as bolded key terms, topic headings, and extracted and highlighted concepts, also known as concept signaling, to help students focus attention on information they need to encode and retain. Evidence shows that cuing important lecture points in the classroom can increase retention of cued material (Scerbo, Warm, Dember, & Grasha 1992). Written cues are much more effective than spoken cues. Lecturers can help students encode important lecture points by using visual aids, such as bullet points in PowerPoint slides, to highlight key content.

PowerPoint is not the only means of signaling key lecture points. The use of the chalkboard, whiteboard, or overhead transparencies to outline lecture topics serves dual functions as advance organizers and as signals for key concepts. Distributing copies of visual displays enables students to focus their attention on the meaning of the material rather than on note taking. The use of visual aids can shift the student's responsibility from simple note taking to deeper levels of processing.

Taking five minutes at the start of the lecture to preview topics to be covered can prime students to recognize important material in the lecture. Titsworth (2001) found that embedding verbal signals during the lecture — such as, "Now I will present a definition of ..." and "Now we will turn to consider the theories of ..." — improved student retention of lecture material. The use of a lecture guide can also help students focus on important content the lesson covers (Ogden, 2003).

Elaborating Meaning

Deeper processing through elaborative rehearsal leads to more enduring memories. Elaborative rehearsal involves focusing on the meaning of the material rather than mere repetition or rote rehearsal. For example, we may be more successful in learning the principles of classical and operant conditioning when we relate these principles to examples from daily life.

Many students process information superficially. They may hear the instructor's words and copy down a few choice remarks but may not become engaged in thinking or reflecting about the material in a way that would promote deeper processing.

To promote effective learning in the classroom, instructors need to engage students and help them become more active learners. Lectures need not be passive forms of instruction, but instead can incorporate interactive components that encourage students to take a more active role in the learning process. The use of interactive exercises, small group projects, demonstrations, and other active learning exercises help maintain students' focus as well as provide opportunities to strengthen and expand upon new learning.

The most effective lectures engage students by promoting active learning through student participation, use of rhetorical questions, small group activities, self-assessment exercises, and informal debates. The lecture format is a group experience, which means it has great potential for encouraging participation and interaction among group members (Pence, 1996-1997). The effective lecturer facilitates participatory activities to involve students more directly in the learning process. For example, lecturers can

Association for Psychological Science

structure cooperative learning exercises in which pairs or groups of students work together on solving a problem.

Readers interested in active learning and interactive learning exercises may consult sources on problem-based learning (Willis, 2002), active learning and cooperative learning (Keyser, 2000), collaborative learning (Giordano & Yost Hammer, 2000), teaching tips (McKeachie, 2002), and active learning (Sutherland & Bonwell, 1996).

The process of elaborating meaning applies more broadly to presenting information in different formats so that learning does not become context-bound. New learning is a fragile commodity that needs to be strengthened and reinforced if it is to lead to enduring memories. In other words, lecturers should not assume that because concepts are clearly conveyed in class, they will be processed and imprinted in long-term memory.

As with textbook writing, lecturers need to think creatively in presenting information repeatedly through different channels, both to elaborate and to reinforce new learning. A combination of learning aids, including written materials like handouts, visual aids like PowerPoint or overhead transparencies, and interactive classroom exercises can broaden the learning environment beyond listening and note taking.

Effective lecturers come prepared with a clear outline, well-organized notes and learning aids — such as videotapes, PowerPoint slides, CD-ROMs, and so on — but they do not give a speech or read from their materials.

Evaluating Progress

Many instructors do not discover until exam time that students are not "getting" major points. Leaving 5 minutes at the end of the lecture to briefly review key points and present study questions helps students evaluate their progress. Instructors may also use interim quizzes to identify students who may be struggling at an early point in the semester.

Handouts

Handouts complement and reinforce oral learning that occurs from lecturing. The use of handouts also minimizes the need for rote note taking. Lecturers can leave large margins and spaces in their handouts so that students are able to write additional notes or sidebars to these materials. Handouts can include related information, embedded examples, and study questions, all of which help students encode important points and elaborate the meaning of the material.

Speed and Pacing

A common complaint among students is that instructors go too fast (Forrester-Jones, 2003). Beginning instructors often find their rate of speech increasing in proportion to their anxiety level. Experienced instructors may find themselves racing the clock to cover all the intended lecture material. I find it helpful to prioritize information beforehand. I include information I feel I must cover in the first part of the lecture and hold more expendable material until the end. I often carry over to the next lecture the material I was not able to cover. We need to bear in mind that any learning that occurred earlier in the lecture is likely to be forgotten in a rush to cram as much information as possible into the end of the class.

Graph It!

Graphs and diagrams are powerful and intuitively appealing ways of presenting scientific findings and illustrating relationships between variables. Evidence supports the learning benefits of visual displays. For example, a recent study showed that learning was enhanced when information about the human circulatory system was presented in diagram form as compared to presenting the same information in narrative form (Ainsworth & Loizou, 2003).

Conclusion

We should use psychology to teach psychology. We can apply concepts and principles developed and honed in research studies of learning and memory to become more effective instructors and to assist our students to become more effective learners.

References and Recommended Readings

Ainsworth, S., & Loizou, A. (2003). The effects of self-explaining when learning with text or diagrams. *Cognitive Science, 27*, 669-681.

Beard, R.M., & Hartley, J. (1984). *Teaching and learning in higher education* (4th ed.). London: Paul Chapman.

Benjamin, L.T. (1991). Personalization and active learning in the large introductory psychology class. *Teaching of Psychology, 18*, 68-74.

Forrester-Jones, R. (2003). Students' perceptions of teaching: The research is alive and well. *Assessment & Evaluation in Higher Education, 28*, 59-69.

Giordano, P.J., & Yost Hammer, E. (2000). In-class collaborative learning: Practical suggestions from the teaching trenches. *Teaching of Psychology, 26*, 42-44.

Iidaka, T., Anderson, N.D., Kapur, S., Cabeza, R., & Craik, F.I.M. (2000). The effect of divided attention on encoding and retrieval in episodic memory revealed by positron emission tomography. *Journal of Cognitive Neuroscience, 12*, 267-280.

Keyser, M.W. (2000). Active learning and cooperative learning: Understanding the difference and using both styles effectively. *Research Strategies, 17*, 35-44.

McKeachie, W. J. (2002). *McKeachie's teaching tips: Strategies, research, and theory for college and university teachers* (11th ed.). Boston: Houghton Mifflin.

Murray, J.P., & Murray, J.I. (1992). How do I lecture thee? *College Teaching, 40*, 109-113.

Nevid, J.S., & Lampmann, J. L. (2003). Effects on content acquisition of signaling key concepts in text material. *Teaching of Psychology, 30*, 227-229.

Ogden, W. (2003). Reaching all the students: The feedback lecture. *Journal of Instructional Psychology, 30*, 22-27.

Pence, H.E. (1996-1997). What is the role of lecture in high-tech education? *Journal of Educational Technology Systems, 25*, 91-96.

Scerbo, M.W., Warm, J.S., Dember, W.N., & Grasha, A.F. (1992). The role of time and cuing in a college lecture. *Contemporary Educational Psychology, 17*, 312-328.

Sutherland, T. E., & Bonwell, C.C. (Eds.). (1996). *Using active learning in college classes: A range of options for faculty.* San Francisco: Jossey-Bass.

Titsworth, B.S. (2001). The effects of teacher immediacy, use of organizational lecture cues, and students' notetaking on cognitive learning. *Communication Education, 50*, 283-297.

Willis, A.S. (2002). Problem-based learning in a general psychology course. *Journal of General Education, 51*, 282-292.

Effective Teaching When Class Size Grows

Todd Zakrajsek
Central Michigan University

CLASS SIZES SEEM TO increase every year, through the combining of course sections into a few large sections or through class size creep, from 18 students to 25 or even 30. Whether adding a few students, or moving from 30 to 200, faculty must reconsider individual meetings with students, term papers with multiple drafts, and other time-intensive practices. As soon as you feel that you can no longer teach the course the way it has been taught in the past, it is time for reflection.

Faculty responses to increased class sizes often resemble Kubler-Ross's (1969) stages of grief and loss: denial ("There is no way to in-crease the size of this class and maintain academic integrity!"); anger ("I can't believe they did this, administrators don't care about stu-dents or faculty!"); bargaining ("If I teach 20 percent more students without additional compensation, what do I get in return?"); depres-sion ("How am I ever going to teach this class in a meaningful way again?"); and finally acceptance ("OK, my class is larger. How do I deal with the hordes?").

Getting through these stages can be traumatic; however, class size is not the major deterrent to positive learning environments. In fact, perception of what constitutes an acceptable class size is relative. A teacher of 150 students would love to teach the class with only 50 students, whereas someone who has just been told her class is moving from 20 to 50 may experience an overwhelming feeling of dread. The number of students is important, but the attitude of the teacher in dealing with the class size makes the difference.

When class size increases, teachers can do many things to enhance students' learning opportunities. One way is to use Chickering and Gamson's (1991) seven principles for good practice in undergraduate education as a guide:

- Encourage student-faculty contact
- Encourage cooperation and reciprocity among students
- Encourage active learning
- Give prompt feedback
- Emphasize time on task
- Communicate high expectations
- Respect diverse talents and ways of learning

Incorporating these practices into your course may be difficult for any size class, but most faculty, even if they have no knowledge of these seven principles, quickly note that increases in class size negatively impact one or more of these areas. "I can no longer get to know my students, students feel like they are just a number, it is impossible to do anything but lecture, and it takes too long to provide feedback on tests and papers," faculty complain. The following tips for how to teach well when class size increases address five of these principles (Chickering & Gamson, 1991).

Student-Faculty Contact
Learn Students' Names and Something About Your Students

Small classes allow teachers to learn students' names relatively quickly, a primary method to developing contact with them. Faculty often state that as class sizes increase it becomes impossible to learn students' names and to get to know them. Do not give up. There are wonderful methods available to learn student names. To find some, type "learning student names" into any search engine.

Most faculty can learn all student names for classes of 40 to 50. Determine how many you can learn and try for that number, regardless of the class size. I once taught 200 students and, because I could not learn everyone's name, I did not try to learn any. A wise colleague reminded me that I usually learn all names for classes of 50 and that learning one quarter of the names in class was certainly better than a few. In the end, I learned the names of close to half, which positively changed the classroom atmosphere. I was able to quiet disruptive students by calling on them by name, and students were stunned that I expended the effort to learn their name in such a large class.

Student anonymity is a problem in many contexts, so learn as much as you can about as many students as possible. When students feel like a face in the crowd, it is easier for them to be disruptive, argue about trivia, arrive late or leave early, miss class, and disengage. A good way to get to know students is to arrive at class early; use five minutes to get your material ready and then spend five to 10 minutes talking to students before class begins. As students tend to sit in the same area for each class, focus your discussion with a group in different areas each class period.

Civility

With larger classes a wider variety of disruptive behaviors have a better chance of emerging (often a function of the number of students attending class). Cover ground rules the first day and ask the class what they expect of you in maintaining classroom civility. Then discuss what you expect of them. In adjusting to a larger class, some policies work and others fail. Learn from your mistakes and move on. In a class of 150, the odds are good that a cell phone will ring unless you start each class with a quick statement to turn ringers off. I have used statements such as, "the cabin doors are now closed, please turn off and stow cell phones and other electronic devices until we have reached our destination." Keep good humor and remind the students immediately if they engage in behavior that is distracting or disruptive.

Especially problematic as class size grows are students getting ready to leave before the class officially ends, distracting both to the teacher and other students. This packing up can be avoided if you state at the beginning of the course, and when the behavior occurs, that this is rude behavior and that you will end on time.

Student Feedback

The best information regarding how well the new, larger course is going is to periodically ask your students and have them write short feedback statements at the end of class (Angelo & Cross, 1993). Ask them to write on one topic at a time, such as the extent to which they struggled with any specific aspect of the class or what material they felt was covered in too much detail. Give the students only one or two minutes to write. Then, and this is most important, during the next class discuss two or three issues they brought up. Students will write if they feel you use what they write. The good news is that you do not have to read all comments. In a class of 150, select 50 or so and look for themes to discuss briefly in the next class. You demonstrate that you care about their opinions, which is particularly impressive in a large class.

Cooperation and Reciprocity Among Students

It is important to create a collegial feel, even when the class appears to be a large mob. Have students get into groups of four on the first day and learn at least one thing about everyone in the group. Following 10 minutes of discussion, call on a few individuals and have them introduce the three other people in their group. Tell your class you will increase expectations by one name every week (i.e., in the second week they should be able to introduce four, and in the third, five). I often start class by calling on two students to see if they can introduce the requested number of classmates. I use small bags of chips, candy bars, and fruit as reinforcers that lighten the mood and make it a bit safer for shy students to introduce themselves to classmates.

Students knowing students has benefits. They can email each other for missed course material and announcements, have better discussions when participating in active learning techniques, and tend to be more respectful of one another. For additional feedback, assign short writing assignments and have students proofread for each other. You could give an assignment and ask the students to put their name at the top of the first page. They then list the name of the first reviewer and the second reviewer. Good reviews mean fewer grammatical errors and perhaps better coverage of the material, which helps you to read the papers faster. You even could give reviewers points for a job well done, and when final papers are full of errors, reviewers could be marked down. This allows for more writing, even as the number of students increases.

Active Learning

Concept Tests

The most common comment faculty make as class size increases reflects a sense of change (the class used to be smaller and by implication better) and hopelessness: "The only way I will be able to teach the class is by lecturing." Although it is difficult to coordinate group projects in large classes, several ways exist to get students actively engaged. One of the most common is "concept tests," developed by Mazur (reviewed by Crouch & Mazur, 2001). The instructor presents a "mini-lecture" of about 15 minutes. A multiple-choice question is then presented on a projector for the class. The instructor then asks students "How many think 'a' is the correct answer, how many think 'b' is, and so on. If most students answer correctly, move to the next block of material. If many students get the question incorrect (the cutoff is up to you), ask the students to "convince your neighbor of your answer." Then, after a period of one to two minutes, again ask which answer is correct. Most students will get it correct following peer discussion. If they still struggle, a short lecture can address the correct answer and why the alternatives are incorrect. A lot of learning and collaboration can take place in five minutes. This procedure brings much energy to the classroom with students discussing various aspects of the test question and content.

Problem-Based Learning

An instructor also can bring problem-based learning to a class of any size. Present a "real world" problem that students must use course material to solve, and allow students to work together in teams of two or three to arrive at a possible solution.

Pair-Share

In a think/write pair-share exercise, the instructor presents a prompt that stimulates thinking or requires integration or application of course material and requests students to work individually either by thinking or writing for one minute. Do not merely ask students to list something or recreate a simple fact. After a minute, ask students to "pair" with someone and discuss possible responses. Then, call on students to see what answer or solution the "pair" identified.

Not all students will participate, but not all are participating during a small seminar or lecture either. As long as a great majority participates, there is no harm in a few sitting quietly during the activity. A teacher can get to know those quiet students better by asking them what they think of the material.

Prompt Feedback: Grading Rubrics Can Help

Providing prompt feedback is perhaps the most challenging aspect of larger classes. Teachers need to assess their level of commitment — what they can do well — and, if they decide to keep assignments that are time intensive in grading, find mechanisms to speed up the process. Essay responses on examinations and term papers seem impossible when classes grow too large. It may not be possible to grade 200 long term papers at the end of the semester. Although I agree the task is difficult, do not discount all writing for large classes. I recently taught a section of introductory psychology with 200 students with five examinations containing four one-half page essay responses per exam. Using a scoring rubric, it took only four to five hours to grade the essays.

Grading rubrics (Stevens & Levi, 2005; or type "grading rubrics" into an Internet search engine) speed up grading and increase both the reliability and validity for both papers and essay responses on exams. A rubric is a scoring template for written responses. To construct one, identify the three to five most important aspects of the written work to be graded. For a brief review of a research article, they might be: summary of major points, description of methods, major conclusions drawn by the author, and overall response by the student. Each of these four areas is allocated a number of points based on importance. Simply read the paper, allocate points for each area, and total the points. Use of rubrics reduces the amount of writing you need to include, reduces bias as a result of one especially strong or weak aspect of the writing, and, by giving the rubric to the students at the time of the assignment, provides structure and guidance, reducing uncertainty. And better papers equal faster grading. A positive additional outcome is that grade grievances tend to decrease.

Respecting Diverse Talents and Ways of Learning

Do More Than Lecture

Incorporate active learning into the class. The standard lecture method works well for auditory learners and linear thinkers. To assist in the learning for others, consider including visuals and class discussions. With overhead projectors and increasing numbers of "mediated classrooms," it is easier to do so. Visual models, short video clips, and other stimulus materials are commonly found on the Web. Most textbook publishers also include multimedia suggestions from the Web tied to your course text.

Discussion

Perhaps the most challenging aspect of increased class size is handling discussions well. Teachers need good facilitation techniques to keep the conversation going, minimize personal attacks, and keep students involved and on task. I have seen many wonderful discussions in large sections (see Stanley & Porter, 2002); it simply takes a keen eye and practice. Watch the discussion as you would with any class, but keep in mind that with larger classes comes more variability, and, therefore, very different viewpoints.

Conclusion

Having your class size increase is a challenge, but then so is teaching in general. Overall, the most important consideration is to stop and think about what is possible and not possible, something we should do in all classes. If your class sizes jump, the discouragement you feel is natural, but you can do more than lecture. You can assess student learning in many ways besides multiple-choice exams and maintain interpersonal interactions with students in an atmosphere where everyone feels part of the group. Hold onto your standards and teaching goals. Seek out and talk to colleagues about what they do in their classes. Ask two or three who have taught a class the size you have just been given to offer tips for handling the hordes. Take advantage of the many resources on this topic. Keep in mind that although a larger class means potentially more work, it also means more opportunities to meet and get to know students, and to touch their lives.

References and Recommended Readings

Angelo, T.A., & Cross, K.P. (1993). *Classroom assessment techniques: A handbook for college teachers* (2nd ed.). San Francisco: Jossey-Bass.

Crouch, C.H., & Mazur, E. (2001). Peer instruction: Ten years of experience and results. *American Journal of Physics, 69,* 970-977.

Chickering, A.W., & Gamson, Z.F. (1991). Applying the seven principles for good practice in undergraduate education. *New Directions for Teaching and Learning, 47,* 5-12.

Kubler-Ross, E. (1969). *On death and dying.* New York: MacMillan.

Stanley, C.A., & Porter, M.E. (2002). *Engaging large classes: Strategies and techniques for college faculty.* Bolton, MA: Anker.

Stevens, D.D., & Levi, A.J. (2005). *Introduction to rubrics: An assessment tool to save grading time, convey effective feedback and promote student learning.* Sterling, VA: Stylus.

Beyond the Grade:
Feedback on Student Behavior

BRIAN L. BURKE
LESLIE B. GOLDSTEIN
Fort Lewis College

Good communication is as stimulating as black coffee,
and just as hard to sleep after.
Anne Morrow Lindbergh (1991, p. 121)

FEEDBACK IS A SPECIAL case of the general communication process that constitutes part of our ethical duty as psychology instructors (Ethical Standard 7.06; APA, 2002). Although instructors generally use grading tests and assignments as their primary academic feedback to students, value exists in other forms of feedback as well. For instance, some student behaviors that may warrant feedback include:

- Sally was unprepared for class discussions because she had not done the readings.
- Ralph often came 10-15 minutes late to class.
- Kyle monopolized the instructor's office hours to complain and argue about grades.
- John interrupted the instructor frequently to call out comments or ask questions.
- Karen rarely spoke in class despite having many excellent ideas to share.
- Todd dominated class discussions, often telling long-winded stories about his family.
- Jill missed classes, assignments, and tests, which the syllabus stated could not be made up.

Two Functions of Feedback on Student Behavior

Feedback to students serves two distinct yet potentially complementary functions: (a) fostering students' individual growth, and (b) maintaining a productive classroom environment for the benefit of all students.

Student Growth

Instructors are in a unique position to provide feedback that assists students in their academic performance and helps them to grow, mature, and learn about themselves. For instance, Sally is more likely to increase her academic engagement if an instructor gives her effective feedback regarding her lack of preparation. Often such feedback may help students form a positive self image and increase their sense of efficacy both within and beyond the classroom (Milan, Parish, & Reichgott, 2006).

Classroom Environment

College teachers owe it to all students in a class to not let other peers dominate, disrupt, or demand special privileges (Wilson & Hackney, 2006), like Ralph, whose frequent lateness taints the classroom environment for everyone. A skilled instructor who handles the situation respectfully may be able to accomplish two goals simultaneously: teaching difficult students how they present to others (which may help them interpersonally) and concomitantly protecting the class from undue intrusions.

Setting the Stage for Feedback: Three Ideas

There are two main steps in the feedback process: setting the stage and feedback delivery. If we want to set the stage so that students hear our feedback, it is crucial to first establish rapport with them (e.g., Buskist & Saville, 2004). Here are three ideas for enhancing rapport with students as we set the stage for feedback delivery.

"Please See Me"

Rapport starts with the way instructors ask students for a meeting. Specifically, students who receive a note on their test saying "Please see me" are more likely to be offended, angry, or anxious than students who receive the following, more explicit note: "I would like to help you understand this material. Please see me" (Perrine & King, 2004). Students who receive the clearer note are more likely to be grateful and perceive the instructor as helpful and caring, leading to the potential for a more productive meeting.

Two examples of explicit notes teachers can write to students (or say if they prefer to communicate verbally) in a private communication are:

- "You are not currently passing the class. Please come see me in my office to work on improvement." [Goal: give students feedback about their academic work.]
- "Lately you have seemed frustrated in this class. Please come to my office to discuss what we can do to improve your experience in this course." [Goal: give students feedback about some facet of their academic behavior.]

The Individual Feedback Meeting

Rather than singling out specific students via a note, teachers may find it valuable in small classes (if they are lucky enough to teach any) to schedule a mid-semester meeting with each student individually. Some instructors build the meeting times into their course syllabus. In these meetings, teachers can give specific behavioral feedback regarding performance in the course, including "growth edges" such as encouraging those who are quiet to participate more actively in class or asking dominating students to limit their calling out. What makes these meetings useful is that instructors can share corrective feedback face to face in a safe setting and can build the topic of "feedback" into the course content itself (especially in psychology classes such as Counseling Skills or Group Dynamics). To further enhance the meeting, teachers can encourage students to give them concrete feedback about their performance (the way they come across in the classroom), and how the course is working for the students.

Empathic Highlights

Actively listen. Once students arrive at an instructor's office for a meeting, either in response to a request to talk with them or at their own request, teachers can build rapport through reflective listening. The first step in this process entails actively listening to the student's story or point of view, which will emerge during the dialogue. As the student responds to the teacher's open-ended questions, teachers can ask themselves "What are the main points here?" or "What is most important to this student?" (Egan, 2006) and try to form a hypothesis or educated guess about what the student is thinking and feeling.

Express your understanding. After teachers grasp the key elements of what the student has said, the next step is to express an empathic understanding in a form such as "You feel ... [guess how the student might be feeling] because ... [paraphrase the situation that you think gave rise to these feelings]." Empathic highlights would likely be useful with Kyle, the grade complainer, to whom an instructor could say something like, "I understand that you feel disappointed because you did not receive the grade you were hoping for," which may diffuse some of his anger and grade-related arguing. Using empathic highlights conveys respect for the student's experience and thus even translate into increased student motivation and learning (Wilson, 2006).

Feedback Delivery: Two General Strategies

Once teachers have successfully set the stage and established rapport with a student, here are two strategies they can use to deliver effective feedback regarding the student's behavior.

The Assertive Statement

Giving behavioral feedback requires a type of assertiveness (Paterson, 2000), except instead of the classic "I-statements," instructors are often speaking on behalf of the class — so they can say "the class" or "the other students" to give the statement more social power. The steps to crafting an effective assertive statement are:

♦ Describe the student's behavior objectively, using concrete information and focusing on the behavior rather than on the person (Brinko, 1993; Egan, 2006).e.g., "When you interrupt me and call out in class..."

♦ Describe how the student's behavior impacts you and/ or the other students in the class.e.g., "...I am unable to respond to you" or "...it is disruptive to the other students."

♦ Specify one or two observable behavior changes a teacher would like the student to make, e.g., "If possible, instead of interrupting, I would prefer if you could write down your questions or comments to discuss with me after class."

♦ Finally, provide specific positive feedback to the student whenever they successfully perform the requested behaviors; this will bolster their self-efficacy (Egan, 2006). e.g., "I appreciate your not interrupting me today. Do you have any questions for me?"

The Bleep Sandwich

Feedback is more effective when negative information is "sandwiched" between positive information (Brinko, 1993). For instance, one of us requested a meeting with John after the first week of class during which the student interrupted the instructor about 10 times to call out or ask questions. He conveyed the following to John in the meeting (note the assertive statement embedded between positive feedback statements):

I enjoy your contributions to the class already, John, and it is clear that you are a bright and motivated student. There have been many times in the first week, however, when you called out inappropriately in class and this is disruptive to me and the other students. If you have your hand up and I choose not to call on you, it is because my goal for the class is to give everyone a full chance to participate in class discussion. In those instances, instead of calling out, would it be possible for you to write your questions down to ask me after class? That way, I'd be able to give your good questions the attention they deserve.

John responded by stating that he had received similar feedback in other classes but without constructive suggestions for how to change the disruptive behavior. He employed the idea of writing down his questions and subsequently reported that this strategy worked well for him in many of his classes.

Feedback Delivery: Specific Strategies

Once the two main steps in the feedback process — setting the stage and feedback delivery — have been implemented, there are more specific considerations to keep in mind depending upon which of the two functions of feedback are being addressed.

Student Growth

Teaching Responsibility

Students' receptivity to feedback (and hence growth) may be undermined by their tendency to blame others for their behavior. The essential first step in feedback with such students is assisting them in assuming responsibility for their own situation. Teachers can explain to students that, even if 99 percent of the problems in the class are due to other students, the main issue they can help them with is the 1 percent that they can directly control. For instance, when a teacher gave corrective feedback to Karen that she had been passive in class despite her obvious intelligence, she complained of dominant classmates (like Todd) who prevented her participation. After empathizing with her frustration, the teacher said: "I understand that most of this situation may be out of your control, and I will certainly do my part to reign in the dominators. I wonder also, what can you do, Karen, to get more out of this class?" Karen acknowledged that her own shyness was a factor, and her teacher brainstormed possible remedies with her, such as seeking counseling or starting with simple questions in class (e.g., requesting clarification) to work gradually toward increasing her classroom participation. Teaching responsibility also was effective with Kyle, the grade complainer, who came to realize that some of his frustration was due to his own lack of study skills (a solvable problem) rather than the tests or grading system.

Teaching Students How They Present

Another important component in helping students grow as individuals is to provide them with honest feedback about how they present to others—in other words, how the student is perceived by the instructor or the other students in the class. Todd's (the dominating student) teacher gave him feedback only after building a sound relationship with him outside the classroom. She explained to him that, while she enjoyed his passion, many students indicated that they found Todd's stories excessive and wanted to hear more from the instructor and other students. She then asked Todd to monitor his storytelling more carefully in class (e.g., only telling one story per week and writing the others down to hand in after class), which he did. Todd later shared that this feedback helped him connect with other students more easily.

Classroom Environment
The Exception Contract

Inevitably, life impacts students during the academic semester, and a teacher may legitimately decide to make an exception for a student in crisis. What a teacher may not know at the time is that this student will repeatedly be in "crisis" and will ask for more exceptions, and other students will inevitably notice this unfair situation. Some instructors have students sign a contract when they make a one-time exception stating: "I am aware that the instructor is making an exception this one time and I will not ask for more exceptions this semester for any reason." In our experience, this strategy has been effective on two counts: it conveys a clear message to the student (and the class) that the exception will not be a pattern, and it gives the instructor concrete documentation of the agreement, which is a good idea in dealing with problem students.

Pattern Detection

If teachers find themselves teaching a student who continually undermines the classroom environment, it may be useful to learn more about this student so they can provide accurate and more effective feedback. If instructors have access to the student's transcript or know which classes he or she has taken, they can ask past teachers about any strategies that were helpful for that student (such as the feedback to John, above). Note that this suggestion is permissible under The Family Education Rights and Privacy Act of 1974 (FERPA), because there is a legitimate educational interest at stake (see http://www.epic.org/privacy/education/ferpa.html, subsection b1A).

Putting the Pieces Together: Jill

Jill was a student for whom pattern detection came in handy. She was a difficult student throughout her Personality class, missing classes, assignments, and tests with alarming regularity and demanding special privileges and exceptions due to her many "crises." Her teacher's mistake as a young instructor was not providing careful feedback to Jill using the steps we have outlined. Jill decided to take another class with this teacher, likely due to his initially permissive stance with her. Fortunately, the second time, the instructor detected the pattern the first week of class and immediately sent Jill the following email; the specific strategies used are noted in squared parentheses in italics following each sentence:

> I appreciate having you in my class this semester, Jill, as I very much enjoy your participation and interest [*begin with positive feedback*]. I just want to be clear with you about the lateness, absence, and makeup policies for the class. In this first week, you arrived late to class twice, missed one class, and handed in your homework a day late [*assertive statement – step 1: specify the problem*

behavior]. When you come late, it is disruptive to me and the entire class, and it is unfair to the other students for me to accept your late assignments [*assertive statement – step 2: describe the behavior's impact on the other students*]. If you want to make a full contribution to the class and receive the grade you deserve, it is important that you do your best to attend class more regularly and hand in assignments/homework by the due dates [*assertive statement – step 3: outline the desired behavior change*]. I understand that this may feel frustrating to you because you frequently have difficult situations in your life that are out of your control [*an empathic highlight*]. While I enjoy your participation and your academic potential [*end with positive feedback*], if you are not able to make this class a priority, it would be best to drop the class while you still can do so easily. If you decide to commit to Abnormal Psychology this semester despite the difficulties you are facing outside the classroom [*teach responsibility*], please reply to this email indicating that you fully understand these conditions [*a modified exception contract*].

Jill elected to stay in the class and improved virtually all problem behaviors, with her teacher complimenting her each time she came to class early and handed in her assignments on time.

Conclusion

Giving behavioral feedback to students that goes beyond their course grade is a critical skill for instructors. Not only is it valuable to help students develop and grow interpersonally, but it also is educators' jobs to protect other students from the destructive behaviors of a few individuals. Both goals — to educate and to protect — can be simultaneously achieved by employing effective strategies, such as crafting assertive statements, giving "bleep sandwiches," implementing specific contracts, and teaching students to be responsible for their own classroom behaviors.

References and Recommended Readings

American Psychological Association. (2002). *Ethical principles of psychologists and code of conduct.* Washington, DC: Author.

Brinko, K.T. (1993). The practice of giving feedback to improve teaching. *Journal of Higher Education, 64,* 574-593.

Burke, B.L. (2007). For the "grader" good: Considering what you grade and why. In B. Perlman, L. I. McCann, & S. H. McFadden (Eds.), *Lessons learned: Practical advice for the teaching of psychology* (Vol. 3, pp. 125-134). Washington, DC: Association for Psychological Science.

Buskist, W., & Saville, B.K. (2001). Rapport-building: Creating positive emotional contexts for enhancing learning and teaching. In B. Perlman, L.I. McCann, & S.H. McFadden (Eds.), *Lessons learned: Practical advice for the teaching of psychology* (Vol. 2, pp. 149-155). Washington, DC: Association for Psychological Science.

Egan, G. (2006). *The skilled helper: A problem-management and opportunity-development approach to helping* (8th ed.). Pacific Grove, CA: Brooks/Cole.

Lindbergh, A.M. (1991). *Gift from the sea.* New York: Pantheon.

Milan, F.B., Parish, S.J., & Reichgott, M.J. (2006). A model for educational feedback based on clinical communication skills strategies: Beyond the 'feedback sandwich'. *Teaching and Learning in Medicine, 18,* 42-47.

Paterson, R. J. (2000). *The assertiveness workbook: How to express your ideas and stand up for yourself at work and in relationships.* Oakland, CA: New Harbinger.

Perrine, R.M., & King, A.S. (2004). Why do you want to see me? Students' reactions to a professor's request as a function of attachment and note clarity. *Journal of Experimental Education, 73,* 5-20.

Wilson, J.H. (2006). Predicting student attitudes and grades from perceptions of instructors' attitudes. *Teaching of Psychology, 33,* 91-95.

Wilson, J.H., & Hackney, A.A. (2006). Problematic college students: Preparing and repairing. In W. Buskist & S. F. Davis (Eds.), *Handbook of the teaching of psychology* (pp. 233-237). Malden, MA: Blackwell.

Make Your Teaching and Your Life More Enjoyable

LEE I. MCCANN
BARON PERLMAN
University of Wisconsin-Oshkosh

*This job is miserable; the workload is unbearable,
there are too many students, and there are not enough
hours in the day to do all the things I need to do. I am
so tired and burnt out I can hardly get up to go to work
in the morning!*

HAVE YOU EVER HEARD anyone say something along these lines, or worse, said something like this yourself? Well, we are government employees, and we are here to help you. There are steps you can take to make your work more satisfying and your life more enjoyable.

It seems like over the years many faculty members do roughly the same thing semester after semester while continually undertaking additional responsibilities— a recipe for stress and unhappiness. We are all familiar with the conditions in academia that help to siphon the joy and meaning out of our lives: things such as teaching the same classes over and over, too many needy students, too much committee work, insufficient resources, piles of paperwork, and time pressures and deadlines. We cannot solve all of your problems, but we do have some suggestions accumulated over our nearly 75 (combined) years of teaching, and we hope some of them will help you to increase your enjoyment of life and academia, so you have more to give to your teaching and students.

Try a New Approach to Your Teaching

Teaching the same class or classes can become repetitious, even if you love the subject. If this is happening to you, you may just soldier on, continuing to try your best in the same old ways. However, to make the next semester more enjoyable, you might try one of the following ideas.

Include something in each class period that is fun for you and your students. Doug Bernstein (2005) says that when he is ready to talk about obedience to authority he asks his students to give him a standing ovation, has them keep trying until he gets a sufficiently gratifying response, and uses this activity as an example of the subject at hand. That satisfies our definition of fun. The use of cartoons or various types of active learning should work, too.

Experience Life as a Student

Attend a lecture or presentation on a topic you know little about and take notes as if you had a test the next day, or try writing one of the papers you have assigned to your students. This should refresh your memory of what life is like on the other side of the lectern, and as a result you may find yourself writing more on the board, speaking slower, or reemphasizing major points.

Rearrange Your Teaching Schedule

Teaching at different times of the day or changing to longer or shorter class periods or a night class is a simple way to add variety to your life.

Change Your Assignments

Assign your students to give presentations or engage in group work, or ask them to write papers on new or different topics.

Change Your Mode of Delivery

Change the proportions of PowerPoint presentations, overheads, lecture, or discussion in each class period, or try a day with no technology and just lecture. Move around the room more and lecture from different locations, or change how you teach a particular topic.

You Also Might:

- ♦ Ask students for specific feedback on your teaching;
- ♦ Review syllabi from others who teach the same class;
- ♦ Invite guest lecturers to your class, or volunteer to do the same for a colleague;
- ♦ Attend a teaching conference, or read some teaching journals or books;
- ♦ Team-teach a class with a colleague;
- ♦ Teach a new course;
- ♦ Try a field trip;
- ♦ Get your students involved in service learning;
- ♦ Teach an on-line class;
- ♦ Change your textbook;
- ♦ Keep a teaching journal.

Take Advantage of New Opportunities

If you are in a rut, there are any number of alternatives you might consider trying outside of the classroom to add something new and different to your academic life.

Take a Sabbatical Leave or Attend an Interesting Short Course

Sabbaticals are a tried and true method of getting away from the normal routine, completing research or retraining, and recharging your batteries. Auditing a course you have always been interested in is another option. Dr. McCann has found the Chautauqua Program of short courses run by the National Science Foundation a pleasant way to see and learn new things that can enhance his teaching. Consider applying to grade Advanced Placement Psychology exams. Although grading essays does not sound either interesting or stimulating, it is — as hard as that is to believe.

Collaborate With Colleagues on a Research Project

Getting two or more people involved in the same research activities can make the work easier, better, and more interesting. We know from experience that two heads are better than one and that working with someone will improve your experimental designs, stimulate you to get the work done since your colleague expects you to do so, and suggest new variables to consider.

Attend Conferences

Attending a conference can be counted on to suggest new teaching or research ideas. Consider attending presentations in areas you normally might avoid, or going to a conference you have not been to before. Some years ago, we decided to attend a teaching conference rather than the more research oriented gatherings we normally frequented. Our lives have not been the same since.

You also could:

- ♦ Temporarily exchange positions with someone on another campus;
- ♦ Seek new committee or administrative assignments;
- ♦ Try a new area of research;
- ♦ Become active in a professional or national organization;
- ♦ Get more involved in your community.

Take Better Care of Yourself

Teaching can consume larger and larger portions of our lives, often to the degree that we cannot find enough time to take care of ourselves as we should. If you take care of yourself, your mental CEO will work better and more efficiently, and you should get more work done in less time.

Get Regular Exercise

We once had a dean who appeared in the gym at noon nearly every day, even though he had endless responsibilities and meetings. When asked how he managed to exercise so consistently, he said, "Exercise is the first thing I put on my calendar." This is about the best advice one could receive on how to make the time for an activity that is known to reduce stress, improve nearly every aspect of health, and create more energy for our other daily tasks.

Get Enough Sleep

This is easier said than done. However, health experts are starting to say that sleep is as important to health as exercise and diet. The current research suggests that insufficient sleep decreases cognitive efficiency. We heard a presentation where the speakers maintained that getting enough sleep increases your efficiency and accuracy so much that you can do more in less time and accomplish at least as much during a shorter work day as you would in a longer day following insufficient sleep. As an added bonus, you will feel a lot better.

Decrease the Work You Take Home

Working at home grading papers, creating lectures, writing papers, or doing committee work makes you feel (correctly) that your job is taking over your life. Rescheduling your day to allow some time to actually work with your office door closed will decrease the work you take home and help separate "life" from work.

Enjoy Your Accomplishments

Pat yourself on the back when you complete a task, clear off your desk, or accomplish something significant. Take a minute to relax and enjoy the pleasant feelings you deserve. You might even reward yourself with a short break, walk, or visit with a colleague. Another idea is to develop specific short and long-term goals for the things you want to accomplish in your career and life.

Get Away From It All

Set aside time for light reading, a play, movie, concert, sports, or hobby. A vacation or just a short drive can give you a change of environment and some relaxation. Even an occasional walk around campus can clear your mind. Some people recommend REAL leisure, finding time to do absolutely NOTHING.

Spend More Time With People

Create a network of people with similar teaching or research interests or with whom you simply enjoy spending time. Having someone to talk with, and to discuss your common interests has a variety of benefits, including access to new ideas and useful advice, evaluation of your own work and plans, and an opportunity to relax and escape the normal routine. Schedule in time to see friends more often — perhaps a weekly lunch. Make it a point to get to know new faculty in and outside of your department.

Improve Your Work Environment

Minimize clutter. A disorganized or cluttered work environment makes tasks appear more numerous and adds to the difficulty of doing them efficiently. While some of the following may not seem worth the time, remember that we are looking for long-term efficiency, not an immediate solution for the problem du jour.

- Clean out your office;
- Clean off your desk at the end of each day;
- Get small things off your to-do list ASAP;
- Do the most unpleasant task on your to-do list first;
- Do not procrastinate;
- Concentrate on whatever you are doing — do not multi-task;
- Empty the trash can and remove ancient files from your computer;
- Look at e-mail only once or twice a day;
- Take time to do it right;
- Plan ahead. Look to see what is coming on your calendar and in your classes for the next week or two and avoid the rush to get tasks done at the last minute.

Say No More Often

Academics get many requests to serve on committees, advise independent study projects in areas where they have little interest, and attend social functions. An unattainable, ideal approach would be to try to do only things you like to do. Failing that, you can at least try to decrease the number of activities in which you really do not want to be involved.

Enhance Your Office

Spend some time and a little money to make the place more pleasant. A small stereo, soft lighting from a new lamp, a nice rug, and comfortable chair can make your office much more pleasant, and more welcoming for students.

Hire Student Help

As you probably recall with painful clarity, students often work for minimum wage. If you can manage it, hire a student a few hours a week to do filing, organizing, or run errands to free up your time for more important tasks.

Minimize Negative Experiences
Avoid Negative People

Avoid constant contact with the discontented. Recreational gripers may have entertainment value, but they keep your attention focused on the negative side of life and the negative interpretation of every event. Likewise, minimize contact with people who annoy you. Life is too short to endure this form of water torture.

Learn How the System Works

When they need to interact with the dark side of the force (administration), many teachers drown in the resulting red tape. The next time you need to wade into this swamp, ask a wise old head for advice on how to proceed effectively and efficiently. Over time, if you take some of this advice and get around the campus a bit more, you will become familiar with the system, and save a lot of time and annoyance. Learning how the system works is not a waste of time.

Save Your Silver Bullets.

There are things that might be changed with varying degrees of effort. Pick your battles, and spend time only on important issues. Charging every windmill in sight will take a lot of time and emotional energy, generate stress and unhappiness, and undermine your credibility when you have a legitimate complaint.

Do Not Worry About Things You Cannot Change

There are occasional irritations in academic life (believe it or not), and dwelling on these major or minor stupidities will not improve your mental health. If you cannot change something, staying annoyed is not a good solution. Do not try to solve every problem yourself; call attention to it and if nothing happens, move on. Some things simply have to be endured, ideally with a good dose of humor, bemusement, or sarcasm. Remember that administrators and rules come and go; this, too, shall pass — in the fullness of time.

Conclusion

Don't just sit there — take more control of your academic life and your surroundings, and make your life and work more satisfying. There is nothing better than a job you like doing. Most teachers got into teaching because they loved it. Do what it takes to keep it that way, and make the remaining years of your professional life as satisfying as they can be.

References and Recommended Readings

Baker, E.K. (2004). Caring for ourselves as psychologists. Retrieved August 12, 2007, from http://www.e-psychologist.org/index. iml?mdl=exam/show_article.mdl&Exam_ID=1&Article_ID=1

Bernstein, D.A. (2005). Was it good for you, too?: Keeping teaching exciting for us and for them. In B. Perlman, L.I. McCann, & W. Buskist. (Eds.), *Voices of experience: Memorable talks from the National Institute on the Teaching of Psychology.* (pp. 111-118). Washington, DC: Association for Psychological Science.

Lloyd, M.A. (1999). As time goes by: Maintaining vitality in the classroom. In B. Perlman, L.I. McCann, & S.H. McFadden, (Eds.), *Lessons Learned: Practical advice for the teaching of psychology* (Vol. 1, pp. 7-10). Washington, DC: Association for Psychological Science.

Part V

Themes Across Psychology

"Exporting" Psychology: Communicating the Value of Our Field to Students

ROBERT A. BARON
Rensselaer Polytechnic Institute

IN 1974, I WAS A YOUNG associate professor at Purdue and believed that I was doing just what I was supposed to be doing — teaching large courses, working with students, and conducting research. In fact, I had recently received a grant from the National Science Foundation (NSF) to conduct research on the effects of heat on aggression (the so-called "long, hot summer" effect). My students and I performed many laboratory studies in which we carefully varied temperature to observe the effects on human behavior. Then, for a change of pace and to test the generalizability of our work, we moved outside the laboratory and observed horn-honking by motorists on hot and cool days. As we expected, more honking occurred on hot days than on cool ones, and I presented these findings at a convention. The effect was totally unexpected: A major storm suddenly broke around my head.

At that time, U.S. Senator William Proxmire was awarding "prizes" — the Golden Fleece — to faculty members in any field who, in his opinion, excelled in wasting taxpayers' money. (For more information about the Golden Fleece Award's impact on psychology, see "All That's Gold Does Not Glitter," *Observer*, June 2006, and "Scientists Provide a Civics Lesson for Politicians," *Observer*, December 2006) I woke up to find that I had received one of these prizes, which focused on our single field study while ignoring our careful laboratory experimental work. In essence, the Senator claimed we had spent the entire grant on this single field demonstration. In fact, that particular study was conducted without cost and used no university or NSF funds. But the Senator did not seem to know — or care!

The day after the original news story broke, my dean phoned and, to his everlasting shame, told me not to talk to reporters or defend myself in any way. I heard his message clearly, but I could not accept it. How could I let anyone — even a U.S. Senator — disparage my reputation? I did talk to reporters and tried to explain the purpose of our research. Many reporters accepted my comments and joined in strong condemnation of Senator Proxmire. Even the highly respected *Washington Post* published an editorial severely criticizing Proxmire's tactics. The NSF, which had supplied funds that supported my research, was pleased with this outcome, and as a result, I was invited to become a Program Director there.

I accepted and when I arrived in Washington, DC, all was fine. But then Reagan defeated Carter for the Presidency, and within a few months my program (social and developmental psychology) experienced a 75 percent budget cut. Many of my colleagues seemed to believe that this cut resulted from members of the Reagan administration being anti-science. However, after meeting several of the representatives they sent to the NSF, I had a different impression. In my view, they had cut my division's budget and program not because they were against scientific research; in fact, they actually increased funding for many other programs. Rather, they cut our funds because they truly did not understand the nature of psychology, that it was largely scientific in orientation and adopted systematic methods of research similar to those used in other fields. At that point, I experienced a painful realization. Perhaps this distressing outcome was, to some extent, our fault! Perhaps we (psychologists) had not done a good job of communicating the true nature and immense value of psychology to our students and others. Those thoughts, which recurred during my two years at the NSF, played an important role in my thinking about what we, as teachers of psychology, should do in our courses. Up until that time, I had truly enjoyed teaching (and had received high ratings from my students). But now, I began to wonder, "Can I do better? Can I focus more on explaining the value of psychology to students — thereby winning friends for our field?" This idea was stimulated, in part, by the fact that most of my students were not psychology majors, but were from other fields (e.g., engineering, science, management, and nursing). In fact, for some, especially the engineering students, our courses were among the few electives they could take. I found myself wondering if we didn't owe them more than an interesting course based on our own expertise. Shouldn't we also be communicating as clearly as possible the value and usefulness of psychology — a goal first stated persuasively by George Miller (1969)?

I shifted my own teaching and research in major ways, and ultimately these changes led me into a career path in which I have been, to some extent, an exporter of our field, attempting to communicate not only psychology's content but also its essential value to people who are not going to become psychologists. As a result, during the 25 years since my "awakening," I have taught students in every conceivable field, including those enrolled in MBA programs, special programs for executives, and graduate students in fields such as finance, communication, and philosophy. In teaching these students, I have tried to be a true exporter of psychology, illustrating the intrinsic value of our field and the many ways it can be put to excellent use by non-psychologists. After explaining why I believe this is an important goal, I will turn to some strategies for becoming better exporters of our field in our teaching.

Why Should We Seek to Export Psychology?

There are two key reasons why we should want to export psychology. First, it is the right thing to do. Psychology is scientific in orientation and approach but has always had a dual nature with science as one aspect and application as the other. Our field always has sought knowledge of human behavior in order to contribute in positive ways to human welfare. Thus, we have an obligation to communicate the value of psychology to our students and to help them understand the many ways they can benefit by using it in their own lives and work. The benefits of such exportation, I believe, are immense. The principles and findings of psychology can help students lead richer, fuller lives and attain greater success in their chosen careers. A few examples from my own courses help illustrate these points. The questions listed below can all be answered by the knowledge and findings of psychology. They cannot, to the best of my knowledge, be answered readily by any other field or body of information.

♦ Is using a cell phone really dangerous when driving? If so, how can these dangers be reduced — assuming people will not readily give up their phones?

- Is punishment effective in disciplining children? When? How should it be used?
- Why do we find certain characteristics attractive in others? Is this the result, at least in part, of our inherited biological nature?
- Are performance appraisals at work fair? If not, how can they be improved?
- How can individuals "win the battle of the bulge" and control their weight?
- How can we best resist the harmful effects of stress?
- How can we, as individuals, become truly happy?
- What makes people suited to becoming entrepreneurs?
- How can we resist the many persuasive attempts to which we are exposed every day?
- Should depression be treated primarily with drugs? Or is therapy more effective?

These are just a small sample of the many practical questions to which psychology can be applied, and the more we discuss such questions and explain the role of psychology in dealing with them, the richer the experience our students will have in our courses and the more they will appreciate the value of psychology as a tool for improving their own lives.

This is one important reason to export our field, but there is another equally compelling one: Being exporters of our field will help us gain the friends and supporters we need to guarantee the continued progress and advancement of psychology. If my two years at the NSF taught me anything it is that we cannot take such support for granted! Each year, millions of people take courses in psychology. Do they leave these experiences as believers in our field? Many do, but many others, my experience tells me, do not. These skeptics do not believe we can use scientific methods to understand love, memory, the cognitive abilities of children, the effects of stress on health, the nature of psychological disturbances, or a host of other topics. They retain doubts about the value of our research. It is imperative that we reach these skeptics and convince them. If we do not, they will be the people who, in the future, vote against government support for psychological research, resist having psychology included in their local schools' curricula, and seek to limit psychologists' rights within the health care system. Can we afford such adversaries? My experience at the NSF tells me that we cannot and that we should adjust our teaching to reach out to these people and convince them of our field's essential value.

How Can We Export Psychology? Some Specific Tips

Aside from using examples such as those presented above, how can we compellingly illustrate that psychology is interesting and enormously valuable? How can we promote its acceptance and use by people who will not spend their lives studying psychology? I have no simple answers, but here are two techniques that have worked in my own classes.

Bring in Guest Lecturers From Other Fields and From Outside the University

I often invite individuals from other fields to my classes to discuss how they use psychology in their work. They provide vivid examples that psychology is an invaluable tool used by people in many walks of life. Over the years, I have had guest lecturers from such fields as medicine, accounting, business, law, engineering, and marketing. Most are not professors, but they talk about topics of interest to students and about which they know a great deal. In my invitation, I always try to make it clear that my primary goal is to illustrate how important knowledge of human behavior is in a wide range of fields. The results are often outstanding.

Recently, a stock broker visited class. He did not talk about the stock market or about finance, nor did he offer advice on how to make quick profits. He discussed the role of emotions in investment decisions. His main point was that emotions often get in the way of such decisions and influence people to take actions that are not rational from a business perspective. As he explained it, one reason many people make common investment errors (such as rushing to buy when markets are approaching a peak or selling in panic just when markets are near a bottom) is that they let their emotions rule their decisions. As psychologists, we know that affective reactions exert a powerful influence on many aspects of cognition, and I often discuss this topic in my classes. But most students do not appreciate how strong or general such effects can be. As my guest speaker described examples from his own experience, I could see many students, including the hardcore skeptics, moving toward the conclusion: "Gee, there really is something to this behavioral stuff after all...."

I have been fortunate to team-teach a course with a Nobel Prize-winning physicist, Ivar Giaever. The course focuses on innovation and creativity, and my role is to describe the psychological aspects of these topics. Ivar, as a world-renowned scientist, talks about creativity in science and how it has reshaped our world. Perhaps the best part of working with Professor Giaever is when he says something like this to the class: "Listen carefully to Professor Baron because what he tells you is very important. Physics is central — it helps us understand the universe. But knowing about people — that may be even more important to you in the future...." Truly, I am flattered, but more importantly, this shows students that my faith in psychology is not misguided — it truly is valuable, and this fact is apparent to intelligent people as far removed from our field as Nobel-Prize-winning physicists!

There are many ways of demonstrating the value of our field to students. Guest lecturers do not have to be Nobel-Prize winners. It is important only that they use psychology in their own lives and recognize its value and that they are from other fields and outside the university.

Use Short Cases and Exercises

I am not a fan of the case method of teaching. It goes against my own training in scientific psychology. Occasionally, however, I like to clip an interesting newspaper article and reproduce it for use as a short case (example or illustration is probably a better term). Recently, I presented an article dealing with the founder of a new chain of pharmacies in Mexico, Victor Gonzalez. He is unusual for a businessperson — he is high in extraversion, has a great sense of humor, and is something of a maverick. (His own family, prominent in Mexico, objects strongly to some of his tactics!) The point of the article, which students discuss in groups, is that the success of his new business is due, in part, to his personality. Specifically, I ask members of the class to discuss questions like these: "What aspects of his personality do you think are most important? Why?" and "Do you think he would have been so successful if he were low rather than high on these aspects of personality?" After reading this case, even the doubters from engineering or science begin to grasp the important role that individual difference variables play in a wide range of settings.

The main point is this: short cases that illustrate the application of psychology's principles and findings in situations outside the laboratory or university can be useful, and I recommend their use as part of our broad array of teaching procedures.

An Optimistic Conclusion — Of Course!

If we truly believe — as I think most of us do — that our field is not only fascinating but also tremendously valuable and useful, our task is a happy one. As teachers of psychology, we can help large numbers of people outside our field to appreciate its value. By doing so, we contribute to their future happiness and success and also to psychology's future growth and development. Perhaps the famous missionary Mother Teresa put it best when she said (1975): *"We ourselves often feel that what we are doing is just a drop in the ocean. But if that drop was not in the ocean, the ocean itself would be less because of that missing drop..."* (p. 58). I agree. Our individual contributions to the goal of exporting psychology may seem small, but together they do make a difference. The benefits will be real for our students, for society, and for psychology itself

References and Recommended Readings

Baron, R.A. (2006). Opportunity recognition as pattern recognition: How entrepreneurs 'connect the dots' to identify new business opportunities. *Academy of Management Perspectives, 20,* 1–16.

Miller, G.A. (1969). Psychology as a means of promoting human welfare. *American Psychologist, 24,* 1063–1075.

Mullins, P. (2004). Using outside speakers in the classroom. In B. Perlman, L.I. McCann, & S.H. McFadden (Eds.), *Lessons learned: Practical advice for the teaching of psychology* (Vol. 2, pp. 119–126). Washington, DC: Association for Psychological Science.

Svinicki, M.D. (1999). *Teaching and learning on the edge of the millennium: Building on what we have learned.* Hillsdale, NJ: Erlbaum.

Teresa, Mother. (1975). *A gift for God: Carriers of Christ's love.* New York: Columbia University Press.

The 10 Commandments of Helping Students Distinguish Science From Pseudoscience in Psychology

Scott O. Lilienfeld
Emory University

"Professor Schlockenmeister, I know that we have to learn about visual perception in your course, but aren't we going to learn anything about extrasensory perception? My high school psychology teacher told us that there was really good scientific evidence for it."

"Dr. Glopelstein, you've taught us a lot about intelligence in your course. But when are you going to discuss the research showing that playing Mozart to infants increases their I.Q. scores?"

"Mr. Fleikenzugle, you keep talking about schools of psychotherapy, like psychoanalysis, behavior therapy, and client-centered therapy. But how come you've never said a word about sensory-motor integration therapy? My mother, who's an occupational therapist, tells me that it's a miracle cure for attention-deficit disorder."

The Pseudoscience of Popular Psychology

If you're like most introductory psychology instructors, these sorts of questions probably sound awfully familiar. There's a good reason: much of the popular psychology "knowledge" that our students bring to their classes consists of scant more than pseudoscience. Moreover, our students are often fascinated by dubious claims on the fringes of scientific knowledge: extrasensory perception, psychokinesis, channeling, out-of-body experiences, subliminal persuasion, astrology, biorhythms, "truth serum," the lunar lunacy effect, hypnotic age regression, multiple personality disorder, alien abduction reports, handwriting analysis, rebirthing therapy, and untested herbal remedies for depression, to name but a few. Of course, because some of these claims may eventually be shown to contain a core of truth, we should not dismiss them out of hand. Nevertheless, what is troubling about these claims is the glaring discrepancy between many individuals' beliefs in them and the meager scientific evidence on their behalf.

Yet many introductory psychology instructors accord minimal attention to potentially pseudoscientific topics in their courses, perhaps because they believe that these topics are of, at best, marginal relevance to psychological science. Moreover, many introductory psychology textbooks barely mention these topics. After all, there is already more than enough to cover in psychology courses, so why tack on material of doubtful scientific status? Furthermore, some instructors may fear that by devoting attention to questionable claims they will end up sending students the unintended message that these claims are scientifically credible.

Benefits of Teaching Students to Distinguish Science from Pseudoscience

So why should we teach psychology students to distinguish science from pseudoscience? As personality theorist George Kelly (1955) noted, an effective understanding of a construct requires an appreciation of both of its poles. For example, we cannot grasp fully the concept of "cold" unless we have experienced heat. Similarly, students may not grasp fully the concept of scientific thinking without an understanding of pseudoscientific beliefs, namely those that at first blush appear scientific but are not.

Moreover, by addressing these topics, instructors can capitalize on a valuable opportunity to impart critical thinking skills, such as distinguishing correlation from causation and recognizing the need for control groups, by challenging students' misconceptions regarding popular psychology. Although many students find these skills to be "dry" or even deadly dull when presented in the abstract, they often enjoy acquiring these skills in the context of lively and controversial topics (e.g., extrasensory perception) that stimulate their interest. Students often learn about such topics from various popular psychology sources that they seek out in everyday life, such as magazine articles, Internet sites, and television programs.

Indeed, for many beginning students, "psychology" is virtually synonymous with popular psychology. Yet because so much of popular psychology consists of myths and urban legends, such as most people use only 10 percent of their brains, expressing anger is usually better than holding it in, opposites attract in interpersonal relationships, high self-esteem is necessary for psychological health, people with schizophrenia have more than one personality, among a plethora of others, many students probably emerge from psychology courses with the same misconceptions with which they entered. As a consequence, they often depart college incapable of distinguishing the wheat from the chaff in popular psychology.

Teaching students to distinguish science from pseudoscience can prove immensely rewarding. Foremost among these rewards is producing discerning consumers of the popular psychology literature. Indeed, research evidence supports the efficacy of teaching psychology courses on pseudoscience and the paranormal. For example, Morier and Keeports (1994) reported that undergraduates enrolled in a "Science and Pseudoscience" seminar demonstrated a statistically significant reduction in paranormal beliefs relative to a quasi-control group of students enrolled in a psychology and law class over the same time period (see also Dougherty, 2004). They replicated this effect over a two-year period with two sections of the course. Wesp and Montgomery (1998) found that a course on the objective examination of paranormal claims resulted in a statistically significant improvement in the evaluation of reasoning flaws in scientific articles. Specifically, students in this course were better able to identify logical errors in articles and provide rival explanations for research findings.

The 10 Commandments

Nevertheless, teaching students to distinguish science from pseudoscience brings more than its share of challenges and potential pitfalls. In my introductory psychology course (in which I emphasize strongly the distinction between science and pseudoscience in psychology) and in my advanced undergraduate seminar, "Science and Pseudoscience in Psychology," I have learned a number of valuable lessons (by first making just about every mistake about which I'll warn you).

In the following section, I summarize these teaching tips, which I refer to as the "10 Commandments" of teaching psychology students to distinguish science from pseudoscience. To avoid being accused of failing to separate Church from State, I have worded all of these injunctions in the positive rather than the negative to distinguish them from the (only slightly better known) biblical 10 Commandments. I urge readers of this column to inscribe these commandments on impressive stone tablets to be mounted outside of all psychology departments.

First Commandment

Thou shalt delineate the features that distinguish science from pseudoscience. It's important to communicate to students that the differences between science and pseudoscience, although not absolute or clear-cut, are neither arbitrary nor subjective. Instead, philosophers of science (e.g., Bunge, 1984) have identified a constellation of features or "warning signs" that characterize most pseudoscientific disciplines. Among these warning signs are:

♦ A tendency to invoke ad hoc hypotheses, which can be thought of as "escape hatches" or loopholes, as a means of immunizing claims from falsification.

♦ An absence of self-correction and an accompanying intellectual stagnation.

♦ An emphasis on confirmation rather than refutation.

♦ A tendency to place the burden of proof on skeptics, not proponents, of claims.

♦ Excessive reliance on anecdotal and testimonial evidence to substantiate claims.

♦ Evasion of the scrutiny afforded by peer review.

♦ Absence of "connectivity" (Stanovich, 1997), that is, a failure to build on existing scientific knowledge.

♦ Use of impressive-sounding jargon whose primary purpose is to lend claims a facade of scientific respectability.

♦ An absence of boundary conditions (Hines, 2003), that is, a failure to specify the settings under which claims do not hold.

Teachers should explain to students that none of these warning signs is by itself sufficient to indicate that a discipline is pseudoscientific. Nevertheless, the more of these warning signs a discipline exhibits, the more suspect it should become.

Second Commandment

Thou shalt distinguish skepticism from cynicism. One danger of teaching students to distinguish science from pseudoscience is that we can inadvertently produce students who are reflexively dismissive of any claim that appears implausible. Skepticism, which is the proper mental set of the scientist, implies two seemingly contradictory attitudes (Sagan, 1995): an openness to claims combined with a willingness to subject these claims to incisive scrutiny. As space engineer James Oberg (see Sagan, 1995) reminded us, we must keep our minds open but not so open that our brains fall out. In contrast, cynicism implies close-mindedness. I recall being chastised by a prominent skeptic for encouraging researchers to keep an open mind regarding the efficacy of a novel psychotherapy whose rationale struck him as farfetched. However, if we foreclose the possibility that our preexisting beliefs are erroneous, we are behaving unscientifi-cally. Skepticism entails a willingness to entertain novel claims; cynicism does not.

Third Commandment

Thou shalt distinguish methodological skepticism from philo-sophical skepticism. When encouraging students to think criti-cally, we must distinguish between two forms of skepticism: 1) an approach that subjects all knowledge claims to scrutiny with the goal of sorting out true from false claims, namely methodologi-cal (scientific) skepticism, and 2) an approach that denies the possibility of knowledge, namely philosophical skepticism. When explaining to students that scientific knowledge is inherently tentative and open to revision, some students may mistakenly conclude that genuine knowledge is impossible. This view, which is popular in certain postmodernist circles, neglects to distin-guish knowledge claims that are more certain from those that are less certain. Although absolute certainly is probably unattain-able in science, some scientific claims, such as Darwin's theory of natural selection, have been extremely well corroborated, whereas others, such as the theory underpinning astrological horoscopes, have been convincingly refuted. Still others, such as cognitive dissonance theory, are scientifically controversial. Hence, there is a continuum of confidence in scientific claims; some have acquired virtual factual status, whereas others have been resoundingly falsified. The fact that methodological skepticism does not yield completely certain answers to scientific questions and that such answers could in principle be overturned by new evidence does not imply that knowledge is impossible, only that this knowledge is provisional. Nor does it imply that the answers generated by controlled scientific investigation are no better than other answers, such as those generated by intuition (see Myers, 2002).

Fourth Commandment

Thou shalt distinguish pseudoscientific claims from claims that are merely false. All scientists, even the best ones, make mistakes. Sir Isaac Newton, for example, flirted with bizarre alchemical hypotheses throughout much of his otherwise distinguished scientific career (Gleick, 2003). Students need to understand that the key difference between science and pseudoscience lies not in their content (i.e., whether claims are factually correct or incorrect) but in their approach to evidence. Science, at least when it operates properly, seeks out contradictory information and — assuming that this evidence is replicable and of high quality — eventually incorporates such information into its corpus of knowledge. In contrast, pseudoscience tends to avoid contradictory information (or manages to find a way to reinterpret this information as consistent with its claims) and thereby fails to foster the self-correction that is essential to scientific progress. For example, astrology has changed remarkably little over the past 2,500 years despite overwhelmingly negative evidence (Hines, 2003).

Fifth Commandment

Thou shalt distinguish science from scientists. Although the scientific method is a prescription for avoiding confirmatory bias (Lilienfeld, 2002), this point does not imply that scientists are free of biases. Nor does it imply that all or even most scientists are open to evidence that challenges their cherished beliefs. Scientists can be just as pigheaded and dogmatic in their beliefs as anyone else. Instead, this point implies that good scientists strive to become aware of their biases and to counteract them as much as possible by implementing safeguards against error (e.g., double-blind control groups) imposed by the scientific method. Students need to understand that the scientific method is a toolbox of skills that scientist have developed to prevent themselves from confirming their own biases.

Sixth Commandment

Thou shalt explain the cognitive underpinnings of pseudoscientific beliefs. Instructors should emphasize that we are all prone to cognitive illusions (Piatelli-Palmarini, 1994) and that such illusions can be subjectively compelling and difficult to resist. For example, class demonstrations illustrating that many or most of us can fall prey to false memories (e.g., Roediger & McDermott, 1995) can help students to see that the psychological processes that lead to erroneous beliefs are pervasive. Moreover, it is important to point out to students that the heuristics (mental shortcuts) that can produce false beliefs, such as representativeness, availability, and anchoring (Tversky & Kahneman, 1974), are basically adaptive and help us to make sense of a complex and confusing world. Hence, most pseudoscientific beliefs are cut from the same cloth as accurate beliefs. By underscoring these points, instructors can minimize the odds that students who embrace pseudoscientific beliefs will feel foolish when confronted with evidence that contradicts their beliefs.

Seventh Commandment

Thou shalt remember that pseudoscientific beliefs serve important motivational functions. Many paranormal claims, such as those concerning extrasensory perception, out-of-body experiences, and astrology, appeal to believers' deep-seated needs for hope and wonder, as well as their needs for a sense of control over the often uncontrollable realities of life and death. Most believers in the paranormal are searching for answers to profound existential questions, such as "Is there a soul?" and "Is there life after death?" As psychologist Barry Beyerstein (1999) noted (in a play on P.T. Barnum's famous quip), "there's a seeker born every minute" (p. 60). Therefore, in presenting students with scientific evidence that challenges their paranormal beliefs, we should not be surprised when many of them become defensive. In turn, defensiveness can engender an unwillingness to consider contrary evidence.

One of the two best means of lessening this defensiveness (the second is the Eighth Commandment below) is to gently challenge students' beliefs with sympathy and compassion and with the understanding that students who are emotionally committed to paranormal beliefs will find these beliefs difficult to question, let alone relinquish. Ridiculing these beliefs can produce reactance (Brehm, 1966) and reinforce students' stereotypes of science teachers as close-minded and dismissive. In some cases, teachers who have an exceptionally good rapport with their class can make headway by challenging students' beliefs with good-natured humor (e.g., "I'd like to ask all of you who believe in psychokinesis to please raise *my* hand"). However, teachers must ensure that such humor is not perceived as demeaning or condescending.

Eighth Commandment

Thou shalt expose students to examples of good science as well as to examples of pseudoscience. In our classes, it is critical not merely to debunk inaccurate claims but to expose students to accurate claims. We must be careful not merely to take away student's questionable knowledge, but to give them legitimate knowledge in return. In doing so, we can make it easier for students to swallow the bitter pill of surrendering their cherished beliefs in the paranormal. Students need to understand that many genuine scientific findings are at least as fascinating as are many scientifically dubious paranormal claims. In my own teaching, I have found it useful to intersperse pseudoscientific information with information that is equally remarkable but true, such as lucid dreaming, eidetic imagery, subliminal perception (as opposed to subliminal persuasion, which is far more scientifically dubious), extraordinary feats of human memory (Neisser & Hyman, 2000), and appropriate clinical uses of hypnosis (as opposed to the scientifically unsupported use of hypnosis for memory recovery; see Lynn, Lock, Myers, & Payne, 1997). In addition, we should bear in mind the late paleontologist Stephen Jay Gould's (1996) point that exposing a falsehood necessarily affirms a truth. As a consequence, it is essential not only to point out false information to students, but also to direct them to true information. For example, when explaining why claims regarding biorhythms are baseless (see Hines, 2003), it is helpful to introduce students to claims regarding circadian rhythms, which, although often confused with biorhythms, are supported by rigorous scientific research.

Ninth Commandment

Thou shalt be consistent in one's intellectual standards. One error that I have sometimes observed among skeptics, including psychology instructors who teach critical thinking courses, is to adopt two sets of intellectual standards: one for claims that they find plausible and a second for claims that they do not. The late psychologist Paul Meehl (1973) pointed out that this inconsistency amounts to "shifting the standards of evidential rigor depending on whose ox is being gored" (p. 264). For example, I know one educator who is a vocal proponent of the movement to develop lists of empirically supported therapies, that is, psychological treatments that have been shown to be efficacious in controlled studies. In this domain, he is careful to draw on the research literature to buttress his assertions regarding which psychotherapies are efficacious and which are not. Yet he is dismissive of the research evidence for the efficacy of electroconvulsive therapy (ECT) for depression, even though this evidence derives from controlled studies that are every bit as rigorous as those conducted for the psychotherapies that he espouses. When I pointed out this inconsistency to him, he denied emphatically that he was adhering to a double standard. It eventually became apparent to me that he was casting aside the evidence for ECT's efficacy merely because this treatment struck him as grossly implausible. Why on earth, he probably wondered, should inducing an epileptoid seizure by administering electricity to the brain alleviate depression? But because surface plausibility is a highly fallible barometer of the validity of truth claims, we must remain open to evidence that challenges our intuitive preconceptions and encourage our students to do so as well.

Tenth Commandment

Thou shalt distinguish pseudoscientific claims from purely metaphysical religious claims. My final commandment is likely to be the most controversial, especially for skeptics who maintain that both pseudoscientific and religious beliefs are irrational. To appreciate the difference between these two sets of beliefs, we must distinguish pseudoscience from metaphysics. Unlike pseudoscientific claims, metaphysical claims (Popper, 1959) cannot be tested empirically and therefore lie outside the boundaries of science. In the domain of religion, these include claims regarding the existence of God, the soul, and the afterlife, none of which can be refuted by any conceivable body of scientific evidence. Nevertheless, certain religious or quasi-religious beliefs, such as those involving "intelligent design" theory, which is the newest incarnation of creationism (see Miller, 2000), the Shroud of Turin, and weeping statues of Mother Mary, are indeed testable and hence suitable for critical analysis alongside of other questionable naturalistic beliefs. By conflating pseudoscientific beliefs with religious beliefs that are strictly metaphysical, instructors risk needlessly alienating a sizeable proportion of their students, many of whom may be profoundly religious, and (paradoxically) undermining students' critical thinking skills, which require a clear understanding of the difference between testable and untestable claims.

Conclusion

Adherence to the Ten Commandments can allow psychology educators to assist students with the crucial goal of distinguishing science from pseudoscience. If approached with care, sensitivity, and a clear understanding of the differences between skepticism and cynicism, methodological and philosophical skepticism, the scientific method and the scientists who use it, and pseudoscience and metaphysics, incorporating pseudoscience and fringe science into psychology courses can be richly rewarding for teachers and students alike. In a world in which the media, self-help industry, and Internet are disseminating psychological pseudoscience at an ever-increasing pace, the critical thinking skills needed to distinguish science from pseudoscience should be considered mandatory for all psychology students.

References and Recommended Readings

Beyerstein, B.L. (1999). Pseudoscience and the brain: Tuners and tonics for aspiring superhumans. In S.D. Sala (Ed.), *Mind myths: Exploring popular assumptions about the mind and brain* (pp. 59-82). Chichester, England: Wiley.

Brehm, J. (1966). *A theory of psychological reactance.* New York: Academic Press.

Bunge, M. (1984, Fall). What is pseudoscience? *Skeptical Inquirer, 9,* 36-46.

Dougherty, M.J. (2004). Educating believers: Research demonstrates that courses in skepticism can effectively decrease belief in the paranormal. *Skeptic, 10*(4), 31-35.

Gilovich, T. (1991). *How we know what isn't so: The fallibility of human reason in everyday life.* New York: Free Press.

Gleick, J. (2003). *Isaac Newton.* New York: Pantheon Books.

Gould, S.J. (1996, May). *Keynote address, "Science in the age of (mis) information."* Talk presented at the Convention of the Committee for the Scientific Investigation of Claims of the Paranormal, Buffalo, NY.

Hines, T. (2003). *Pseudoscience and the paranormal: A critical examination of the evidence.* Buffalo, NY: Prometheus.

Kelly, G.A. (1955). *The psychology of personal constructs, Vols. 1 and 2.* New York: Norton.

Kida, T. (2006) *Don't believes everything you think: The six basic mistakes we make thinking.* Amherst, NY: Prometheus Books.

Lilienfeld, S.O. (2002). When worlds collide: Social science, politics, and the Rind et al. child sexual abuse meta-analysis. *American Psychologist, 57,* 176-188.

Lilienfeld, S.O., Lohr, M., & Morier, D. (2001). The teaching of courses in the science and pseudoscience of psychology. *Teaching of Psychology, 28,* 182-191.

Lilienfeld, S.O., Lynn, S. J., & Lohr, J. M. (2003). *Science and pseudoscience in clinical psychology.* New York: Guilford.

Lynn, S.J., Lock, T.G., Myers, B., & Payne, D.G. (1997). Recalling the unrecallable: Should hypnosis be used to recover memories in psychotherapy? *Current Directions in Psychological Science, 6,* 79-83.

Meehl, P.E. (1973). *Psychodiagnosis: Selected papers.* Minneapolis, MN: University of Minnesota Press.

Miller, K. (2000). *Finding Darwin's God: A scientist's search for common ground between God and evolution.* New York: Cliff Street Books.

Morier, D., & Keeports, D. (1994). Normal science and the paranormal: The effect of a scientific method course on students' beliefs in the paranormal. *Research in Higher Education, 35,* 443-453.

Myers, D.G. (2002). *Intuition: Its powers and perils.* New Haven: Yale University Press.

Neisser, U. & Hyman, I.E. (2000). *Memory observed: Remembering in natural contexts.* New York: Worth Publishers.

Piatelli-Palmarini, M. (1994). *Inevitable illusions: How mistakes of reason rule our minds.* New York: Wiley.

Popper, K.R. (1959). *The logic of scientific discovery.* New York: Basic Books.

Roediger, H.L., & McDermott, K.B. (1995). Creating false memories: Remembering words not presented in lists. *Journal of Experimental Psychology: Learning, Memory, and Cognition, 21,* 803-814.

Ruscio, J. (2002). *Clear thinking with psychology: Separating sense from nonsense.* Pacific Grove, CA: Wadsworth.

Sagan, C. (1995). *The demon-haunted world: Science as a candle in the dark.* New York: Random House.

Shermer, M. (2002). *Why people believe weird things: Pseudoscience, superstition, and other confusions of our time.* New York: Owl Books.

Stanovich, K. (1997). *How to think straight about psychology* (4th ed.). New York: Harper Collins.

Tversky, A., & Kahneman, D. (1974). Judgment under uncertainty: Heuristics and biases. *Science, 185,* 1124-1131.

Wesp, R., & Montgomery, K. (1998). Developing critical thinking through the study of paranormal phenomena. *Teaching of Psychology, 25,* 275-278.

Student Research in Psychology Courses

JASON A. WILLIAMS
Gonzaga University

A FOUNDATION CLASS for every undergraduate psychology program is some form of "research methods." Not only does this class provide students with tools to design experiments, but perhaps more importantly it teaches them to think critically and skeptically about psychology and more broadly about being better consumers of information and hence better citizens. In this post post-modern era, where the claim is that "you have your evidence, I have mine; all are equal," a research methods class is a critical venue for emphasizing what science is and what it is not. An effective tool to convey this information lies in having students actively conduct research as a course requirement. Currently, roughly 60 percent of methodology classes require students to engage in a research project lasting two weeks or more (Perlman & McCann, 2005). Given my personal experience with and without this component, I hope to see this number increase. Whether you are contemplating initiating this approach or are a veteran, hopefully one or more of the following tips will improve your classroom experience. A number of these tips may prove useful in other courses that involve data collection, or they may motivate an addition of such a component in these classes (e.g., Introductory Psychology).

Institutional Review Board (IRB)

Collecting data from human participants should entail a consultation with the appropriate IRB (National Institute of Health, 2006). There are some old-timers who still claim that collecting classroom data is a pedagogical exercise, and that if it is not going to be published you do not need IRB approval. However, if you go down this road, you preclude your students from presenting or publishing any interesting findings. I would advise everyone to engage the IRB — better safe than sorry, and with undergraduates sometimes adopting some independent methods you are not aware of, the legal coverage cannot hurt.

The IRB is often a busy committee, and it is not going to want to review hoards of student proposals each semester. If possible, cut a deal. At Gonzaga, the agreement is as follows: the instructor of the research methods class must take the NIH online certification (http://www.nihtraining.com), which gives the authority to approve any minimal-risk projects in the classroom. At the end of each semester, the instructor must send a list of the titles of the projects to the IRB. This feedback is painless and fast. You are covered legally, and you can reject inappropriate student ideas out of hand ("I am sorry but depriving people of sleep and measuring its effect on sexual activity is not minimal risk Joe...").

Group Projects and Social Loafing

Unless you have *very* small classes, you are going to have to utter the words that 90 percent of students hate: "You will be working in small groups this semester." Groups of three to four students per project work best; anything larger and there is too much diffusion of responsibility. The dark side of group projects is, of course, social loafing. One practice I have found effective is to have students do all written work independently. A final grade based solely upon these assignments (essentially drafts of the introduction, methods, results, and discussion, and an assembled paper at semester's end) results in a clean indication of individual merit. I do not grade individual contributions to research design, the creation of experimental materials, etc. (being easily divisible tasks, social loafing should be relatively rare, Sharon & Sharon, 1976; Steiner, 1972).

However, if one does choose to grade these less tangible aspects of the project, some form of peer feedback evaluation is probably essential. Although knowing such evaluation is forthcoming is a deterrent to loafing, end-of-semester assessments of these evaluations can be tricky, and grade adjustments should be made only with a strong consensus. Designing questions that minimize personality differences and assess direct contribution is helpful in determining the nature of the group dynamics but is still subject to personal bias. Group members who receive negative feedback from others are likely to claim they were actively excluded from participation despite their best efforts. A good compromise is a peer-evaluation system (and the resultant loafing-deterrence effect), followed by a conservative adjustment policy.

From past experience, I address the issue of sharing on the syllabus: no group member is *required* to share any resources (e.g. references for the literature review), although they are not *prevented* from doing so. A previous lack of clarity on this issue has resulted in within-group conflict, with students placing uncomfortable demands on other students.

Assigning Groups

Will you let students choose the composition of their own groups, or will you assign them? In addition to immediate self-selection, another possibility is to allow students to get to know each other early in the semester through class exercises and to subsequently choose groups. If one does allow self-selection, I advise designing some process whereby students can "divorce" each other at any time with specific rules about what must be shared and how work will be completed. Friends (or lovers) at the beginning of the semester may no longer be so at the end, and group dynamics may become unworkable. As I find splitting up groups too unwieldy, I do not allow such divisions and instead rely on initial random assignment to groups. Individuals may not necessarily like each other, but they can usually maintain a formal enough relationship to get the project done. If possible, I actually employ a faux random assignment that balances groups based on my perceived assessment of ability and motivation.

Choosing a Research Topic

Lower-division students typically have little idea of what constitutes a psychologically interesting and logistically pos-sible project for a semester. The first decision here is whether to "seed" the idea pool or not. The most direct approach to seeding is providing access to a file of past projects, "do-able" research areas, journals of undergraduate research, etc. Students are quickly directed to fertile ground for projects, minimizing false starts, and then subsequently "tweak" or otherwise alter an existing experiment to explore new ground. One problem with this approach lies with the subsequent experimental design process. A project too similar to an existing experiment allows for much of the heavy lifting of design process to be retrieved from prior research. If this is the case, an artificial prohibition is probably necessary to encourage working through the process of research design.

For this reason, I do not mind having students engage in research that is not conceptually sound or that an experienced researcher might find uninteresting if their work entails arriving at completely original operational definitions and having to address numerous potential confounds from scratch. For me, working through the methodological problems is more important than content. Therefore I have students develop ideas cold.

I initially describe minimal risk and then allow 30 minutes or so of class time to generate ideas. We briefly discuss possibilities, with members from all groups piping in, and then I send them on their way. Most really good ideas will come outside the classroom over time. Three subsequent class meetings are scheduled to hone in on a "do-able" experiment. Groups propose their ideas, and along with input from classmates, are guided toward workable projects.

Addressing Three Problems With Proposals

Once a topic area is ethically in the ballpark, inevitably the next obstacle concerns proposals that are much too specific, much too general, or of questionable psychological interest.

Too Specific

Employ the up-down technique. The first step is to pull them up a layer by determining the theoretical question that might be answered by their study. Once this question is identified, the second step is go back down a layer, determining the most efficient way to answer this question, which often has little resemblance to the initial proposal. Nevertheless, the result is a proposal that the group feels they invented, and for which they take ownership.

Example: "We want to study whether males or females push the elevator button more often."

Up-Response: "Well what are you really trying to study?" Some possibilities to draw out might be: are males or females more impatient, or are there gender differences in the belief that technology often fails?

Down-Response: "Okay, if we are trying to evaluate patience, is there an easier, better way to measure it?" Students then come up with operational definitions until a project is workable. Pedagogically, this interactive process allows students to directly address the relationship between theory, constructs, and operational definitions and is complemented by a lecture I conveniently schedule just prior to this process.

Too General

In this case, simply state that no one experiment could address the question they pose, and narrow them down to a specific population, context, etc. This process is relatively painless. If you provide them with a few alternatives, they will usually arrive at others of their own.

Questionable Interest

Informing them that performing a literature review would take *much* more time for an off-the-wall topic is usually sufficient to deter them. A simple refusal works too. Often, however, one can find some related issue with which groups can work, and again, for which they can take ownership.

A final thought — some projects are so ubiquitous that you may create a list that simply rules them out. The classic "studying with or without music" comes to mind. Although it probably is workable in terms of literature reviews and having students design methodology, it may be unworkable in terms of your sanity overseeing the project for the umpteenth time.

Structure

For many research methods classes employing data collection, the final goal is an APA-style paper reporting the research. This can be a daunting task unless some form of division occurs throughout the semester. At scheduled due dates (after discussing each), I collect drafts of the introduction, methods, results, and discussion, which are graded and returned. Assigning a grade is necessary to encourage effort at these stages, but I reserve the bulk (75 percent) of the final grade for the final paper. This allows some rigorous criticism and grading of the drafts that motivates subsequent performance, without prematurely precluding students from a decent overall grade. The final paper is due at the end of the semester, graded according to a tally sheet provided to the students with the initial syllabus.

Collecting Data

During the proposal process I strongly encourage groups toward collection of data during specified class periods — I reserve a time from the lab and one from the lecture for data collection. This allows two possible times for students in other courses to be participants (for extra credit), and provides two ready-made groups for between-participant designs. It also is safer. If data collection is in the classroom or laboratory, you know what is going on. In the field, who knows? Experimental designs where participants are tested individually are tricky unless one has a dedicated space for such projects. If one has this luxury, on-line participant sign-up software can often streamline this process.

I often discourage observational studies, as I want students to work through the problems associated with operationalizing true independent variables. However, if you allow them, I would again emphasize the ethical issues that occur without informed consent. Safest is to forbid both altering the environment or any interaction with the observed person.

Analyzing Data

Whether to assign students to analyze their own data depends on your teaching philosophy, student preparation, the size of class, the strength of your department statistics program, and so forth. I meet with each group and walk them through the inferential statistics, but if your students have a statistics background, it is probably better to let them go at it themselves. At a minimum, assign them the descriptive statistics. Let them collate the data and see if there are differences in group means. They collected the data; let them have the fun of first discovery!

Presentations and Publication

There are outlets for student publication (e.g., *Journal of Psychology and Behavioral Science*; *Journal of Undergraduate Research*; *Psi Chi Journal of Undergraduate Research*), and at many teaching universities, such an outcome is beneficial for tenure/promotion review. Keep in mind, if you collected data without IRB approval, this will not be an option. The promise of publication is also a carrot that motivates students throughout the semester to have cleaner research. They likely will not hit the jackpot, but then again they just might.

Many universities have regular poster sessions where undergraduates present experimental findings. If so, consider making this a course requirement, as it has a number of merits. The public nature of the project increases motivation, students make a physical poster, and they gain confidence in public presentation and speaking. Often regional conferences exist for undergraduate poster sessions, allowing networking with other students and faculty, and further adding to their comfort in public presentations. Another possibility is scheduling a poster session for the last day of class where faculty and interested students drop by and discuss the projects.

Final Thoughts

After shifting to an approach where students design, run, analyze, and interpret experiments while working in small groups, my methods class has improved greatly; students are more interested and engaged in lecture material, and the changing nature of the projects keeps the content fresh every semester. Subsequent to this change, student ratings for the class have broadly increased (a full point on a seven-point scale) and are now on par with my other classes. As an added bonus, one enters a cooperative and collaborative relationship with one's students. No longer only engaged in evaluation, one becomes a teammate in the common goal of scientific inquiry. I always feel a special bond with psychology majors who have taken my methods class for just this reason— we have worked together, and discovered something together.

In addition to the lab, the lecture component of the class can also improve. Discussions of particular techniques are no longer abstract hypotheticals, but rather tools students think about with regard to their own studies. Discussing within- versus between-participant designs now becomes relevant to the student's particular experience. When one discusses counterbalancing, one can use examples right from class, rather than an abstract or historical example. I strongly recommend employing active research components into lab sections of methodology courses and incorporating student projects into lecture material. Give it a try — implementation is easier than you think, and you will be pleasantly surprised by the results.

References and Recommended Readings

Atkinson, J.M. (1982). Understanding formality: The categorization and production of formal' interaction. *British Journal of Sociology, 33*, 86-117.

Cartwright, D. (1968). The nature of group cohesiveness. In D. Cartwright & A. Zander (Eds.), *Group dynamics* (3rd ed., pp. 91-109). New York: Harper & Row.

Horner, D.T., Stetter, K.R., & McCann, L.I. (1998). Adding structure to unstructured research courses. *Teaching of Psychology, 25,* 126-128.

Journal of Psychological and Behavioral Sciences 2006, Farleigh Dickinson University, Retrieved May 24, 2006, from http://view.fdu.edu/default.aspx?id=784

Journal of Undergraduate Research 2006, U.S. Department of Energy, Office of Science, Retrieved May 24, 2006, from http://www.scied.science.doe.gov/scied/JUR.html

Lott, A.J., & Lott, B.E. (1965). Group cohesiveness as interpersonal attraction: A review of relationships with antecedent and consequent variables. *Psychological Bulletin, 64,* 259-302.

National Institute of Health 2006, Regulations and Ethical Guidelines. Retrieved May 24, 2006, from http://www.nihtraining.com/ohsrsite/guidelines/graybook.html#app3

Perlman, B., & McCann, L.I. (2005). Undergraduate research experiences in psychology: A national study of courses and curricula. *Teaching of Psychology, 32,* 5-14.

Psi Chi Journal of Undergraduate Research 2006, Psi Chi, Retrieved May 24, 2006, from http://www.psichi.org/pubs/journal/submissions.asp

Sharan, S., & Sharan, Y. (1976). *Small group teaching.* Englewood Cliffs, NJ: Educational Technology.

Steiner, I.D. (1972). *Group processes and productivity.* New York: Academic.

Teaching Quantitative Reasoning: How to Make Psychology Statistically Significant

NEIL LUTSKY
Carleton College

HOW CAN PSYCHOLOGY contribute to the public good? The Human Capital Initiative (HCI) report, prepared with the assistance of APS, cites an important means of doing so: *helping people to improve their statistical reasoning.* "The goal of learning statistical reasoning" it notes, "should be to develop better statistical 'instincts,' not just knowledge of particular statistical procedures" (Human Capital Initiative, 1998, p. 24).

Those instincts are crucial to contemporary life, for, as the National Council on Education and the Disciplines (Steen, 2001, p. 1) observed, "The world of the twenty-first century is a world awash in numbers." Although data are not always used well (e.g., Best, 2004), data-based claims are nonetheless a staple of policy debates, advertisements, medical news, educational assessments, financial decision-making, and everyday conversation, as well as of pure and applied research in psychological science. In sum, our students need sharp statistical instincts to navigate psychology and to contribute to life beyond it.

Are we as faculty in higher education doing enough to help students develop quantitative values and skills? According to colleagues in mathematics, the answer is no. In a 1998 report, "Quantitative Reasoning for College Graduates," the Mathematical Association of America suggested, "too many educated people... are quantitatively illiterate." Some mathematicians hold their own discipline partially responsible. Lynn Steen (2004) of St. Olaf College has cogently argued that the postsecondary mathematics curriculum channels college students away from quantitative study. Psychology, then, has the opportunity to help undergraduates develop needed statistical instincts.

Psychology's Special Role in Promoting Quantitative Reasoning (QR)

There are at least four reasons why psychology as a discipline is well-suited to contribute to undergraduate education in QR.

Psychology Has Wide Exposure to Undergraduates

Approximately 1.2 million students take introductory psychology courses annually (M. Sugarman, McGraw-Hill Publishers, personal communication, June 1, 2005) and nearly 75,000 graduate each year with a degree in psychology (American Psychological Association, 2005).

Psychology Has a Natural Affinity for QR

As the historian of statistics Stephen Stigler has shown, statistics and psychology are "inextricably bound together" (1999, p. 189). (Unfortunately, Stigler rejects the hypothesis that psychologists were so much quicker to adapt statistics because they were smarter than other social scientists; he might be wrong of course!)

Psychology Has Rich Incentives to Hone Students' QR Instincts

Not only is quantitative reasoning an essential component of training in a psychology major (see Task Force on Undergraduate Psychology Major Competencies, 2002), it is important to public understanding of contemporary psychological research and practice.

Psychologists Can Appreciate the Educational Rationale for QR Across the Curriculum

We recognize that students need to encounter a broad array of stimulus conditions calling for QR if they are to develop and strengthen generalized QR cognitive tendencies. Psychology represents one of a number of content areas besides mathematics in which QR might naturally come into play for students.

What is QR?

In literatures addressing quantitative reasoning and literacy, many authors attempt to specify lists of skills or outcomes constituting QR (e.g., Steen, 2001). Although there is variation among lists, most lists include the following: descriptive and inferential statistics, chance and probability, graphical presentations of data, modeling, and research design and methods. At my own institution, these are embedded in a broader goal: *helping students learn to use and evaluate quantitative information in a principled way in accounts of phenomena and in the construction of arguments.* This intertwining of QR with argument in learned and public discourses builds upon a theme articulated by psychologist Robert Abelson in 1995, "the purpose of statistics is to organize a useful argument from quantitative evidence, using a form of principled rhetoric" (p. xiii). In our approach, we do not only view statistics as a form of argument. We also view argument in general as potentially involving a form of statistics. Within this framework, QR involves 1) appreciating the value of quantitative approaches to understanding; 2) being willing to use QR electively in constructing an argument; 3) knowing or knowing how to find or generate relevant quantitative information; 4) evaluating implicit and explicit quantitative claims in light of relevant standards and critical issues; and 5) representing and communicating quantitative information or evaluations in a clear, informative, and responsible manner.

QR in the Classroom

How can we help move our students toward quantitative literacy? In what follows, I will concentrate on suggestions for general or service psychology courses where teachers of psychology encounter the largest number of students. Students majoring in psychology are repeatedly called upon to use QR through statistics and methods courses, laboratories, readings, and research in psychology (Messer, Griggs, & Jackson, 1999). Whether psychology majors develop generalized statistical instincts, however, remains an open question. The suggestions below, then, might be used profitably across the psychology curriculum.

Focus Student Attention on Quantitative Information

Quantitative information is a content staple of basic psychology texts and class presentations on psychology. However, students may not attend carefully to numbers, figures, and tables they encounter in these sources. An instructor can elicit such attention by highlighting key quantitative findings, walking students through the interpretation of tables and figures, and discussing when and why a particular degree of quantitative precision is warranted in psychology. An instructor can reinforce these points by telling students that examinations will assess their knowledge and use of meaningful quantitative information in psychology.

Invite Students to Interpret Quantitative Findings

A key QR goal is that students learn to interpret research results and recognize critical questions they ought to raise about quantitative claims. An instructor can facilitate this by presenting a quantitative stimulus in class — such as a graphic or table of results on a slide — and asking students to make sense of quantitative findings in a discussion or brief in-class writing assignment. The simple question, "What is this quantitative stimulus telling us?" will get students thinking about quantitative information and relating that information to key arguments in a psychological literature. The natural follow-up question, "What additional information would be useful to evaluate this quantitative presentation (e.g., graphic)?" can encourage critical thinking about quantitative claims and generate new research ideas.

Teach Students to Seek Quantitative Information

Students need to learn how to find and evaluate quantitative information relevant to psychology, for example, when they consider the cross-cultural or ecological validity of research results or learn about the epidemiology of mental disorders. Even basic quantitative facts about world population and literacy may help set psychology in context. It may be useful to collaborate with a local college librarian to develop instruction for students about finding sources of relevant quantitative information. Likewise, instructors can provide students a description of the standards employed in psychology to evaluate the adequacy of an informational source (e.g., peer review). An instructor could then expect students to use these skills to frame any oral or written presentations they are assigned.

Involve Students in Data Analysis

One method of getting students to learn and think about statistics is to give them a reason to use statistics. This is common in statistics and research methods courses in psychology, where students write research proposals and complete canned and novel empirical projects. It is also possible to involve general psychology students in data analysis through course laboratories or data set projects.

In my introductory course, for example, students complete two web-based research modules. In one, they take personality and happiness measures and then pose an empirical question answerable from the course data set to which they have contributed. Students then conduct a simple statistical analysis to answer their questions and submit short research reports. A benefit of projects such as these is that they give the instructor a meaningful context in which to assign the statistics appendix of an introductory text and to provide guidance on using and interpreting quantitative findings.

Require Students to Write About Data

Commonly, when students are asked to find quantitative information or to analyze data, they are also called upon to write about what they have discovered. Translating numerical information into words can be an effective means of strengthening statistics students' computational and interpretive skills (Beins, 1993). Beins suggests asking students to write in jargon-free terms about quantitative information found in almanacs, psychology journal articles, and other sources. Because written work in psychology, even at the introductory level, commonly addresses quantitative information, students need to be taught when and how to present and use quantitative arguments. Writing about quantitative information should stimulate students to think about both the meaning of technical concepts (e.g., confidence intervals, statistical significance) and principles that apply to the effective communication of technical information and the construction of arguments. Miller (2004) and Tufte (2001) provide two excellent sources for instructors wanting to address these issues.

At my own institution, we are in the midst of a Department of Education Fund for the Improvement of Postsecondary Education (FIPSE) project (QUIRK, 2005) in which teams of faculty are reading course papers from across the curriculum to study how students incorporate or neglect relevant quantitative information in written arguments. For example, we have found that students are needlessly ambiguous, using words like "many" or "often" to represent a quantitative claim without providing supporting specifics (how many?). One goal of our project is to use what we learn to help faculty develop course work, writing and speaking assignments, and instruction that will teach students to use and present quantitative information more effectively.

Relate QR to Topics in Psychology

Instructors can relate the psychological science of everyday judgment and perception to issues in quantitative reasoning. For example, a presentation can contrast the cognitive tendencies to overgeneralize from single cases and to notice illusory correlations to concerns in formal statistical reasoning such as a reliance on incomplete data (see Lawson, Schwiers, Doellman, Grady, & Kelnhofer, 2003, for an elaboration). In this way, a discussion of a psychological phenomenon may help students appreciate the value of systematic QR.

Model QR and Make the Case for QR

We as faculty need to model QR for students. For example, when we present, assign, or encounter case studies or anecdotes we need to remind our students to ask how representative of some category a particular instance is. We need to draw student attention to the questions we would ask when we discuss quantities (e.g., questions about outliers, subgroups, and variability when we think about averages). We need to demonstrate how we use quantitative information to illuminate phenomena, construct responsible arguments, and express caution about what we believe we know.

The larger social significance of QR may be obvious to most psychologists, but probably not to students. I find it useful to remind students that quantitative reasoning is not only fundamental to psychology as a discipline but is also pertinent to a wide variety of professional and public discourses students will encounter and even rely upon in their lives (e.g., Poundstone, 2003). When I teach general psychology courses, for example, I encourage all students, whether they intend to major in psychology or not, to take a statistics course during their undergraduate careers, and I tell them why I believe such a course would be worthwhile.

QR for Psychology Faculty

Although psychology faculty tend to be well-trained in statistics, we may be less familiar with the broader conversations occurring about QR as a fundamental goal of undergraduate training and how colleges and universities are attempting to address that goal. Because we may have an important role to play, we should consider becoming more involved in those discussions. Here are suggestions for doing so.

Read the Literature

There is a growing popular and educational literature on quantitative literacy and reasoning. I highly recommend recent books by Lynn Steen (2001, 2004) and Joel Best (2004), as well as the classic series on graphics by Edward Tufte (e.g., 2001).

Join the Networks

Link up with faculty across disciplines who are interested in QR. Good places to start are the National Numeracy Network, which has its web home at www.math.dartmouth.edu/~nnn, the Mathematical Association of America's portal for quantitative literacy at www.maa.org/ql/index.html, and the Statistical Literacy website, www.statlit.org. Lynn Steen also maintains a web list of higher education programs that address quantitative literacy and reasoning at www.stolaf.edu/people/steen/papers/qlprogs.pdf.

Get Involved in a Campus QR Initiative

Psychologists have the potential to play an important role in curriculum and faculty development and assessment efforts to address QR, and such participation may, in turn, enhance attitudes toward psychology as a scientific discipline. Teachers of psychology have served as consultants for other faculty at their institution on QR, helped draft curricular definitions and standards for QR, developed methods for assessing students' QR, and led campus workshops on integrating QR into the curriculum. Teachers have also configured their statistics and methods courses in psychology to meet QR standards at institutions that have a QR requirement.

Conclusion

There is a movement afoot in higher education to raise both appreciation for and the quality of training in QR. Psychology and psychologists have important roles to play in this initiative, both as teachers and as participants, in local and national educational communities.

References and Recommended Readings

Abelson, R.P. (1995). *Statistics as principled argument.* Hillsdale, NJ: Erlbaum.

American Psychological Association. (2005). Number of psychology degrees conferred by level of degree: 1970-2000. Retrieved June 2, 2005, from http://research.apa.org/general01.html

Beins, B.C. (1993). Writing assignments in statistics classes encourage students to learn interpretation. *Teaching of Psychology, 20,* 161-164.

Best, J. (2004). *More damned lies and statistics.* Berkeley: University of California Press.

Human Capital Initiative (1998). Decision making and statistical reasoning. *Observer, 11*(2), 23-25.

Lawson, T.J., Schwiers, M., Doellman, M., Grady, G., & Kelnhofer, R. (2003). Enhancing students' ability to use statistical reasoning with everyday problems. *Teaching of Psychology, 30,* 107-110.

Lutsky, N. (2002). Come, putative ends of psychology's digital future. In S.F. Davis & W. Buskist (Eds.), *The teaching of psychology: Essays in honor of Wilbert J. McKeachie and Charles L. Brewer* (pp. 335-345). Mahwah, NJ: Erlbaum.

Mathematical Association of America. (1998). *Quantitative reasoning for college graduates.* Retrieved August 12, 2007, from http://www.maa.org/past/ql/ql_preface.html

Messer, W.S., Griggs, R.A., & Jackson, S.L. (1999). A national survey of undergraduate psychology degree options and major requirements. *Teaching of Psychology, 26,* 164-171.

Miller, J.E. (2004). *The Chicago guide to writing about numbers.* Chicago: University of Chicago Press.

Poundstone, W. (2003). *How would you move Mount Fuji? Microsoft's cult of the puzzle.* Boston: Little, Brown, and Company.

QUIRK. (2005). *Carleton College quantitative inquiry, reasoning, and knowledge project.* Retrieved August 12, 2007, from http://apps.carleton.edu/collab/quirk/

Steen, L.A. (Ed.). (2001). *Mathematics and democracy: The case for quantitative literacy.* Princeton, NJ: National Council on Education and the Disciplines.

Steen, L.A. (2004). *Achieving quantitative literacy.* Washington, DC: Mathematical Association of America.

Stigler, S.M. (1999). *Statistics on the table: The history of statistical concepts and methods.* Cambridge, MA: Harvard University Press.

Task Force on Undergraduate Psychology Major Competencies. (2002). *Undergraduate psychology major learning goals and outcomes.* Retrieved June 2, 2005, from www.apa.org/ed/resources.html

Tufte, E.R. (2001). *The visual display of quantitative information.* Chesire, CT: Graphics Press.

Teaching Biology in a Psychology Class: Using Case Stories and Other Methods to Delight Yourself and Your Students

JOEL L. SHENKER
University of Virginia

ADMIT IT, YOU DON'T like teaching biology in your psychology class. It's not that it's unimportant, but reading and talking about it can be so ... well, not fun. Many of us who teach psychology have a limited biology background, and unless a course is specifically about biological psychology, most students do not expect to learn about nerve cells or ion channels. When did someone ever say, "I want to study psychology to master the cytoarchitectonics of the brain's cortical modules"?

When we teach biology in psychology courses, I think that we often forget principles of good teaching and effective public speaking. The result is class sessions that are overly detailed and poorly digested. We try to: 1)cover too much in less time, with multisyllabic jargon while talking more and faster, 2) cover material only once and in only one way, 3) focus on "trees" rather than the "forest," 4) involve students less and use overwhelming visual aids, and 5) use few examples or demonstrations. The only time that teachers and students are in concert is in a collective sigh of relief as the ordeal ends.

The purpose of this column is to help restore basic principles of good teaching and public speaking to teaching biology in a psychology class. However, the ideas below could apply to any teaching.

Remember the Rules of Public Speaking

Whether you teach in a discussion-oriented or a lecture format, when you lead your classroom sessions, you must employ fundamentals of good public speaking. One framework comes from speechwriter James C. Humes. From studying great orators, Humes (1996, 2002) describes basic principles of public speaking: start strongly, talk plainly, have a theme, paint a picture, and end emotionally. Let us review each rule separately, and consider using them more frequently as we teach biology in our psychology classes.

Rule 1: Start Strongly

Speeches should start with an impressive, captivating, memorable moment. There is plenty of time later to blend in thanks to the fine folks of the [organization name] who invited you, fond recollections of how you and [organization's founder] are good friends, praise for last night's dinner of [local cuisine] that the [region] is famous for, and compliments to the folks of [nearby town only locals know] who were so warm to you years ago. Rather than lead with these momentum-sapping platitudes, great speakers grab our interest right up front.

In covering biological material, one way to start strongly is to describe a person with a neurological problem. Such a case story is a teaching vehicle to make abstract concepts more real and identifiable — giving a face, as it were, to the material. You can summarize a real case from the literature (e.g. read issues of *Neurocase* or *Neuropsychologia*, or skim through a neuropsychology or behavioral neurology textbook) or build a hypothetical case from classic signs and symptoms in a textbook. For example, consider how you might teach the biology of vision. You could show a picture of the parts of the eyeball, name and describe them, then show the retina and describe how light comes in and gets transduced, then tell how visual fields split as information goes into the brain.

Yawn. Snore. REM Sleep. Try This Instead:

A 60-year-old woman saw her doctor for an exam. She had developed "blurred vision" a month ago. "Maybe I need new glasses," she offered, "but, the only time I have trouble seeing is when I read — the words just don't seem real." When the doctor tested her vision, she never reported any visual stimuli presented in her right visual field, no matter which eye she used. She could still see in her left visual field, so she could catch a ball thrown to her and could walk around the office without bumping into things. She could not read any words, but she could see the letters and point to them. She could write perfectly, but as soon as she did, she asked, "What does it say?" Apparently, she could not read the very words she had just written! A brain magnetic resonance imaging study confirmed a stroke affecting her left occipital lobe, including fibers of the back part of the corpus callosum.

This story describes a classic behavioral neurology syndrome, *alexia without agraphia*. Note how you can use this story to teach the biology of vision. Ask students to throw out ideas about what was wrong, such as: "What could she do? What could she not do? Let's look at the biology of vision and try to understand her." Then, always referring back to *this* lady, you can still go to the same pictures you were going to show before ("Let's look at her eyeball ... now let's look at her retina ..."). In this way, something abstract and remote is made real, concrete, and part of a story, and students want to know about it.

Other ways to start strongly might be to make material personal. For example, when I get migraine headaches, sometimes I lose vision in one visual field a few minutes before the headache (a well-known phenomenon). I might ask the class to guess why, then I have them look through diagrams of "my" visual system and ask for their comments along the way. I have an MRI picture of my brain I can show them, too. Who can resist commenting on their teacher's brain?

Or, start strongly by framing class with some questions: "Today we are discussing the biology of memory. What is memory? What does a mind need to do to make memory happen? What does a brain need to do? How might this/these fail? What would it be like to have a memory disorder?" You can then tie these questions to a case of, say, transient global amnesia.

Rule 2: Talk Plainly

The "talk plainly" rule dominates history's great speeches. Scholars argue over the exact words of Abraham Lincoln's Gettysburg Address. We do know, however, that of the approximately 240 words of the speech, about 75 percent were one-syllable words. Lincoln knew that speaking well requires speaking plainly and clearly. Consider if Martin Luther King's "I have a dream" had instead been "It is my fervent desire, not yet realized, but, I envision, will henceforth come to fruition." Not so catchy. Similarly, John Kennedy's "Ask not what your country can do for you, ask what you can do for your country" is a better call to action than "Eschew nationalistic hedonism in favor of its altruistic opposite."

There are three especially important applications of the talk plainly rule when teaching biological material.

Use Simple, Regular Words

Medical students learn words like *cardiac* and *hepatic* and *renal* when English already includes heart and liver and kidney. Do not follow in kind. Whenever possible, use the perfectly wonderful English words that you and your students already know. Talking plainly does not make you sound dumb; it makes you understood.

It is important to avoid using jargon when it is not needed, when its only purpose is to make you sound smart. But there are terms that a discipline uses and a nomenclature that students must therefore learn. So, at times you may have no choice but to use words that seem like jargon to students. For example, in discussing ions inside and outside of a nerve cell, you may need to say *sodium* and *potassium* and *membrane*. If you do need to use jargon (and be sure you really do need to), then explain it, define it, or discuss its origin (e.g. corpus callosum means "hard body"). (A medical dictionary such as *Stedman's* [2000] is an excellent resource.) Then, for a time, keep referring back to that common ground each time you use the term. For example, when I introduce the term *polarity*, I say, "Polarity just means a difference. Whenever you hear 'polar,' think 'different'." Then each time I use the "polar-" root again, I reprise the definition: "Normally, a nerve cell is electrically polarized, that is the electricity inside is *different* than outside," ... "Nerve cells do new things when they are depolarized — that is, when the inside and outside become less polar, or less *different*."

Use Simple Style

Second, the "talk plainly" rule also refers to the level of your discourse, the style of your language. Must you really say, "The intracytoplasmic ionic milieu, in contrast to the extracellular one, establishes a transmembrane polarity which is intracellularly negative"? The real message is: "The electrical charge inside a cell is negative compared with the outside." Just say that.

Cut Detail

The "talk plainly" rule dictates the topics you address in class. Here, you should mercilessly cut detail. Harshly decide what is not necessary and stick to the main points. You do not need to cover everything. Give your students the skeleton, and let them add the meaty details during at-home study. Occasionally in class you can, and should, highlight a point with more details. Doing so adds interest and shows how to pursue higher levels of analysis, but do not let the details become the main point of your class time.

Other applications of the "talk plainly" rule include:

- For every visual aid, have one clinching explanation ("The main point of this picture is ...").
- Rather than showing one complicated diagram, break it into many pictures that each makes a main point.
- Punctuate whenever possible by organizing material into lists, or by taking a complicated process and organizing it as a step-by-step sequence.
- Be truthful. There is a lot of material you may not know either because no one knows, or because it is outside your knowledge. Do not try to oversell what you do not know. If there are holes in the story, admit it. Use such moments as opportunities: Start a discussion, explore what the answer might be or how one could find out, or come back to class next time and report on what you've learned.

Rule 3: Have a Theme

A good dictionary contains most of the great works of literature. All the words are there, they're just not sequenced as they are in a real book. How things are bound together makes all the difference. Similarly, in good oral presentations, the parts fit together. There must be a theme, not just a list of nonconverging statements.

In a typical class session, there are a relatively few discrete concepts that students learn. So, carefully pick the few points that you want to teach, pick them well, and then make these themes hold your class session together.

State a Theme Explicitly

It helps to be clear on what the theme is. Consider again the biology of vision. There, a challenging topic is how visual information splits into visual fields that go to opposite sides of the brain. A bad way to teach this topic is just to show the classic diagram showing where pathways cross over or not, where synapses are, and what happens after damage at various places. This approach shows important details but is vague on how it all hangs together.

Instead, try starting by stating a theme: "Each half of the brain likes to construct a representation for the opposite side of space." Repeat it for emphasis and highlight the word "space." From that theme, you can now make sensible predictions. Of course, motor control would cross over essentially 100 percent, and skin sense information would cross over 100 percent. And, entirely predictably now, one would not want each eyeball to send all information to the opposite side of the brain, as each eyeball sees both the left and right sides of the world. Instead, we need to know from where each piece of retina gets its light. Picture an eyeball in horizontal cross-section, with rays of light coming through the pupil. From this, it is clear that the left eye's nasal retina (i.e. inner half) "sees" the left side of the world, and the right eye's nasal retina "sees" the right side of the world. Again: "Each half of the brain likes to construct a representation for the opposite side of space." So, fibers from each eye's nasal retina must cross to the opposite side of the brain. By contrast, the left eye's temporal retina "sees" the right side of the world, and the right eye's temporal retina "sees" the left side of the world. Yet again: "Each half of the brain likes to construct a representation for the opposite side of space." So, fibers from each eye's temporal retina go to the same side of the brain. Talk it through with the pictures.

A great way to make a class revolve around a theme is to refer back to a case story, perhaps one that you started class with that day ("start strongly"). Can you see how much more interesting the last paragraph becomes if you were discussing the alexia-without-agraphia lady, or my pre-migraine visual loss?

Show Students the "Forest"

Otherwise, the details they get are just so many "trees." Of course, this strategy is important for all teaching, as long-term memory relies on semantic encoding. With biological material, the dictum is even more important. Here, the material is, by nature, remote from one's experiences. Students are well practiced with using language, engaging in social discourse, responding to punishment, and feeling emotions. They can relate to these "real" topics. But most will never see an ion or a cell or, for that matter, a brain. These things are just not "real" in the same sense that the rest of a psychology course can be. You need to make these things semantically meaningful, to stress basic points, to show the forest.

One way to show the forest is to tie biological material with other areas of psychology. Explicitly link biology to some aspect of behavior or mentation. Never just show a brain structure. Instead, discuss the aspects of behavior that depend on this part of the brain. Do not just show ions and ion channels. Rather, talk about how drugs may affect these things to cause psychological changes. Similarly, bring up biology in other areas of your course. In talking about food selection and hunger in a unit on motivation, for example, mention research on hypothalamic mechanisms of hunger and satiety or how hormonal interactions between the gut and brain alter eating behavior. These methods allow students to relate topics to each other, and see the "forest" of psychology.

Teach the Same Idea More Than Once, but in Different Ways Each Time

As students extract the basic thrust of each repetition, they begin to understand the tie that binds, the theme that unites. You might alternate between a forest-level description of a process and a trees-level description, between text and graphics, between examples and principles.

Rule 4: Paint a Picture

Recall how Winston Churchill proclaimed the start of the cold war: "From Stettin in the Baltic, to Trieste in the Adriatic, an iron curtain has descended across the continent." These words labeled the conflict with a concrete image, an icon that the world used for decades. In speaking, the words we use get people to think thoughts. When words also get people to imagine scenes, their thoughts become more concrete, their meaning more crystallized and, ultimately, better remembered.

In teaching biological material, an obvious application of the "paint a picture" rule is to use visual aids. You have many opportunities to do so. You can present experiments with cartoons or photographs showing methods, stimuli, techniques, and data. Photographs and schematics can show brain structures at different levels of detail or from different viewpoints. You can show pictures of materials used to test neurology patients, perhaps along with samples of patients' output. The judicious use of videos and class demonstrations can help "paint a picture" by the live images they create.

You can get many such media easily. Ask colleagues to share materials, access source material from your textbook publisher, scan images from a book or article, create your own graphics with simple computer software, or download materials from an almost limitless supply on the internet (e.g. try a Google search, clicking on "images" to narrow the search). In using visual aids, I make three suggestions.

Understand the Point of Using Visuals

Often, you could say what you want without a picture. Using an actual picture helps to seal the deal. It should make what you say easy to imagine and understand and, ultimately, remember.

Present the Same Material Differently

Especially when showing anatomical pictures, try to show images from different viewpoints (top, bottom, side) or using different artistic styles (cartoons, schematics, actual photographs). This method gives people a chance to get the main point and to build a three-dimensional perspective on otherwise unfamiliar objects.

Use Visual Aids as Complements

Visual aids should complement what is said, not compete with it or take the place of it. Minimize details so the main point is clear, use a minimum of words, trim or edit images so that they inform rather than noisily distract. Each picture should make one or at most two basic points.

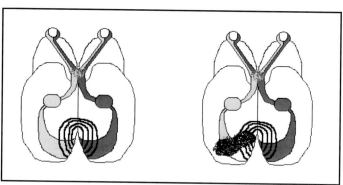

Figure 1

Association for Psychological Science

Let us consider how nicely a figure can work by returning to the alexia-without-agraphia patient from above. I used the simple Paint program pre-installed on most PCs to draw the two figures shown in Figure 1. On the left is a normal brain. It shows, schematically, the general flow of visual information as it enters the retina and goes into the brain. Left visual field, or LVF, information is in dark gray; right visual field, or RVF, information is in light gray. The use of this diagram makes it easier to follow the words-only descriptions (above) for how visual fields cross. Now look at the diagram on the right, with a lesion in the back part of the left hemisphere. By folding in a discussion of hemispheric specialization, you can now explain the patient. Damage to her left visual pathway caused RVF loss. She also had damage to her corpus callosum (the thick black lines). Thus, although she could still see in her LVF, this information could not go to the more linguistically competent left hemisphere. So, she could not read. She could still write because the language production systems for this function were themselves undamaged.

Rule 5: End Emotionally

The phenomena of serial position effects remind us that the start and end of class are more likely to be remembered than what happens in between. Strong speakers, unlike old soldiers, do not just fade away. Instead, strong speakers end by making people emotional, motivated, and ready to rise adoringly as if a reflexive autonomic response! (Well, maybe not that enthusiastic.)

In teaching biology in a psychology class, many of the suggestions above help end class on a motivational or emotional note. I sometimes pass out copies of my brain MRI and ask students to come back next time with the structures labeled, or with an outline of where to give me a stroke so I cannot lecture but could still give grades. Or, tell me what is "wrong" with my brain (there are some benign examples!).

You might end class with a case story. Ask students to be ready next time to say how a brain injury could produce the signs and symptoms. Or, ask them to describe carefully the person's impaired versus preserved functions, and how they could test their ideas. Or, ask them to compare the case at the end of class to one that started the class.

Like a soap opera you can't stop watching, ending class in these ways gives students feelings and questions. In this way, they leave motivated to read, study, do assignments, and come back for more.

References and Recommended Readings

Banich, M.T. (2003). *Cognitive neuroscience and neuropsychology* (2nd ed.). New York: Houghton-Mifflin.

Goldberg, S. (1979). *Clinical neuroanatomy made ridiculously simple.* Miami, FL: Medmaster.

Heilman, K.M. (2002). *Matter of mind.* New York: Oxford.

Humes, J.C. (1996). *Winston Churchill's method of public speaking.* Philadelphia: University of Pennsylvania.

Humes, J.C. (2002). *Speak like Churchill, stand like Lincoln: 21 practical secrets of history's greatest speakers.* New York: Crown Publishing.

Jozefowicz, R.F., & Holloway, R. G. (1999). *Case studies in neuroscience.* Philadelphia: FA Davis.

Rolak, L.A. (2001). *Neurology secrets* (3rd ed.). Philadelphia: Hanley & Belfus.

Sacks, O. (1970). *The man who mistook his wife for a hat and other clinical tales.* New York: Harper & Row.

Stedman, T. (2000). *Stedman's medical dictionary* (27th ed.). Philadelphia: Lippincott, Williams, and Wilkins.

Integrating Psychology and Law Into Undergraduate Instruction

RANDY K. OTTO
University of South Florida
SOLOMON M. FULERO
Sinclair Community College

UNDERGRADUATE INTEREST in psychological applications to the law has perhaps never been greater. Recent real cases that have involved aspects of psychology and law include the Central Park jogger case, in which four teenaged boys gave videotaped confessions that now appear to have been false (see Kassin, 2002). Due in part to both fictional (*Silence of the Lambs, Profiler, CSI*) and nonfictional (e.g., *Court TV, Dateline, 48 Hours, Forensic Files*) representations in the media, undergraduates are increasingly interested in learning about how psychology may be utilized in and by the legal system and about associated educational and career opportunities (Fulero et al., 1999). For example, students invariably mention wanting to learn about being a "profiler." Faculty can take advantage of student interest in the popular media's portrayal of forensic psychology to teach psychological concepts that have a place in the legal process (e.g., memory, perception, psychopathology, cognition, group processes) in a wide variety of subdisciplinary areas — clinical, cognitive, community developmental, industrial/ organizational, physiological, and social psychology.

In this column, we identify a variety of ways that faculty can enhance student learning and interest by using forensic psychology in the undergraduate curriculum. Although there is not universal agreement about exactly what is encompassed by "law and psychology" or "forensic psychology," we define these terms broadly to include any application of psychological research, theory, or practice to the legal system or legal issues (see Wrightsman & Fulero, in press).

Curriculum Options

Integrate Legal Applications Into Existing Courses

Instructors can simply integrate legal applications of psychological principles into standard psychology courses already in existence. This is easy, as one is hard pressed to identify a psychology specialty area that is not relevant to, or cannot be applied to, some legal issue (see Table 1). This approach has several advantages:

- ♦ It does not necessitate review and acceptance of new courses by the college or university,
- ♦ It does not require instructors to teach an area and a set of concepts with which they are unfamiliar,
- ♦ It provides opportunities for demonstrating applications of scientific psychology in real world contexts,
- ♦ It exposes students to forensic applications that they would not otherwise experience, and
- ♦ It serves as a "teaser" for more specialized forensic offerings that may exist within the department.

Develop Specialized Courses and Seminars

A second way to increase undergraduates' exposure to law and psychology is by offering focused courses. There are two primary types, each of which has its own advantages and limitations.

Survey courses in psychology and law. Survey courses are challenging insofar as they require instructors to lecture about aspects of psychology in which they may not be expert. For example, a clinical psychologist may feel uncomfortable lecturing about the group psychology and decision-making research relevant to jury behavior, whereas a social psychologist may consider it a stretch to discuss authoritatively the specific physiology underlying development and use of the polygraph or the use or misuse of psychological tests in forensic evaluations. In reality, however, such challenges are not that different from those posed to the many psychology professors who teach introductory psychology and must become "expert" in areas they may not have covered since their own undergraduate days.

Developing and offering an introductory course in law and psychology is made easier by the relative large number of

Courses	Topics
Clinical Psychology	• Forensic assessment • Treatment of special populations (e.g., offenders, victims) • Important legal cases defining patient rights
Cognitive Psychology	• Accuracy of eyewitness identification • Repressed memory debate • Ability of persons to understand the law (e.g., impact and comprehensibility of jury instructions) • Efficacy of specialized interview techniques employed in the legal system (e.g., cognitive interviewing, hypnosis)
Community Psychology	• Behavior of prison and jail inmates • Efficacy of various interventions in reducing delinquent and criminal behavior (e.g., prevention programs, boot camps, substance abuse treatment in drug courts and correctional settings • Community attitudes and knowledge about specific crimes and change of venue surveys • Assessing impact of changes in the legal system
Developmental Psychology	• Impact of abuse and neglect on children or older persons • Impact of divorce on children and families • Accuracy of children's accounts of legally significant events • Legally relevant decision-making capacities of children, adolescents, adults, and older persons
Industrial-Organizational Psychology	• Issues related to selection of high risk occupations applicants (police, etc.) • Discrimination in employment selection and identification of selection techniques with disparate impact
Physiological Psychology	• Utility of the polygraph • Sex offender assessment
Social Psychology	• Persuasion, coercion, and false confessions • Jury behavior and decision making • Jury selection and trial consultation • Sex differences in perception of sexual harassment • Effects of discrimination and prejudice in the legal system (e.g., arrest and criminal charging, transfer of minors to adult court, sentencing, imposition of the death penalty) • Testing legal assumptions (e.g., evaluating, deterrent effects of criminal sanctions, identifying "legal fictions")
Statistics	• Efficacy and errors associated with various types of profiling approaches (e.g., terrorist profiles, hijacker profiles, drug courier profiles) • Utility of various methods (e.g., Receiver Operating Characteristics, classification rates) to assess accuracy of predictions (e.g., re-offense risk, violence risk potential)

Table 1: Integrating Legal Applications Into
Existing Psychology Courses

texts in the area. These texts are typically organized around legal issues (e.g., jury decision making, the insanity defense, corrections, abuse and neglect) that involve matters of psychology. Instructors should review competing texts carefully, as there is considerable variability in the substantive areas covered. For example, the undergraduate texts by Walker and Shapiro (2003), and Ackerman and Otto (in press) are more narrow and focus primarily on applications of clinical psychology to the law, whereas the texts by Wrightsman and Fulero (in press) and Bartol and Bartol (2004) are more diverse and include applications of clinical, social, cognitive, and developmental psychology.

More Focused Undergraduate Courses

An alternative approach is to develop and offer more focused undergraduate courses, typically revolving around a particular psychological specialty and its application and relevance to legal issues, such as eyewitness identification, the psychology of the jury, or law and mental illness. These courses typically have smaller enrollments, adopt a seminar format, and have one or more prerequisites such as completion of a forensic psychology overview course as well as an advanced course in the area of interest (e.g., developmental psychology, abnormal psychology, social psychology, cognition). Although these courses allow instructors to structure the semester or quarter around psycholegal topics of most relevance to their specialty area, they typically require compilation of a reading list or use of books developed primarily for graduate and professional audiences (e.g., Barthel, 1976, is a good supplemental reading for both eyewitness identification and false confessions; Finkel, 1988, for the insanity defense; Lykken, 1998, for polygraphy).

Use the Opportunity to Instruct Students About Larger Issues

Teaching undergraduates about psychology and law can be about more than introducing them to psychological applications in the legal system. In a course syllabus listed on her website (www.udel.edu/soc/vhans/cj346.html#info), Valerie Hans, professor of psychology at the University of Delaware, identifies three general course goals: 1) increasing the student's understanding of the different perspectives and assumptions held by law and psychology about human behavior and the creative tension between the two; 2) demonstrating how psychological research can provide insight into the legal system and its operation; and 3) improving the student's ability to think critically and to evaluate the use of psychology within the legal system. Professor Mark Small of Clemson University suggested that such courses can, at the broadest level, help students understand the diverse contributions psychologists can make in legal settings as "pure scientists" (by conducting research that shapes legal policy), "problem solvers" (by conducting program evaluation and applied research in legal settings), and "technicians" (by delivering psychological services in legal contexts or to persons involved in the legal system; Small, 1993). Taking his suggestion a bit further, instructors can use psychology-and-law offerings as an opportunity to demonstrate the connection between research and practice and the scientist-practitioner approach most useful in clinical pursuits.

Take Advantage of the Applied Nature of the Interface Area

Perhaps the most valuable aspect of instruction in psychology and law is its ability to make clear to undergraduates the value of psychology in real-world settings and applications. This may serve not only to stimulate undergraduates' interest in psychology and law specifically, but in psychology more generally. As a way of further stimulating that interest, instructors should take advantage of numerous teaching aids that will make the course work more interesting and its relevance all the more obvious.

There are a large number of readily available video resources (see Fulero, 2000). For example, the documentary *The Interrogation of Michael Crowe* does a good job of demonstrating adolescents' vulnerability to false confessions, and the Oscar-winning documentary *Murder on a Sunday Morning* makes clear the problems associated with false confessions as well as the limitations of eyewitness testimony (as does, in a more humorous way, the movie *My Cousin Vinny*). The classic movie *Twelve Angry Men* provides a starting point for discussion of persuasion and jury behavior and deliberations, whereas the more contemporary suspense movie, *The Bedroom Window*, shows the problems with eyewitness testimony, perjury, and litigation strategies employed by attorneys, as do the movies *My Cousin Vinny* and the older *The Wrong Man*. In addition to the above, a week rarely goes by without some TV news magazine (i.e., *60 Minutes, 20/20, Dateline, 48 Hours*) focusing on some interesting psycholegal issue (e.g., eyewitness testimony, repressed memory, vulnerability of child witnesses to suggestion, the insanity defense). Court TV is also a valuable resource for trial-related material, and often offers transcripts or tapes for sale.

At least two recent books have focused in whole or in part on psychology-and-law–related films. Bergman and Asimow (1996), in their book *Reel Justice*, review 69 law-related movies, some of which have psychological content. In addition, Wedding and Boyd (1999), in their recent book *Movies and Mental Illness: Using Film to Understand Psychopathology*, discuss films that are relevant to particular DSM-IV disorders and may be relevant to particular cases involving psychological disorders.

Guest lecturers who work in the legal system can also do much to make clear the real-work relevance of what students are studying in the class. After reading about jury behavior and jury selection, students will be fascinated to hear a prosecutor and criminal defense attorney offer their jury-selection and case-presentation strategies. The potential role that psychologists can play in change-of-venue decisions can be demonstrated by having students actually develop and administer change-of-venue questionnaires revolving around criminal cases in the community. Other possible active-learning techniques are the use of focus groups and mock trials (see Berman, 2000, 2004; Perry, Huss, McAuliff, & Galas, 1996).

How much students are learning can be demonstrated by regularly polling them about issues before they are introduced in class readings and lectures. For example, polling students about how frequently they believe the insanity defense is employed by criminal defendants and how successful it is when used, is a compelling way of demonstrating the public's misperception of this psycholegal area (see Borum & Fulero, 1999). The instructor can also provide students with a list of well-known, notorious offenders, and ask them to identify those that employed the insanity defense and how many were successful (students typically overestimate its use and success). Students also can be directed to review case materials of an insanity defense (either via text or video summary), deliberate as juries, and offer verdicts, with the "juries" being provided with different insanity standards.

Querying students about child witnesses and their susceptibility to persuasion, what constitutes sexual harassment in the workplace, behaviors common and uncommon to children who have and have not been sexually abused, and behaviors frequently and infrequently observed among adult victims of sexual assault may serve as a way of introducing them to commonly held misperceptions and identifying roles that psychologists may play in litigation revolving around such issues. Starting the first class of the semester with a mock theft (making sure to stage it in a way that does not risk the safety of class members) and then asking students to complete descriptions of the suspects is an invaluable device to gain students' attention and make clear the real-world impact of the application of psychology to legal issues. Inviting a detective to class to discuss interrogation techniques employed with suspects will help students put the research regarding false confessions in perspective (see Lassiter, 2004). Inviting a polygrapher into class to demonstrate the technique with a live demonstration of its effectiveness with a class volunteer may make consideration of this investigative technique more interesting.

Available Resources

The American Psychology-Law Society (APA Division 41) is an excellent resource for instructors and students interested in psychological applications to the law. Posted on the organization's website (www.unl.edu/ap-ls) are a number of syllabi from undergraduate and graduate courses taught by college and university faculty around the country, as well as an excellent summary of teaching and demonstration materials compiled by professor Edie Greene of the University of Colorado, Colorado Springs. The website also provides a list of graduate programs offering specialty training in law and psychology and an e-booklet that introduces interested undergraduates to different career opportunities in forensic psychology. The organization also allows student memberships at a reduced price that includes receipt of its newsletter and its bimonthly journal, *Law and Human Behavior.*

The section of APA's website devoted to law and psychology issues (www.apa.org/PsycLAW) also provides some helpful resources including access to *amicus curiae* briefs submitted on behalf of the organization, access to guidelines and other position statements of the organization that are relevant to matters of law and psychology, a listing of journals and books devoted to law and psychology, and links to other organizations examining the interchange between law and psychology.

Conclusion

Instructors who wish to provide undergraduate students with material relevant to psychology and law have a wealth of available options. Books, movies, Internet or Web materials, as well as classroom activities and demonstrations can give students an appreciation for the complex application of psychology to legal questions. As psychology and law becomes a more popular undergraduate topic, such applications can both increase student interest and provide an introduction to more focused courses offered later in the undergraduate curriculum.

Editor's Note: This chapter is based, in part, on an invited presentation delivered by Randy Otto at the 2003 meeting of the National Institute on the Teaching of Psychology (NITOP). Direct all correspondence to Randy K. Otto, Department of Mental Health Law & Policy, Florida Mental Health Institute, University of South Florida, 13301 N. 30th St., Tampa, FL 33612, otto@ fmhi.usf.edu.

References and Recommended Readings

Barthel, J. (1976). *A death in Canaan.* New York: Dutton/Plume.

Barton, C., & Bartol, A. (2004). *Psychology and law: Theory, research, and application.* Belmont, CA: Wadsworth.

Bergman, P., & Asimow, M. (1996). *Reel justice: The courtroom goes to the movies.* New York: Andrews McMeel.

Berman, G.L. (2000, March). Can class participation be enhanced? Active learning exercises for undergraduates in a Psychology and Law course. In B. Bennett (Chair), *Active learning techniques for use in a psychology and law course.* Symposium conducted at the meeting of the American Psychology-Law Society, New Orleans, LA. For a copy, e-mail gberman@rwu.edu.

Berman, G.L. (2004, March). What can I do to present a better case? The use of focus group simulations in an undergraduate legal psychology course. In J. Platania (Chair), *Beyond active learning: Developing interdisciplinary and collaborative projects in psychology and law.* Symposium presented at the American Psychology- Law Society, Scottsdale, AZ. For a copy, e-mail gberman@rwu.edu.

Borum, R., & Fulero, S. (1999). Empirical research on the insanity defense and attempted reforms: Evidence toward informed policy. *Law and Human Behavior, 23,* 375-394.

Finkel, N. (1998). *Insanity on trial.* New York: Kluwer/Plenum.

Fulero, S. (2000, March). *Lights, camera, action: The use of films and videos in the undergraduate teaching of psychology and law.* Paper presented at the biennial meeting of the American Psychology-Law Society, New Orleans, LA.

Fulero, S., Greene, E., Hans, V., Nietzel, M., Small, M., & Wrightsman, L. (1999). Undergraduate education in legal psychology. *Law and Human Behavior, 23,* 137-153.

Kassin, S. (2002, November 1). False confessions and the jogger case. *New York Times,* p. A31.

Kressel, N., & Kressel, L. (2002). *Stack and sway: The new science of jury consulting.* New York: Perseus Books Group/Westview Press.

Lassiter, G.D. (2004). *Interrogations, confessions, and entrapment.* New York: Kluwer Academic/Plenum Publishers.

Lykken, D. (1998). *A tremor in the blood: Uses and abuses of the lie detector.* New York: Kluwer/Plenum.

Miller, L.A. (1997). Teaching about repressed memories of childhood sexual abuse and eyewitness testimony. *Teaching of Psychology, 24,* 250-255.

Perry, N.W., Huss, M.H., McAuliff, B.D., & Galas, J.M. (1996). An active learning approach to teaching the undergraduate psychology and law course. *Teaching of Psychology, 23,* 76-81.

Small, M. (1993). Legal psychology and therapeutic jurisprudence. *St. Louis University Law Journal, 37,* 675-700.

Wedding, D., & Boyd, M.A. (1999). *Movies and mental illness: Using film to understand psychopathology.* New York: McGraw-Hill.

Wrightsman, L., & Fulero, S. (2004). *Forensic psychology* (2nd ed.). Belmont, CA: Wadsworth.

Putting Social Justice Into Practice in Psychology Courses

STEVEN A. MEYERS
Roosevelt University

PEOPLE WHO ADVOCATE for social justice believe all members of society should have equal rights and access to opportunities. Although its values, assumptions, and approaches may differ from traditional psychology, social justice has an impact on our discipline. For example, psychologists have studied many topics related to social justice (e.g., prejudice, discrimination, and conformity), and several subfields have coalesced around these issues, including community psychology, multicultural psychology, and the psychology of women. Moreover, the ethical principles of the American Psychological Association (2002) even require psychologists to ensure that their work benefits and respects the rights of all people, regardless of age, gender, gender identity, race, ethnicity, culture, national origin, religion, sexual orientation, disability, language, or socioeconomic status. The standards urge psychologists to remain aware of these factors, avoid discrimination, and oppose unjust practices.

The challenge that many psychology faculty members encounter in this regard is how to integrate social justice themes into their teaching. The discussion of how psychological knowledge can help solve social problems or why social and political factors are important for psychological understanding may not seem to fit within the framework of many of our courses. To assist psychology professors who are uncertain about how to proceed, I summarize four general teaching tips by which faculty can meaningfully address social justice in their classes.

Link Your Content With Social Justice Themes

Social justice can be promoted by the content you teach. However, the desire to emphasize topics such as societal inequalities can be complicated because text material and core concepts within many subfields often ignore such issues. Here are two ways to bridge the gap.

Explain to Students That Psychology Is Not Always Value Free

Modern psychology is often framed as a science that uses empirical methods to advance knowledge about the mind, the brain, and behavior in an objective manner. However, students should also understand that psychologists' worldviews shape the questions we pose in research, the strategies we use to answer those questions, and how we understand phenomena.

For example, most psychological research uses quantitative methods. Students learn to conduct quantitative studies in research methods courses; instructors most often rely on quantitative findings to inform their lectures. Psychology instructors can teach about qualitative research that models greater power-sharing between researchers and participants through its open-ended questioning and community immersion (Kidder & Fine, 1997). Moreover, qualitative research can advance social justice by amplifying the voices of research participants, particularly people who have been mischaracterized by psychology and broader society, such as women, people of color, and sexual minorities.

Students also become aware that psychology can be value-laden when professors help them:

- Question whether important phenomena or research findings addressed in class are relevant or even applicable across different groups of people.
- Discuss whether foundational research involved representative samples and review whether findings have been replicated across gender, race, and social class.
- Examine if the experiences of historically disenfranchised people are reflected in the questions asked.

Widen Your Inquiry to Address Sociocultural and Sociopolitical Contexts

Our field often emphasizes individual-level functioning instead of broader social, cultural, and political forces. A focus on social justice means that professors seek out new connections that relate course topics to issues of social importance and inequalities. This coverage draws attention to potential applications of psychological knowledge and the ways in which it can create change. Consider the following illustrations for organizing a class session:

♦ How does a lack of safe neighborhoods affect children's well being? (Developmental Psychology)

♦ What are the effects of gender-based pay inequities on corporate climate? (Industrial/Organizational Psychology)

♦ How does social class shape access to psychological and psychiatric services? (Abnormal Psychology)

♦ How can principles of operant and classical conditioning be used to change attitudes toward members of ostracized groups? (Learning/Cognitive Psychology)

♦ Why were lobotomies performed disproportionally on women? (Biopsychology)

♦ Are the Big Five personality dimensions universal given the role of gender and culture in identify formation? (Personality)

I generated each of these topics by asking the question, "What are the implications of traditional course information for society and the disenfranchised?" Consider the influence of culture, class, gender, and similar categories on the material that you traditionally cover.

Examination of these issues can be deepened through newspaper articles, state and federal budgets, biographies, interviews, and literature. Similarly, course content can be connected to social issues by inviting speakers or community representatives into the classroom. Some guests may be experts (e.g., local elected officials, social service professionals), whereas others may share their personal and relevant experiences (e.g., people who are homeless, people with HIV/AIDS). Expanding the scope of inquiry increases students' awareness about social problems, promotes empathy for marginalized groups, and encourages students to question the status quo.

Develop Assignments That Facilitate Awareness and Action

Promote Students' Self-Examination During In-Class Activities

In-class, interactive exercises are a powerful vehicle for promoting students' awareness of the complexity and pervasiveness of inequalities. Adams, Bell, and Griffin (1997) present curriculum designs and modules that address and challenge racism, sexism, heterosexism, ableism, classism, and anti-Semitism. Representative activities that target racism include placing students in small groups to identify the aspects of their own racial/ethnic heritage about which they are proud, review patterns in their personal relationships regarding people from different backgrounds, articulate ways in which society supports racism, encourage frank and respectful dialog between students of different races, and identify ways to take action.

Help Students Talk With Others Who Are Different Through Interview Assignments

Students can learn more about the scope of oppression by interviewing people from marginalized groups, visiting their neighborhoods, and exploring the quality of services (e.g., schools, hospitals, housing, transportation, recreational facilities, and stores) that are available in their communities in contrast to those of privileged groups.

Encourage Students to Speak Out for Change In Social Action Projects

It is increasingly important for psychology students to understand the connections between research, practice, and public policy. These linkages often have social justice implications. Psychology professors can create class assignments that can impact others on a political level, such as having students explore pending state and federal legislation and to advocate for disenfranchised people by writing opinion editorials or letters to legislators. Students can use the Internet to research relevant policy when formulating their responses. The Library of Congress maintains Thomas (http://thomas.loc.gov/), an online resource providing federal legislative information to the public, including congressional bills, resolutions, roll call votes, and committee reports. Students can search key words related to course content (e.g., children, brain, prejudice, mental illness) to determine an advocacy agenda. The Public Policy Office of the American Psychological Association (http://www.apa.org/ppo/) is also an invaluable resource. Most germane are links pertaining to public interest policy that address supporting children, women, ethnic and sexual minorities, disabled people, and older adults (http://www.apa.org/ppo/pi/). Similarly, the website sponsored by Psychologists Acting with Conscience Together (http://www.psyact.org) provides information and advocacy tools on topics related to poverty, violence, education, human rights, and mental health. With content-relevant, social justice-oriented information, students can speak out against oppression and effect change.

Use Service Learning as a Core Assignment

Service learning, in which students volunteer with under-served or marginalized populations and connect their site experiences to coursework, can be a transformative experience that furthers social justice, has a positive impact on reducing stereotypes, facilitates cultural and racial understanding, and enhances civic responsibility. Service learning is most successful when students have opportunities for reflection and critical analysis through written assignments and class discussions that tie course concepts with field experiences.

Although students and faculty commonly find sites that allow direct contact with people in need (e.g., assisting in hospitals or mental health facilities, tutoring at-risk children, volunteering in community centers that serve lower-income populations), a commitment to social justice also involves attending to broader, societal dynamics evident in the placement. As such, students can reflect on the challenges faced by people who are served by the organization because of societal inequalities or may volunteer at a site that focuses on advocacy or policy reform. Activities may also involve students assisting a community organization or group by using psychology-relevant skills, such as completing a needs assessment or evaluating the effectiveness of a program.

Create Campus-Based Assignments to Promote Social Justice

Other action-oriented assignments can be campus based, such as contributing to university newspapers, creating or participating in relevant co-curricular activities, or conducting campus-wide education projects (distributing literature, encouraging political action among students). Consider the following illustrations:

- ♦ Students in a psychology of women course organize a "Take Back the Night" demonstration on campus.
- ♦ Child development students lobby university officials for the creation of a subsidized, on-campus child care center for children of students and employees.
- ♦ Social psychology students create a new campus organization to promote interfaith and interracial dialog and invite community leaders to catalyze discussions.
- ♦ Industrial/organizational students organize a protest of a mega-store that engages in unfair labor practices and gender bias in its hiring and pay.
- ♦ Research methods students conduct a campus-wide survey of attitudes toward LGBT students and present their analyses to university officials to support programming that promotes tolerance and inclusiveness.

Increase Your Use of Egalitarian Teaching Methods

Social justice also can be promoted by how you teach, regardless of what you teach. Instructors who are concerned with social justice often question conventional notions of authority in college classrooms because it may parallel or reinforce how power is exercised more broadly in society. For example, Friere (1970) criticized the "banking model" of instruction in which professors maximize their control by exclusively determining course content and relying on lectures to transfer information from themselves to their students.

Equalize Power in the Classroom

Try to create more collegial environments when you teach and facilitate interactions among students by using collaborative methods. This approach encourages students to have greater input and control. It also underscores the importance of students' values, priorities, and beliefs in the teaching and learning process. On a practical note, Enns and Sinacore (2004) recommend using the following:

- ♦ Responsive goal-setting, to provide students with a voice in deciding which topics are emphasized within the course.

- Cooperative learning, to encourage students to interact with others (especially those who have a different background in terms of race, ethnicity, social class, age, gender, or sexual orientation) through problem-based learning, laboratory exercises, and group activities (see Ware & Johnson, 2000 for many concrete examples).
- Instructor self-disclosure as appropriate, to model openness.

These teaching methods have been shown to increase college students' educational success, and African American and Latino students actually benefit the most in terms of grade improvement and college retention rates (Kuh, Kinzie, Cruce, Shoup, & Gonyea, 2006).

Reflect On Your Own Attitudes and Experiences

For many instructors, the process of creating an inclusive classroom involves a close examination of their own attitudes toward race, class, and gender and consequently assessing how these beliefs affect their teaching. For example, professors may not ordinarily think about how students of color or from lower income backgrounds may be hesitant to challenge them during a Socratic dialog or attend office hours because of their socialization and previous experiences with authority figures.

Troubleshoot as Needed

Some students can feel threatened by the topic of social justice because it challenges their worldview. Professors may encounter students who appear bored, skeptical, or hostile to this material. This potential difficulty underscores the need for faculty to use student-centered approaches to teaching and for professors and students to create safe environments by listening empathically, communicating respectfully, self-disclosing thoughtfully, including all students in discussions, and tolerating differences of opinion. There are also several ways to respond to such student challenges:

"Why Are We Talking About This Stuff In a Course About Psychology? This Isn't What We're Supposed to Cover!"

First, instructors who incorporate social justice often need to explain that psychology aims to understand and help all people, regardless of their race, age, gender, ethnicity, socioeconomic status, or sexual orientation. In fact, psychologists have misrepresented or excluded women and many minority groups in their research and theorizing for decades (Guthrie, 2003); this situation needs to be actively corrected today for the sake of accuracy and fairness. Second, professors can explain that it is important for all students to feel that course material is relevant. Examining the representation and experiences of historically disenfranchised groups is critical, especially for an increasingly diverse undergraduate population. Third, a social justice orientation allows students to make a difference in the lives of others. Most students initially believe that psychologists help others only through psychotherapy at the individual level; however, professors can explain that a social justice approach teaches them about how to affect change on the macro level by advocacy and social action.

"This Is All Liberal Rhetoric and I'm Not a Liberal. Why Should I Listen to This?"

Although liberals are often concerned with social justice, the movement traces its origins far beyond contemporary progressive politics. The Hebrew Bible exhorts followers to care about the well-being of and justice for the poor (Leviticus 25:8-55, New International Version; Proverbs 29:7) and to maintain the rights of the oppressed (Psalm 82). Christian Scripture highlights virtue in marginalized groups (e.g., Parable of the Good Samaritan, Luke 10:25-37) and underscores the need to feed the hungry, clothe the naked, and care for the stranger (Matthew 25:31-46). The roots of social justice also are evident in the writings of philosophers such as Rousseau and Locke. Regardless of their ideological convictions, students should understand that psychological knowledge coupled with a social justice focus helps them to become more informed and engaged citizens.

Ultimately, psychology professors can tailor the inclusion of social justice in a way that respects their content area, their personal beliefs, and the characteristics of their students and institutions. Some faculty may implement these steps gradually or in part. For example, students often welcome the participatory teaching styles reviewed earlier; they are also likely to be receptive to completing flexible social action projects or learning about and helping poor children. Regardless of the precise implementation, addressing social justice encourages students to understand individuals and psychological processes within a broader framework. It also provides psychology professors with a window to help create a fairer and more tolerant society.

Association for Psychological Science

References and Recommended Readings

Adams, M., Bell, L.A., & Griffin, P. (Eds.). (1997). *Teaching for diversity and social justice: A sourcebook.* New York: Routledge.

American Psychological Association. (2002). Ethical principles of psychologists and code of conduct. *American Psychologist, 57,* 1060-1073.

Enns, C.Z., & Sinacore, A.L. (Eds.). (2004). *Teaching and social justice: Integrating multicultural and feminist theories in the classroom.* Washington, DC: American Psychological Association.

Friere, P. (1970). *Pedagogy of the oppressed.* New York: Continuum.

Guthrie, R.V. (2003). *Even the rat was white: A historical view of psychology* (2nd ed.). Boston: Allyn & Bacon.

Kidder, L.H., & Fine. M. (1997). Qualitative inquiry in psychology: A radical tradition. In D. Fox & I. Prilleltensky (Eds.), *Critical psychology: An introduction* (pp. 34-50). Thousand Oaks, CA: Sage.

Kuh, G.D., Kinzie, J., Cruce, T., Shoup, R., & Gonyea, R.M. (2006). *Connecting the dots: Multi-faceted analyses of the relationships between student engagement results from the NSSE, and the institutional practices and conditions that foster student success.* Bloomington: Center for Postsecondary Research, Indiana University.

Prilleltensky, I., & Nelson, G. (2002). *Doing psychology critically: Making a difference in diverse settings.* New York: Palgrave Macmillan.

Ware, M.E., & Johnson, D.E. (Eds.). (2000). *Handbook of demonstrations and activities in the teaching of psychology* (2nd ed., Vols. 1-4). Mahwah, NJ: Erlbaum.

Part VI

Beyond the Text
and Classroom

Building a Sense of Community in Undergraduate Psychology Departments

Cheryl E. Sanders
Mark E. Basham
Pamela I. Ansburg
The Metropolitan State College of Denver

IMAGINE YOU ARE A student sitting among 300 others in your psychology class. You look around and wonder, "How am I going to fit in? Will I ever make friends in this department? Will my professors ever know my name?"

Although feelings of disconnectedness are common among students, these experiences do not have to occur. Building a sense of community within a department can accomplish a great deal: decrease the number of students who feel lost; ameliorate students' feelings of anxiety, depression, and loneliness; and improve personal growth, motivation, and retention rates (Bailey, Bauman, & Lata, 1998; Cartland, Ruch-Ross, & Henry, 2003; Lounsbury & DeNeui, 1996). In addition, students who feel connected to their department exhibit a decline in classroom disruptiveness and an increase in remorse when they are not prepared for class (Royal & Rossi, 1996). Further, a well-developed sense of community provides an incentive for alumni to recommend their department to high school students and provide psychological, social, and economic support for the institution (Lounsbury & DeNeui, 1996). Overall, a strong sense of community within a department improves the quality of the educational experience. Moreover, it is enjoyable to teach in a department in which faculty, staff, and students are connected.

Practical Ideas on Community Building Within Psychology Departments

Identify Social Leaders

The first step in increasing the sense of community and cohesiveness in a department is to enlist the help of social leaders. The mere presence of strong social leaders increases feelings of community (Zaff & Devlin, 1998). Social leaders are able to identify ways to promote community and inspire others to participate in carrying out ideas (Mumford, Zaccaro, Connelly, & Marks, 2000). Moreover, social leaders persuade others that investing energy in a specific cause (i.e., a psychology department) is akin to investing in oneself (Fiol, Harris, & House, 1999).

Faculty should approach engaged and outgoing students in the classroom to see if they are interested in taking on leadership roles. In addition, faculty can make announcements in classes and post fliers for recruitment; leaders know who they are and will be drawn to the opportunity. It is important that these student leaders have at least one faculty member who can support them and act as a liaison between faculty and students.

Provide Common Physical Space

Providing an area where students can interact with each other and with faculty facilitates community building (Appleby, 2000). Ideally, physical space should be designated as a student lounge. Although some students will use this space for schoolwork, the space also should afford students the opportunity to relax and engage socially. Include comfortable furniture, computers, coffee maker, refrigerator, books and other resource materials, and anything else that makes the space inviting. Students will take ownership of the space if they decorate it. Our student lounge, for example, has posters of the anatomy of a neuron and a portrait of Sigmund Freud. The student lounge provides a useful place to post announcements and photographs of department events. If it is not feasible for the department to offer building space, a common area may involve a picnic area or space in a hallway. What matters most is that students have a place to claim as their own.

Promote Programs That Emphasize Collaboration in Support of Academic and Career Success

Students should feel that in joining a department they are joining a community that will help them succeed. Departments should emphasize to students that collaboration and interaction facilitate academic success and that psychological science is a community endeavor. Hosting regularly scheduled activities — such as those listed below — promotes community.

Have current students maintain an advice book (hard copy or online) for new students on how to succeed in the major. Some suggestions for topics are study techniques for specific classes, lists of helpful resources for content areas (e.g., statistics tutorials on the Web), writing and APA style tips, and general study aids.

- ♦ Host career fairs and graduate school information presentations. These events should occur every semester in order to reach students in varying stages of their educational career. They should be made by a variety of individuals: successful alumni, directors of graduate programs, local faculty, current students, and professionals in the field.

- ♦ Support student clubs and national honor societies such as a local Psi Chi chapter, research club, psychology club, or journal club. Student clubs are one of the most successful avenues to building a sense of community. Department chairs should appoint energetic, knowledgeable, and approachable faculty to seek out institutional support (e.g., club space, funding) or act as advisors (for ideas on promoting active student clubs, see Giordano, Hammer, & Lovell, 2004).

- ♦ Host an annual undergraduate conference where students can present their research projects. Include a keynote speaker and a celebratory luncheon to recognize the presenters. Schedule this event during class time and cancel regularly scheduled classes to promote attendance. Attendance of students who are not presenting supports those who are presenting. It also allows non-presenters a no-risk view of a conference, thereby encouraging future participation.

- ♦ Provide opportunities for students to work closely with faculty mentors. Students can serve as teaching assistants (TAs) and research assistants (RAs) (see Davis, 1999). Build these experiences into the departmental curriculum so students can earn college credits for serving in these roles.

Create Celebratory Rituals That Mark Achievement

Ceremonies and rituals are an important part of developing group cohesiveness (Appleby, 2000; Mullis & Fincher, 1996; Taub, 1998;), as they initiate students into a community and create a sense of pride in membership. In fact, students on campuses that do not offer unique rituals are more likely to complain that they a lack of sense of community (Manning, 1994). Ceremonies and rituals also provide vivid memories that help sustain a feeling of belonging. There are several traditions and ceremonies that departments might adopt.

◆ A Psi Chi induction ceremony allows faculty and students to celebrate student academic achievements. A strong faculty presence is important to communicate that the department values this event. Encourage students to invite family members and friends so that faculty and other students better understand who students are.

◆ An annual ceremony acknowledges student and faculty achievements. Highlight psychology-related internships, research presentations, academic awards, and service awards. To promote appropriate goals to first and second-year students, encourage underclassmen to attend. Hold a luncheon for research assistants, teaching assistants, and faculty mentors to celebrate and discuss their collaborative work. Host a commencement party to recognize graduating majors.

To foster a departmental sense of community, these rituals should be public and include as many members as possible. For example, sophomore and junior psychology majors could be in charge of organizing the commencement party.

Host Purely Social Events

Social events and group recreation lead to an increased sense of community.

◆ Create a student/faculty intramural team, or have an annual recreational event (e.g. softball or volleyball). Our department recently held its first annual faculty versus student bowling tournament, and it was a huge success. For several weeks after the competition students bragged about beating faculty, which has sparked interest in planning similar events.

- Organize social events that occur in conjunction with a conference, a seasonal holiday, or the beginning or end of a semester. For example, host an end-of-the year picnic or holiday party.
- Encourage faculty to host potlucks at their homes or participate in on-campus ones. One possibility is to host an annual progressive dinner where faculty members serve various parts of the meal at their respective homes or in different classrooms on campus (e.g., appetizers at one location, salad at another). It might be fun to have a themed dinner: "An evening in Vienna" as a tribute to Freud or "Beyond Borscht" to celebrate Pavlov's contributions.

Develop a psychology social group that meets bimonthly for social events (e.g., social hours, bowling). Give your group a catchy name. One department has a group called PITFALL (Psychologists In Training For A Life of Learning). Invite faculty to attend.

Collect, Maintain, and Display Artifacts of the Community

Group cohesiveness increases when symbolic representation of the group identity is physically displayed (Elsbach, 2004). Departments should display symbols that present who they are and what they value.

- Create a physical and/or virtual space devoted to student achievements. For example, design a "Wall of Scholars" that acknowledges winners of department awards and display photos of student poster presentations and papers on the departmental website.
- Produce a department newsletter that highlights events and achievements. Involve student organizations in its creation or recruit an editorial board of faculty and students.
- Take pictures at department events and post them on the department website and on the department walls. Maintain a physical or virtual scrapbook so new students understand that departmental involvement is part of the department's culture.
- Display pictures of faculty in a central location to promote familiarity. To increase perceptions of faculty accessibility, consider posting a short biography with each photograph that describes the faculty member's specialty and his or her career path.

Lessons Learned

We cannot be certain which ideas will work to build a sense of community in your department; however, common pitfalls exist that will almost assuredly hinder your attempts. Below are some lessons that our department and others have learned over the years.

♦ A lack of faculty involvement guarantees failure. Although student leaders play a large role in developing a sense of community, their efforts must be reinforced with faculty encouragement, guidance, support, and recognition. Reward faculty involvement by including this type of departmental service as part of faculty evaluations.

♦ Activities should be directly relevant to students. We have included ideas that should be relevant to most undergraduate students; however, departments should tailor activities to meet the interests of their particular student population.

♦ To maximize attendance at any event, publicize it early and often. Use multiple media, including in-class announcements, posters and flyers, mass mailings, email, websites, and discussion lists.

♦ Beware of cliques. The goal is to foster a sense of departmental community, however some of the ideas (e.g., a research club and Psi Chi) can lead to the development of smaller cliques of students. Be vigilant of subgroups, and encourage students to be inclusive of peers. Some departments have instituted a policy of revolving leadership, where officers in a research club or Psi Chi can only serve a single semester or year, thereby minimizing the chances of a small cadre of students monopolizing a club.

Challenges to Consider

Although there are a number of ways to promote a sense of community within a Psychology department, there also are challenges and obstacles.

Number of Psychology Majors and Students

There is probably a minimum size below which a department does not have enough students to implement many of the ideas presented. Smaller departments may need to combine with related departments for some events and/or be selective in choosing which ideas to implement.

Institution Type

More than 80 percent of U.S. college students are commuters (students who do not live in campus dorms) (Horn & Berktold, 1998). Commuter campuses face the challenge of competing with other aspects of their students' lives. Many commuter students are "non-traditional," holding full-time jobs and raising families. Although they tend to have hectic schedules, many still want to feel connected to their learning environment (Orlando, 2000; Taub, 1998). Departments have a responsibility to promote a sense of community with this population by implementing programs that fit their varying schedules. For example, offer events that repeat at morning, afternoon, and evening times.

Residential campuses face other concerns. One problem is competition from other communities on campus such as Greek groups and sports teams. Departments on these campuses will need to implement programs that appeal to their students and provide opportunities not available through other groups.

Diversity

College student populations are becoming more and more diverse (Boyer, 1990). This diversity is a challenge to a sense of community because students of various races, ethnicities, ages, socioeconomic statuses, and sexual orientations have varying needs. In addition, prejudice can hinder community building. Education and information regarding the diversity of the student population should be included in efforts to promote community.

Influence of Technology

The increase in dependence on technology creates an additional barrier to promoting community. Students increasingly replace face-to-face interactions with online communication, allowing themselves to "disengage physically and psychologically from campus community" (Taub, 1998, p. 414). Departments should be aware of the technological habits of their students and utilize them in building communities.

Ethics

Ethical boundaries between faculty and students should be monitored. Both parties need to be aware of the general expectations of their behavior. When faculty are serving in multiple roles — such as instructor, evaluator, sponsor, mentor, or even teammate — ethical issues may arise. Faculty members need to maintain their multiple roles with integrity, being careful not to use their status in a coercive manner or allow personal relationships to contaminate professional decisions. In turn, students need to respect the ethical boundaries that faculty face. Awareness of these issues and open and frank discussions between faculty and students will go a long way towards avoiding problems.

Assessment of Community Building

To maintain a strong sense of community, departments need strategies to detect and combat entropy. Regular assessment of community building efforts is crucial; it reveals the present sense of community and also signals that building a sense of community is a priority.

♦ Solicit student and faculty input through informal conversations and suggestion boxes.

♦ Use a formal assessment instrument to measure department-level attachment. To determine how best to focus efforts, survey classes of all levels. Junior and senior level students may feel connected to the department, freshman and sophomore less so.

♦ If assessments demonstrate a need for increased effort — experiment! Implement some of our suggestions or contact colleagues from other departments to learn about strategies that have worked for them. Try new ideas; if they flop, seek feedback and try again. A small energetic corps can create the momentum that invites others to become invested in building and maintaining a strong sense of community.

Conclusion

Building a sense of community within a psychology department is challenging yet immensely beneficial. Begin by implementing just one or two of the suggested ideas and monitor their success. Identification of social leaders and development of a physical space for students are good places to begin. A few changes will make a big difference in the overall feel of the department. In addition to increased student achievements and positive regard for the department, being a part of a department with a strong sense of community is rewarding for all involved.

References and Recommended Readings

Appleby, D.C. (2000, November). Hoping to build more community in your psychology department? Here's how. *APA Monitor, 31*(10), 38-41.

Bailey, B.L., Bauman, C., & Lata, K.A. (1998). *Student retention and satisfaction: The evolution of a predictive model.* Paper presented at the Annual Forum of the Association for Institutional Research, Minneapolis, MN.

Boyer, E.L. (1990). *Campus life: In search of community.* Princeton, NJ: Carnegie Foundation for the Advancement of Teaching.

Cartland, J., Ruch-Ross, H.S., & Henry, D.B. (2003). Feeling at home in one's school: A first look at a new measure. *Adolescence, 38*, 305-319.

Davis, S.F. (1999). The value of collaborative scholarship with undergraduates. In B. Perlman, L.I. McCann, & S.H. McFadden (Eds.), *Lessons learned: Practical advice for the teaching of psychology* (Vol. 1, pp. 201-205). Washington, DC: Association for Psychological Science.

Elsbach, K.D. (2004). Interpreting workplace identities: The role of office décor. *Journal of Organizational Behavior, 25*, 99-128.

Fiol, C.M., Harris, D., & House, R. (1999). Charismatic leadership: Strategies for effecting social change. *Leadership Quarterly, 10*, 449-482.

Giordano, P.J., Hammer, E.Y, & Lovell, A.E. (2004). Teaching outside the classroom: Sustaining a vibrant Psi Chi chapter or Psychology club. In B. Perlman, L.I. McCann, & S.H. McFadden (Eds.), *Lessons learned: Practical advice for the teaching of psychology* (Vol. 2, pp. 323-332). Washington, DC: Association for Psychological Science.

Harris, B.A. (2006). The importance of creating a "sense of community." *Journal of College Student Retention: Research, Theory, and Practice, 8*, 83-105.

Horn, L.F., & Berktold, J. (1998). *Profile of undergraduates in U.S. postsecondary education institutions: 1995-96.* (NCES 98-084). Washington, DC: U.S. Office of Educational Research and Improvement, U.S. Department of Education.

Johnson, A.M., Rodger, S.C., Harris, J.A., Edmunds, L.A., & Wakabayashi, P. (2005). Predictors of alcohol consumption in University residences. *Journal of Alcohol and Drug Education, 49*(3), 9-18.

Lounsbury, J.W., & DeNeui, D. (1996). Collegiate psychological sense of community in relation to size of college/university and extroversion. *Journal of Community Psychology, 24*, 381-394.

Manning, K. (1994). Rituals and rescission: Building community in hard times. *Journal of College Student Development, 35*, 275-281.

Mullis, F., & Fincher, S.F. (1996). Using rituals to define the school community. *Elementary School Guidance & Counseling, 30*, 243-252.

Mumford, M.D., Zaccaro, S.J., Connelly, M.S., & Marks, M.A. (2000). Leadership skills: Conclusions and future directions. *Leadership Quarterly, 11,* 155-170.

Orlando, C.E. (2000). The collegium: Community as gathering place. *New directions for higher education, 109,* 33-41.

Raphael, C. (2006). Review of interpersonal divide: The search for community in a techonological age. *Journal of Communication, 56,* 864-866.

Royal, M.A., & Rossi, R.J. (1996). Individual-level correlates of sense of community: Findings from workplace and school. *Journal of Community Psychology, 24,* 395-416.

Taub, D.J. (1998). Building community on campus: Student affairs professional as group workers. *Journal for Specialists in Group Work, 23,* 411-427.

Zaff, J., & Devlin, A.S. (1998). Sense of community in housing for the elderly. *Journal of Community Psychology, 26,* 381-398.

Academic Advising and Teachable Moments: Making the Most of the Advising Experience

REBECCA D. FOUSHÉE
Fontbonne University

AS I WRITE THIS, IT'S near the end of the semester, and yet another academic advising period has come and gone. For many busy faculty members, advising time conjures images of extended office hours, multiple meetings with frazzled advisees, and hectic schedules added to the normal routine of classes, research, and administrative or service responsibilities. Although academic advising is frequently underemphasized in yearly faculty activity reports and unappreciated in rank and tenure decisions, it is an integral and necessary part of most faculty positions. Granted, effectively advising students takes a considerable amount of energy, but the potential rewards often outweigh the costs and it is frequently a mutually beneficial exercise for everyone involved. For faculty, the opportunity to enrich undergraduates' college experiences in a venue outside of the classroom can provide a welcome addition to routine academic responsibilities. For students, regular and consistent interaction with a faculty member throughout their academic careers can help them feel more connected to the university during their college years and beyond.

The ways in which psychology departments handle advising have been historically quite varied, and faculty may meet students at different stages, either at the beginning or midway through their college careers. Lunneborg and Baker (1986) originally outlined four different models for handling advising:

The Central Model

In some universities and departments, faculty members do not advise, as a central office on campus handles advising.

The No Faculty Model

In others, undeclared majors are advised in the central office at first, then later in a departmental office supervised by one faculty member within the major.

Part and All Faculty Models

In other, mainly smaller departments, individual psychology majors are assigned to a specific advisor from the beginning of their college career or after declaring the major.

Advising Styles

For both students and faculty, some advising styles are more effective and fulfilling than others, depending on their advising goals.

- *The Hurried Form-Signer.* These advisors are frequently too busy to talk with advisees. They are available to sign forms and identify errors in course selection, but they have little time for anything else, expecting advising appointments to last less than 10 minutes. This type of advising is typically the easiest in time and energy expenditure, but rarely provides positive advising for students.

- *The Detached Authority Figure.* These advisors are not concerned with building rapport or listening to students' needs. They function as an all-knowing source of wisdom regarding courses, career options, or requirements for the major. Students can take or leave their advice. This style is more informative than the form-signer approach but also rarely provides the guidance that students often need or want.

- *The Substitute Parent.* These advisors hover over their advisees and attempt to make decisions for them. They may become overly involved in students' personal lives and are always available and nurturing. However, students may fail to learn how to actively control their own career trajectories and frequently have difficulty making their own decisions.

- *The Mentor.* These advisors provide accurate information and help students identify all possible options for growth and development at each stage of their academic careers. They are available, actively listen, and allow students to make their own decisions and support those decisions, even if they disagree with them. These advisors guide students and simultaneously provide opportunities for independence and personal growth.

♦ *The Trail-Guide.* Over the years, my personal philosophy of advising has evolved into what I consider the "trail-guide" approach, a style most closely aligned with the Mentor. The college years are an exciting, formative, and life-altering journey for most students, providing a critical set of experiences and opportunities that build the foundation for their lives and facilitate their pathway to self-actualization. Regardless of students' individual directions and levels of dedication to achieving their goals, it helps to have at least one person continually present along the way who can guide them on their individual journeys, pointing out pitfalls, providing information about possible pathways, and supporting their professional development.

The Relationship Between Teaching and Advising

Regardless of the particular model your university uses, if you advise, it is important to develop effective advising skills (Ware, 1999). Good advising requires applying effective teaching techniques to the individual advising context (see Appleby, 2001). Good advisors are available to their students, care about their advisees' welfare as much as their classroom performance, and encourage students to engage in active learning, self-reflection, critical-thinking, and decision-making within a broader context than the classroom. These skills are often emphasized in class settings but may be even more valuable as students seek advice and make career-altering decisions about courses, internships, graduate schools, employment options, and research opportunities.

Advising and the Teachable Moment

Given the similarities between advising and teaching, it should come as no surprise that advising provides teaching and learning opportunities similar to those found in the classroom. Although specific definitions of teachable moments are elusive, they usually center around spontaneously generated situations in which we seize on an opportunity — as it arises — to help students enhance their understanding of a concept, theory, perspective, or idea (see Perlman & McCann, 2002, for a brief discussion).

After many years of advising undergraduate and graduate students, I have come to realize that the academic advising context produces a large number of teachable moments. Students seeking advice typically have questions that they hope faculty members can answer. Frequently, these questions relate to broader issues than those arising in the classroom and, more often than not, are unrelated to course material. By adopting an organic approach to advising, we can seize upon these non-classroom teaching opportunities and help shape our majors' career trajectories and perspectives on college life.

One of my most salient encounters with an advising teachable moment happened a few semesters ago with a sophomore advisee. As we discussed his fall semester courses for his upcoming junior year, he was visibly excited about delving into the upper-level psychology curriculum. However, I realized that he had one general education course left — in fine arts. He had clearly saved his favorite core area for last.

> Me: "Well, it looks like you still have an art class left to take."
> Advisee: "I hate art."
> Me: "Hmmm, what don't you like about art?"
> Advisee: "I don't really know exactly, I just know I can't stand it. Do I really have to take it?"

For a few seconds, I pondered: Why *do* we require undergraduate students to complete the general education curriculum including the fine arts area? Does knowing about art enrich psychology majors' lives or create better psychology graduates? After those few seconds of reflection, I realized that our advising conversation had transformed into a clear teachable moment.

So, as they say, *carpe diem.* I took a deep breath and seized the opportunity to discuss the reason for the art requirement. We talked about general and specific knowledge and how they both relate to the well-informed college graduate and world citizen. We discussed the presence of art in everyday life as a form of self-expression for humans. I pointed out that self-expression is fundamental to human psychology and suggested that viewing, hearing, or feeling art enhances our aesthetic experience of the world. I suggested that at least one area of art might be interesting to my advisee. How about music? Photography? Art history? Theater appreciation? Performance or dance? And here, the usefulness of the teachable moment emerged even though all those artsy options were listed in the university catalog; my advisee's schema of the art requirement had previously included only painting or drawing, both of which were of zero interest to him. He came to our meeting dead-set on avoiding "art," but by the end realized that his schema of art had been a bit narrow. Ultimately, my advisee decided on American Popular Music. And during our next advising meeting, I asked him how his semester was going. He informed me that it was going well and mentioned that his music class was his favorite course that semester. I was thrilled that our teachable moment had been transformed into a positive semester-long experience for my advisee.

Maximizing Advising Effectiveness Through Teachable Moments

Depending on the size and structure of your program, you may only see your advisees two or three times per year for advising meetings. That means advisors have limited time to expand on teachable moments during advising. But they do arise, so it's best to be ready for them when they happen. Below are several specific situations in which teachable moments may arise during advising.

Clear Up Misconceptions About Psychology

Often, the first teachable moments emerge early in the advising relationship. Many students declare psychology because of information they've gleaned from television shows, movies, books, or magazines. They may have impressions that psychology only encompasses applied fields within the discipline and may be unfamiliar with the broader, interdisciplinary and academic areas of psychology. They may not realize that psychologists conduct scientific research or that a graduate degree in psychology is a requirement for certain types of jobs. One of the first questions I ask my new advisees is, "What do you want to do with your psychology degree?" Depending on the answers offered — which more often than not include something along the lines of "helping people" — I seize the teachable moment to outline the realities of the discipline, the broad array of career options, and specific strategies and directions for reaching various career goals.

Fine-Tune Realistic Professional or Career Goals

Some colleges and universities have a formal course dedicated to students' professional and career development. For others, these courses are not available, so students may have limited access to career information about psychology. In the latter situation, advisors can step in to bridge the knowledge gap. Typically, this teachable moment emerges in the latter half of students' undergraduate or graduate careers, as they begin preparations for entry into the job market or graduate school. It may start with a student asking questions about the graduate school application process. Or it may arise when students begin assessing their GPAs and resumes. Often, I spend most of my advising sessions with students in their junior year discussing career directions rather than pointing students toward particular course options. These teachable moments often lead to students realistically assessing their future options and fine-tuning their plans for reaching their goals.

Enhance Student Strengths

All students have individual strengths and areas for improvement. Academic advisors are in a unique position in the university community to see the spectrum of advisees' lives inside and outside the classroom. As both faculty mentors and psychologists, we are especially attuned to the unique knowledge base, skills, abilities, and personalities of our advisees. An important part of advising involves paying attention to students' academic and interpersonal strengths and recognizing when a particular course, lab experience, internship, or academic minor may help them. Often, teachable moments during advising can arise when advisors listen to their students talk about their favorite classes or interests. One of my advisees a few years ago raved about her I/O class. Based on her obvious interest, I suggested that she add a business minor and seized the moment to discuss the overlap between the two disciplines. She had never considered that option before, but quickly added the minor, later graduated, and successfully entered a PhD program in I/O psychology. Adding business courses had only reinforced her interest in the subfield.

Be Ethical and Maintain Appropriate Boundaries

Occasionally, students will reveal information within the advising meeting that is beyond the scope of our ability to help them. This revelation may involve a negative personal experi-

Association for Psychological Science

ence, a physical or psychological issue, financial problems, or interpersonal difficulties. In these cases, faculty can seize the teachable moment to guide advisees in the right direction for help. Many colleges and universities have extensive networks of individuals who are specifically trained to handle these issues. Whether students need help from the career center, financial aid, the counseling center, or legal help, we can teach students where to find the most appropriate resources for their situation. Perlman, McCann, and Kadah-Ammeter (2007) provide an excellent perspective on ethical issues that arise when working with students-in-need.

Approach Advisees Holistically

It is tempting to focus only on the teachable moments where students become enlightened by their faculty advisors. Often, however, I have found that we as faculty can equally experience "teachable moments" in which students broaden our own horizons. In today's rapidly changing academic environment, students arrive at college with increasingly divided responsibilities and demands on their time. Appreciating students as individuals, who each have unique personal histories and current life situations to navigate, allows academic advisors to respond and adapt to their changing needs throughout their academic careers. Recognizing that students may have different goals or interests than those of their faculty advisors can create teachable moments in which the mentor learns to step back and let students make their own decisions. In fact, this teachable moment may lead to the realization that advisees need to spread their wings and switch to different advisors who more closely match their career interests.

Challenges in Advising

Sometimes, the teachable moments that arise during advising involve navigating difficult topics. For example, it sometimes becomes clear in advising meetings that students are struggling academically (Foushée & Sleigh, 2004, discuss ways to assist struggling students). During these times, it helps to seize the teachable moment and refer advisees to appropriate campus resources. Or, try discussing individualized study and test-taking strategies, time management skills, and note-taking techniques.

Advisors may also encounter resistant students who visit because they "have to." Here, it helps to build rapport with the advisee first, then later seize teachable moments as they arise, providing information that might allow advisees to see the usefulness of advising meetings.

Working with transfer students may also present unique challenges. As they adjust to a new academic and social environment, transfer students often raise questions about careers, campus life, and course opportunities that lend themselves well to teachable moments.

Some obstacles to teachable moments in advising are structural when departments utilize online, group, or peer advising. In each of these cases, teachable moments can be elusive, as faculty and students are relatively removed from each other. In other departments, faculty may have so many advisees that they can spend little time with individual students, severely limiting the opportunities for discovery. Departments that value advising and its potentials may want to limit or remove these structural obstacles as best they can.

Conclusion

Regardless of the advising style faculty adopt, positively and effectively interacting with advisees requires many of the skills that faculty already utilize in the classroom. The benefits of approaching advising from the perspective of mentor and teacher are enormous both for faculty and students. Grabbing teachable moments and using them to improve future teaching and advising is one of the best ways to increase faculty wisdom and fine-tune skills that enhance the college experience for both advisees and students. For the administration, advising may not be the most glamorous activity listed on faculty activity reports. But for engaged and thoughtful faculty, academic advising can be one of the most rewarding aspects of being a professor.

References and Recommended Readings

Appleby, D. (2001). The teaching-advising connection: Parts I–V. *The Mentor: An Academic Advising Journal.* Retrieved April 7, 2007, from http://www.psu.edu/dus/mentor/

Foushée, R.D., & Sleigh, M.J. (2004). Going the extra mile: Identifying and assisting struggling students. In B. Perlman, L. I. McCann, & S. H. McFadden (Eds.), *Lessons learned: Practical advice for the teaching of psychology,* (Vol. 2, pp. 303-311). Washington, DC: Association for Psychological Science.

Johnson, R.D. (Ed.). (2006). *Teachable moments: Essays on experiential education*. Lantham, MD: University Press of America.

Lunneborg, P.W., & Baker, E.C. (1986). Advising undergraduates in psychology: Exploring the neglected dimension. *Teaching of Psychology, 13,* 181-185.

Perlman, B., & McCann, L.I. (2002). What we need to know about teaching and teachers. In W. Buskist, V. Hevern, & G.W. Hill, IV (Eds.), *Essays from excellence in teaching, 2000–2001* (Chapter 10). Retrieved April 9, 2007, from http://teachpsych.org/resources/e-books/eit2000/eit00-10.html

Perlman, B., McCann, L.I., & Kadah-Ammeter, T.L. (2007). Working with students in need: An ethical perspective. In B. Perlman, L. I. McCann, & S. H. McFadden (Eds.), *Lessons learned: Practical advice for the teaching of psychology* (Vol. 3, pp. 333-342). Washington, DC: Association for Psychological Science.

Ware, M.E. (1999). Academic advising for undergraduates. In B. Perlman, L.I. McCann, & S.H. McFadden. (Eds.) *Lessons learned: Practical advice for the teaching of psychology* (Vol. 1, pp. 187-192). Washington DC: Association for Psychological Science.

What We Can Do to Help Undergraduate Students Not Going on for Graduate Studies

RAYMOND J. GREEN

Texas A&M University-Commerce

"I WANT TO GO TO graduate school and become a professor of psychology." Who doesn't receive a thrill when a promising student declares an intention to become an academic? Is there anything in the world more flattering than someone sharing our ideals, mimicking our behavior, reinforcing our belief that we made "the right career decision" and that we are "really neat people"? Aside from stroking our academic egos and, for some faculty, signaling professorial success, our more pragmatic side may view these students as "more valuable" because they can assist us in our careers. We can honestly say that we are helping students, for example, by providing them with research activities in our lab. They will learn more about research than they could from a textbook, they may get a chance to present research at a conference, and they may even find their name on a publication. However, we are also benefiting by finding an employee who is willing to work for "free."

The reinforcing nature of these students can easily lead us to design classes that are biased toward the needs of the "pre-graduate" student. This may occur unwittingly as we pay more attention to these students inside and outside of class due to the human tendency to interact with people who have similar interests. Or it may even become purposeful when a professor decides to dedicate his or her energies to students who are "serious" about the field. Regardless of the reason, this tendency to aim our lectures and activities toward students going to graduate school may do a disservice to our other students. Most of our students, particularly in first and second year courses, will not pursue master's degrees and even fewer will pursue doctoral degrees in psychology. Thus the question becomes, "How do we serve the needs of undergraduates who are not planning to go to graduate school?" In this article, I will first discuss skills that are likely to increase a person's quality of life, then how a major in psychology can fulfill many of these needs, and finally, I will present some specific activities designed to make students aware of the careers available to them with a bachelor's degree.

What Skills Are Necessary for Success

Although a college education has the potential to enrich a person's life in a myriad of ways, some skills are more likely to lead to success than others. For example, although I am now a master at short-sheeting a bed, it is a skill that has nothing to do with my current position! Two areas of expertise that are closely linked to success after college are work and interpersonal skills. These abilities may at first seem to have little in common, but success in one is likely to influence the other.

Work Skills

What do employers look for in a potential employee? At the most basic level employers want people who are intelligent, can read and write well, and have solid mathematical skills (Landrum, 2001). Appleby (2000) asked employers who were willing to interview psychology graduates about what they were looking for in a good candidate. Social, personal, and communication skills were perceived to be of the greatest value to the employers. More specific examples of these skills include the ability to deal effectively with a wide variety of people, work productively as a member of a team, demonstrate initiative and persistence, hold to high ethical standards, speak articulately and persuasively, write clearly and precisely, and demonstrate appropriate interpersonal skills. There are numerous ways that an instructor can provide students with opportunities to hone these skills.

♦ Assign group projects that cannot be completed successfully unless every member of the group contributes to the task. Corporations lament the inability of many new hires to work successfully in groups. Considering that most academic assignments are completed individually, difficulty working in groups should not be a surprising outcome.

- Help students to develop persistence by providing projects that require the completion of multiple stages.
- Have students hone their oral persuasion skills through in-class debates. Unlike physics or chemistry, psychology is not bound by laws. Instead, our science is full of competing theories providing numerous chances for our students to take a position and forcefully defend it.

Interpersonal Skills

Multiple sources (e.g., Johanson & Fried, 2002; Yancey, 2001) indicate that interpersonal skills are important factors in the workplace. In both studies cited above, recent psychology graduates ranked interpersonal skills as first in importance in their jobs. The question then becomes, what exactly are these interpersonal skills that everyone thinks are so important? Yancey, Clarkson, Baxa, and Clarkson (2003) suggest that the following interpersonal competencies are important: effective communication, the ability to accurately interpret others' emotions, sensitivity to others' feelings, strong conflict resolution skills, and politeness.

However, work success is not the only reason to improve interpersonal skills. From a liberal arts perspective, friendship, love, and civility to our neighbors are important reasons to improve our interpersonal skills. If we want to have a circle of friends who care for us and provide support, intimate others with whom to share our lives, and neighbors from whom we borrow garden tools, we must constantly seek to improve our ability to listen accurately and communicate clearly.

How Psychology Can Help
Competencies That Make Up a Psychology Education

The general principles inherent in psychology content provide the framework needed to improve students' career chances and interpersonal relationships. When professors think about preparing students for graduate study, they think a lot about content issues — do students understand the history of psychology, the major theories in their proposed field of study, and research methodology? However, knowing what year Wundt started his laboratory in Leipzig is unlikely to get someone a job and probably is not the strongest pick-up line either! Does this mean a separate set of courses is necessary for students not interested in pursuing a graduate degree? Not at all.

The APA's Taskforce on Undergraduate Major Competencies recently proposed 10 goals (Halonen, Appleby, & Brewer, 2002) and related learning outcomes for psychology majors that echo this idea. The first goal is to create a knowledge base of psychology. The next four involve the application of psychological concepts to the solution of real world issues (e.g., use of research methodology, application of values). The five remaining goals involve knowledge, skills, and values consistent with a liberal arts education that have the potential to be developed further by psychology. For example, the taskforce argued that communication skills and personal development should be augmented through one's experience as a psychology major. In essence, the suggested goals and outcomes emphasize that psychological content is only one small component of a psychology education. Psychology majors acquire a set of competencies that increases the likelihood that they will be successful in whatever work and personal situations they encounter. Psychology has the potential to fulfill this overarching goal in that it is unique in the breadth of skills that it provides to its graduates (Hayes, 1997).

Emphasize Literacy

In order to secure work, psychology majors should be literate upon graduation (Hayes, 1997). Psychology majors have an advantage over other majors in that they are trained to write in multiple formats. Aside from expressing themselves in essays like students in most majors, they also are frequently required to learn to write reports in pre-established formats as they write experimental/research papers (Hayes, 1997).

To insure the development of these abilities, instructors need to emphasize students' practicing their writing in different formats. One end of this spectrum could include reaction pieces when students express their feelings and thoughts in writing. These papers allow students to learn to write "in their own voice" while being relatively easy to grade. For example, in a social psychology course, students could watch Milgram's *Obedience* film, imagine themselves as subjects, and describe how they would react to the situation. At the other end of the spectrum, research methodology courses frequently require research projects where information must be presented in a very precise format. The expectations for the technical writing that underlies research papers are different from the more prosaic writing that is appropriate for reaction pieces, and students not only become facile with different formats, but also with expressing themselves with different vocabularies and styles.

Emphasize Numeracy

Hayes (1997) also points out that although some other majors may produce students with more mathematical skills, the combination of literacy and numeracy skills found in psychology majors is unparalleled. Although qualitative research is gaining acceptance in the behavioral sciences, psychology still emphasizes quantitative methodology, a key part of which is the use of inferential statistics to make informed decisions about human behavior.

♦ *Assign journal articles as part of the course.* Virtually every journal article provides students with an opportunity to see numbers discussed in the midst of prose but also, even more importantly, to see these numbers interpreted and discussed. To insure that our students become adept at understanding numbers, it would help if we had them read primary sources. Frequently, texts boil down and summarize journal articles, which is a necessary simplification if a large amount of material is going to be covered in our classes. Yet, at the same time, assigning a handful of journal articles each semester is not a large expense for students in terms of time or money.

♦ *Use journal articles as extra credit.* Another avenue to getting students to read more research articles is to provide extra credit assignments for reading primary research sources. One approach I take is to provide students a list of our departmental faculty, direct them to find an article written by a faculty member, and write a 2-3 page article summary. Aside from gaining familiarity with reading and interpreting research, ancillary benefits include students becoming more familiar with the faculty and the idea that professors apply in the "real world" that which is discussed in class.

Ethical Standards and Decisions

In our post-Enron society, there is a focus on whether students, particularly college students, are being provided with the tools to make ethical decisions. Psychology provides an excellent arena for a discussion of ethics. Whether one's preference is an applied or a research setting, psychology is rife with good and bad examples of ethical decision making and ambiguous situations in which the rules are unclear. There are many opportunities to discuss ethics throughout our curriculum.

- ◆ Students in abnormal psychology courses could be presented with the key parts of the APA code of ethics and then be asked to imagine or role-play scenarios where the ethical guidelines would be useful in guiding professional behavior.

- ◆ An exercise for understanding ethics in research would be for a class to appoint a mock Institutional Review Board to evaluate research proposals written by other class members. Although the specific ethical guidelines that they face in their career field may be different, students will receive practice in thinking in terms of ethics.

Ability to Understand Emotions and Behaviors

Psychologists do not have some mystical ability to look inside the hearts and minds of other people, but our students are provided with numerous tools for studying and understanding human emotion and behavior. For example, learning the major theories of personality provides a basis for understanding general tendencies in human behavior, and courses in social psychology provide evidence that casual observers frequently make mistakes in their interpretations of behavior. Most textbook authors say that they highlight these mistakes so that students become aware of them and may perhaps become more effortful and less mistake prone in their processing of social information.

The good news is that these efforts may be paying off. Research indicates that psychology students move somewhat beyond casual observation and explain human behavior less simplistically than natural science students (Fletcher, Danilovics, Fernandez, Peterson, & Reeder, 1986). Although knowledge does not guarantee better interpersonal skill (Hayes, 1997), knowledge of one's perceptual biases may help a person more accurately interpret people's emotions and behaviors. Further, being aware of the perceptual sources of misunderstanding may enhance students' conflict resolution skills.

Use of Psychology in Everyday Life

Faculty get students' attention and make psychology "real" when they share stories about their lives that draw attention to the use of psychology. This moves the discipline from something to be memorized to an approach to living and a useful set of tools.

♦ Students are fascinated and appalled when they discover how findings from research on persuasion are applied to advertising and marketing campaigns. Some of the most captivating explorations of consumer psychology have revolved around how my students make decisions in the grocery store.

♦ If you are feeling brave, elicit stories from the students about their pets. Use these stories to demonstrate to students that learning theory can be used to understand the behavior of our animal companions. I often tell the tale of how my in-laws had an outside dog that would sneak inside at times. They would then entice the dog back outside with a yummy dog bone. It doesn't take students long to figure out why that dog was found more and more often in the house (usually sitting by the back door and drooling in anticipation!).

♦ Did psychology assist you in your parenting and if so, how? Sometimes I kid with my students that my knowledge of psychology increases my neuroses when it comes to parenting. For example, I find myself asking questions like, "Did I respond to my son's needs quickly enough or is he going to develop a sense of mistrust?" If your children's behavior was more interesting or your parenting methods were influenced by your knowledge of Piaget or Erikson, share these moments and anecdotes with your students.

♦ How does the research literature on attraction and proximity explain why students have a crush on the person sitting to their left or in the dorm room next door?

Guiding Toward Appropriate Careers

Although students will come to appreciate the skills gained during their college career, they also want answers to the question "What kind of work can I find with a bachelor's degree in psychology?" Students often ask this in panicked voices that suggest that they believe the answer to the question is "none," or that they better get used to asking, "Do you want fries with that?". In reality, however, the skills described above can be applied to a multitude of careers. Thus, the diversity of careers available to psychology majors suggests that multiple approaches need to be taken to insure that students gain the information required to make intelligent decisions about careers.

Useful Print and Internet Resources

Countless sources list and describe the careers available to psychology majors (see References and Recommended Readings). These lists provide an excellent starting point for students in their exploration of career fields. Although students will profit from these sources, the use of interactive modes of communication may prove more beneficial.

Use Former and Current Students as Resources

Psychology clubs and honor societies can play a role in providing information about potential careers. One option is for Psi Chi chapters to invite alumni to conduct presentations and answer questions about their careers. I attended one of these sessions as an undergraduate and was surprised by how many people had what I considered to be fascinating jobs that did not require going to graduate school and were difficult to categorize as "psychology." In addition, with alumni permission, departmental Web pages can contain biographies and e-mail addresses of former students willing to answer questions about different career tracks.

Include students in the advising process. Seegmiller (2003) designed a peer advising course where knowledgeable students were trained to provide information not only about graduate school but also about careers in psychology. For our purposes, a psychology major or two trained by the college or university placement office to work with peers has great potential. Non-official peer advisement systems already exist at every college, but these unofficial systems may pass on flawed or incomplete information. Training students to advise effectively should only have positive results.

Zechmeister and Helkowski (2001) created a career course that culminated in a student-run career fair open to students not enrolled in the class. Students in the course chose a career to investigate, designed a portfolio containing important information about the career (e.g., opportunities, how to prepare for the career) and then created posters and handouts that were presented at a career fair that was heavily advertised to psychology students. The benefits of this process were that the students in the class became knowledgeable about a career that interested them, and other students became more aware of the fields potentially available to them. One caveat is that Zechmeister and Helkowskis' course was aimed at master's-level careers, but it could easily be adapted to careers appropriate for bachelor's degrees.

Utilize the University's Placement/Career Office

Although there are many things that can be done to assist our students in their search for meaningful employment, we should remember that there is no need to reinvent the wheel. Every college campus has an office of professionals who are trained to help students find work during and after college. Departments need to develop strong relationships with their career/placement offices. Further, certain class assignments can be designed so that they highlight important psychological principles while also providing practical assistance to a student who will soon be looking for employment. For example, industrial/organizational psychology courses provide a perfect excuse for students to practice writing and evaluating resumes. Students can be directed to the placement office for resume templates, at least insuring that you have taught them where the office is located! Mock interviews can be utilized in social psychology classes to highlight the importance of impression formation and to discuss various elements of persuasion.

Conclusion

A large number of psychology majors do not choose to pursue advanced degrees upon graduation, and many of our students will not find jobs in "psychology." Our responsibility is to be aware of and sympathetic to the needs of these students. Although our first instinct may be to focus on students who intend to attend graduate school in psychology, we need to be supportive of, listen to, and spend time with students who are interested in psychology as a liberal arts degree.

Helping students lead productive, ethical lives both in and out of the workplace is an important measure of our success as teachers, and a source of pride faculty often overlook. At the end of the day, or the end of our careers, isn't that what teaching is all about?

References and Recommended Readings

Conard, M.A. (2004). Conscientiousness is key: Incentives for attendance make little difference. *Teaching of Psychology, 31*, 269-272.

Davis, B.G. (1993). *Tools for teaching.* San Francisco: Jossey Bass.

Forsyth, D.R. (2003). *The professor's guide to teaching: Psychological principles and practices.* Washington, DC: American Psychological Association.

Halonen, J.S., Appleby, D.C., & Brewer, C.L. (2002). *Undergraduate psychology major learning goals and outcomes: A report.* Retrieved September 6, 2005, from http://www.apa.org/ed/pcue/taskforcereport2.pdf

Hancock, T.M. (1994). Effects of mandatory attendance on student performance. *College Student Journal, 28*, 326-329.

Houston, J.P. (1976). The assessment and prevention of answer copying on undergraduate multiple-choice exams. *Research in Higher Education, 5*, 301-311.

Jones, C.H. (1984). Interaction of absences and grades in a college course. *Journal of Psychology, 116*, 133-136.

Lepper, M.R., Greene, K.D., & Nisbett, R.E. (1973). Undermining children's intrinsic interest with extrinsic reward: A test of the 'overjustification' hypothesis. *Journal of Personality & Social Psychology, 28*, 129-137.

Lucas, S.G., & Bernstein, D.A. (2005). *Teaching psychology: A step by step guide.* Mahwah, NJ: Erlbaum.

McCabe, D.L., Treviño, L.K., & Butterfield, K.D. (2001). Cheating in academic institutions: A decade of research. *Ethics & Behavior, 11*, 219-233.

Nilson, L.B. (1998). *Teaching at its best: A research-based resource for college instructors.* Bolton, MA: Anker.

Pintrich, P.R. (1994). Student motivation in the college classroom. In K.W. Prichard & R. McLaran Sawyer (Eds.), *Handbook of college teaching: Theory and application* (pp. 23-43). Westport, CT: Greenwood Press.

Royse, D. (2001). *Teaching tips for college and university instructors: A practical guide.* Needham Heights, MA: Allyn & Bacon.

Shimoff, E., & Catania, C.A. (2001). Effects of recording attendance on grades in introductory psychology. *Teaching of Psychology, 28*, 192-195.

Sperber, M. (2005). Notes from a teaching career. *Chronicle of Higher Education, 52*(3), B20-B21.

St. Clair, K.L. (1999). A case against compulsory class attendance policies in higher education. *Innovative Higher Education, 23*, 171-180.

van Blerkom, M.L. (1992). Class attendance in undergraduate courses. *Journal of Psychology: Interdisciplinary and Applied, 126*, 487-494.

Weimer, M. (1993). *Improving your classroom teaching:* (Vol. 1) Newbury Park, CA: Sage.

A Developmental Strategy to Write Effective Letters of Recommendation

DREW C. APPLEBY

Indiana University-Purdue University Indianapolis

IN *THE COMPLETE GUIDE to Graduate School Admissions*, Keith-Spiegel and Wiederman (2000, p. 175) state that letters of recommendation "are taken very seriously, and sometimes are as important as grades and test scores." This statement highlights the essential function letters play in our students' attempts to achieve their post-baccalaureate goals and to the crucial role faculty play in this process. Faculty who have written such letters know how rewarding this process can be, but they also are aware that it is a time-consuming, sometimes difficult, and occasionally frustrating task.

This column provides advice to faculty to help them to write effective letters that can portray their students' capabilities in an honest and compelling manner, increase their students' chances of being accepted into the graduate programs or jobs of their choice, and do not place their authors in litigious jeopardy.

Effective letters are the product of an active developmental partnership between students who request them and faculty who write them. The success of this partnership is determined by the degree to which the following steps have been accomplished:

1. Faculty become aware of the knowledge, skills, and characteristics(KSCs) that potential employers and graduate school admissions committees value in their applicants.

2. Students are made aware of these KSCs early in their education.

3. Faculty provide students with opportunities to develop these KSCs.
4. Faculty create a system for students to provide information about their KSCs that allows letters to be written in a timely, evidence-based, and procedurally correct manner.
5. Faculty become aware of the ethical aspects of letters so they can write honest letters while avoiding legal peril.

Which KSCs Are Valued

Faculty are responsible for teaching more than the content of psychology. They also are responsible for teaching students how to use what they have learned to succeed after graduation. One way to do this is to make students aware of the KSCs valued by employers and graduate school admissions committees and to help them develop plans to attain these KSCs.

Letters and KSCs for Graduate School

Effective letters describe the attributes of their subjects that are valued by the people who read them. Research with two of my students (Appleby, Keenan, & Mauer, 1999) generated the following list of KSCs (in descending order of importance) based on the number of graduate programs that specifically requested letter authors to rate them: 1) motivated and hard-working; 2) high intellectual/scholarly ability; 3) research skills; 4) emotionally stable and mature; 5) writing skills; 6) speaking skills; 7) teaching skills/potential; 8) works well with others; 9) creative and original; 10) strong knowledge of area of study; 11) strong character or integrity; 12) special skills (e.g., computer or lab); 13) capable of analytical thought; 14) broad general knowledge; 15) intellectually independent; and 16) leadership ability.

Tell students they must provide you with specific examples of things they have done during their college careers that will allow you to say they possess these KSCs and enable you to support your statements with specific evidence. Provide students with a form that lists these KSCs and include space for them to describe their supporting behaviors under each one.

Letters and KSCs for Employment

Another study (Appleby, 2000) provided a similar list of KSCs (in descending order of importance) valued by employers who come to campus to interview psychology majors: 1) deals effectively with a wide variety of people; 2) displays appropriate interpersonal skills; 3) listens carefully and accurately; 4) shows initiative and persistence; 5) exhibits effective time management; 6) holds high ethical standards and expects the same of others; 7) handles conflict successfully; 8) speaks articulately and persuasively; 9) works productively as a member of a team; 10) plans and carries out projects successfully; 11) thinks logically and creatively; 12) remains open-minded during controversies; 13) identifies and actualizes personal potential; 14) writes clearly and precisely; 15) adapts easily to organizational rules and procedures; 16) comprehends and retains key points from written materials; and 17) gathers and organizes information from multiple sources. The advice I give my employment-bound students about these KSCs is the same that I give graduate-school-bound students. The forms I have students complete are available; e-mail requests to dappleby@iupui.edu.

Communicate KSCs Early and Provide Students the Opportunity to Develop Them

Include KSCs and information about preparing for the steps necessary to obtain a job or gain entrance to graduate school in the academic advising process. If students are to develop the KSCs necessary to accomplish their post-baccalaureate goals, they must first become aware of them. Without this type of advanced preparation, students are likely to utter the oft-heard phrase, "Why didn't someone tell me I had to ____?" during their senior year, when it is too late to do what they should have done to accomplish their goals.

Psychology departments can provide opportunities for students to develop these KSCs. For example, the vast majority of our students do not apply to graduate school, but they still need written or verbal support from faculty to secure jobs. Providing students with opportunities to function as teaching assistants, research assistants, peer advisors, or psychology club or Psi Chi officers enables them to acquire the KSCs valued by potential employers.

Consider an Academic Course

One departmental strategy to increase students' awareness of these crucial activities (and their resulting KSCs) is to offer a course that systematically exposes students to them early in their undergraduate careers. My "Orientation to a Major in Psychology" syllabus and a sample of one of my student's work also are available by request to dappleby@iupui.edu.

The Process

Students Providing Information

Faculty need a system for students to request letters that allows them to be written in a timely, evidence-based, and procedurally correct manner.

Ask students to provide extensive academic and personal information. I use a system based on Zimbardo's (1987) that requires my students to organize the following information using a manila file folder on which they print their names and 1) a list of all graduate schools or employers to whom they wish me to write a letter with the deadline by which the letter must be received; 2) where the letter is to be sent; 3) whether there is a form to complete in addition to my letter; 4) the specific graduate program or job for which they are applying; 5) their e-mail address and phone number; 6) their resume or *curriculum vitae*; 7) their completed KSC form (which lists all the classes taken from me and the grades earned); 8) recommendation forms with the necessary sections completed; and 9) a stamped envelope with the typed address of each employer or graduate program to which it should be sent, or their own address if I should send the letter to them for inclusion with their application.

It is in the students' best interests to sign the statement waiving their right to see their letter. Graduate schools are more likely to have confidence in the honesty and objectivity of letters whose subjects have not read them (Ceci & Peters, 1984; Keith-Spiegel & Wiederman, 2000).

Ask students to give you their completed folder at least one month before the earliest deadline so you have sufficient time to write a carefully crafted letter. This process enables me to keep all of my letters information organized, which is particularly important during peak letter-writing periods such as Christmas vacation. My students often comment that this system reduces some of the stress of the application procedure by helping them to create a sense of control.

Requesting the Letter

Once students become aware of the nature and importance of letters and are familiar with the information they must provide, the next step is for them to "pop the question." After a student asks for a recommendation, I set up a meeting to explain my letter-request method, during which I stress that "Will you write me a letter of recommendation?" is *not* the right question to ask.

The more appropriate question for students to ask is, "Can you write me a strong letter of recommendation?" Replacing the *will* with *can* and adding *strong* gives faculty the option to diplomatically decline the request, not because they do not want to write a letter, but because they believe their letter could be a potentially negative addition to the student's application. This type of letter is a "kiss of death" (Appleby & Appleby, 2004). A graduate school admissions committee chairperson reports the following:

"[A student] asked me to write a letter of recommendation for her. She informs me that she took my class last semester. I'll have to take her word for it because I don't remember her. If she was in my class, she did nothing to distinguish herself from the other students. Needless to say, I can't comment on her qualifications."

It is crucial to help students understand that strong letters are those whose authors say they know the student well, are willing to make positive statements about the student's KSCs, can support these statements with compelling evidence, and whose letters will be credible to readers.

Inform students that letters included in the application materials for graduate school candidates should not be written by travel agents, ministers, therapists, mothers, and the candidates themselves. Some students are remarkably naïve about the nature of letters and believe that graduate school admissions committees and potential employers are simply interested in reading letters that contain positive comments about the student, regardless of their source.

Faculty are not required to write a letter for a student just because it is requested. If a faculty member does not believe he or she can write a strong letter, it is in the best interest of the student for the faculty member to decline, to explain why the letter could have a negative impact on the student's application, and to help the student find a more appropriate reference author. My most effective defense against having to write negative letters is my letter-request method. Once students discover the type of evidence I need to write a strong letter, those for whom I would have to write a potentially damaging letter either thank me for my honesty and withdraw their request or simply never return the letter-request forms.

Writing the Letter

Address the KSCs most valued by the letter reader early in the letter, thus increasing the positive impacts of a letter using the power of the primacy effect. I begin my letters with a paragraph introducing the subject of my letter, the program for which he/she is applying, and for how long and in what capacity I have known him or her. I end this paragraph by introducing each of the KSCs I will identify and support with evidence in the remaining paragraphs. For example, the following is taken from one of my recent letters.

"I will use this letter to describe Cindy's skills and characteristics in the following areas that are crucial to graduate school success: motivation and work ethic, intellectual ability, maturity and responsibility, research skills, and communication skills. I will also provide you with empirical evidence that she has acquired each of these skills."

"Make every attempt to state facts about a student ... and then support them with criterion-referenced observations" (Swenson & Keith-Spiegel, 1991, para. 3). Heed Swenson and Keith-Spiegel's legal advice to letter writers that any "unfavorable information must be supportable" (1991, para. 5). I am also careful to read the directions to letter writers, which often request answers to very specific questions (e.g., "Do you believe this candidate will be able to survive in a scientifically-rigorous doctoral program?"). Instructions sometimes request the letter writer to address a candidate's weaknesses. I attempt to comply in a positive and developmental manner by describing a KSC the candidate previously lacked, but which he or she has now developed or is in the process of developing.

Letter Length and the Quality of Writing

Write letters of moderate length (i.e., no more than two pages) that exhibit verbal parsimony and felicity of expression. I assume that letter readers are suspicious of extremely short and extremely long letters. An extremely short letter is most likely interpreted as an indication that the writer does not know the letter's subject well or does not have many complimentary things to say about the subject. Extremely long letters are tedious to read, and unless they are written in such a way as to hold the attention of the reader, they may be dismissed as overblown or exaggerated. Graduate admission committees are often faced with hundreds of letters.

Avoid spelling, grammar, punctuation, or capitalization errors. These errors can seriously erode a reader's confidence in the writer's content.

Letters Students Must Include in Their Application Package

When a letter must be included in the student's application package, it is customary for writers to sign their name across the sealed flap of the envelope and then either mail it to the applicant or have them pick up the letter. I prefer to have students pick up their letters to avoid the possibility of loss or delay in the mail.

The Follow-Up Process

It is perfectly acceptable to have students remind you the week before their letters should be mailed. Faculty should be true to their word if they promise to write strong letters and to mail them so they arrive before their deadlines, but faculty and students are all too familiar with stories about strong candidates who were rejected by admissions committees because of missing letters. Timely reminders can save students from worrying more than necessary during the application process, and give a faculty member one more prompt just in case an extra busy workload has produced an inadvertent memory lapse.

Ethics and the Law

Faculty must be aware of the ethical aspects of letters of recommendation so they can write honest letters while avoiding legal peril. According to Swenson and Keith-Spiegel (1991, para. 2), "Libel occurs when false information that damages a person's reputation is written and disseminated to a third party, with some fault on the part of the writer. ... Truth is a defense to an allegation of defamation." These authors present the following suggestions (with clarifying examples) to protect faculty from liability when they write letters:

- State factual information and support it with evidence.
- Support unfavorable information with empirical observations of behaviors.
- Verify the truth of your statements.
- Label opinions as opinions, and offer the basis upon which they were formed.

- Write in a clear and unambiguous manner. Do not use obfuscation to conceal negative information.
- Gain students' consent before you write letters requested by third parties.
- Send information about students only after third parties have officially requested it, and send that information only to those requesting it.

Understand that you are not required to write a letter about students just because a student asking you to do so. Consult your university's attorney if you believe a letter may endanger your legal well-being.

Conclusion

I would be remiss if I did not reiterate one crucial point. Although letters can be difficult, time-consuming, and frustrating, they also can provide a wonderful opportunity for faculty and students to interact in a manner that can enrich and facilitate their teaching and learning partnership. Helping students to understand the nature and importance of letters in a positive and developmental manner — and then providing them with opportunities to develop the KSCs you want to highlight in their letters — can be a mutually rewarding process.

References and Recommended Readings

Appleby, D.C. (2000, Spring). Job skills valued by employers who interview psychology majors. *Eye on Psi Chi, 3*, 17.

Appleby, D.C., & Appleby, K.M. (2006). Kisses of death in the graduate school application process. *Teaching of Psychology, 33*, 19-24.

Appleby, D.C., Keenan, J., & Mauer, E. (1999, Spring). Applicant characteristics valued by graduate programs in psychology. *Eye on Psi Chi, 1*, 39.

Ceci, S.J., & Peters, D. (1984). Letters of reference: A naturalistic study of the effects of confidentiality. *American Psychologist, 39*, 29-31.

Keith-Spiegel, P.K., & Wiederman, M.W. (2000). *The complete guide to graduate school admission* (2nd ed.). Hillsdale, NJ: Erlbaum.

Svinicki, M.D. (1999). *Teaching and learning on the edge of the millennium: Building on what we have learned.* Hillsdale, NJ: Erlbaum.

Swenson, E.V., & Keith-Spiegel, P. (1991). Writing letters of recommendation for students: How to protect yourself from liability. Retrieved May 17, 2004, from http://www.teachpsych.org/otrp/resources/swenson91.pdf

Zimbardo, P.G. (1987). Reducing the agony of writing letters of recommendation. In M.E. Ware & R.J. Millard (Eds.), *Handbook on student development: Advising, career development, and field placement* (pp. 94-95). Hillsdale, NJ: Erlbaum.

Working With Students in Need: An Ethical Perspective

BARON PERLMAN
LEE I. McCANN,
University of Wisconsin-Oshkosh
TAMMY L. KADAH-AMMETER
University of Wisconsin-Fox Valley

Professor Smith, do you have a minute? I need to talk with you. Dr. Jones, can I see you after class for a few minutes? Professor Miller, are you busy tomorrow?

FACULTY MEMBERS interact with students in many ways. They teach, advise, oversee student clubs and honor societies, do collaborative scholarship, help with career and graduate school aspirations, and many times, simply listen or offer advice.

The fact that students' lives are not always idyllic is no surprise to most faculty. Some students just need a sympathetic ear with whom to talk about everyday problems, stressors, or other difficulties and concerns. Although a rare event for many faculty, meeting with a student in serious need — those acutely stressed; anxious; suicidal; depressed; experiencing serious struggles with coursework, racial or cultural differences, or parental expectations — is important and challenging work. Sometimes, students take the initiative and ask to meet with their teachers, but faculty members also reach out to students, even spelling out in their course syllabi that they are available. A faculty member may be the first or only person who recognizes or knows that a student needs support or assistance. They may notice course performance or attendance falling or receive notes from their Dean of Students about students who are ill or have suffered the death of a loved one. Just asking, "how are you doing?" can be a way of forming a connection with such a student.

Faculty and institutions need to maximize the chances that encounters with students are helpful and grounded in an awareness of ethical obligations. As is true of any interaction between someone in authority and someone seeking assistance, there are rules of morality, values, and professional behavior for those in power so that those seeking help receive the respect and assistance they deserve. There is no national code of ethical behavior to which all faculty subscribe and in our experience some faculty members, unfortunately, see ethics not as guidance and wisdom, but as misguided restraints on their behavior and academic freedom. Only American Psychological Association (APA) members must abide by the association's ethics (APA, 2002), although all faculty would best insure students' welfare and dignity if they followed such codes of conduct.

In no area of faculty work is moral, professional behavior more necessary than when interacting with students in need, regardless of how "hurting" the student is — yet most faculty receive little or no training or guidance in how to do so. It is especially important that faculty strive for appropriate boundaries and integrity, maintaining their roles as educators but not becoming therapists.

Tips for Ethically Helping Students in Need

Prepare

Read your institution's guidelines and policies on faculty working with students in need, if they exist, especially before meeting a student. Talk with trusted colleagues about their availability and interest should you need to consult with them and know the referral agencies available to you (e.g., Counseling Center, Multi-Cultural Center, Dean of Students Office, Provost's Office, University Health Center, Campus Police, University Legal Counsel).

We recommend that departments work with their Counseling Center or other trained staff to help faculty members with their listening skills and professionalism when working with students in need. Such training and discussions, more useful and different than simply distributing a handout, can be especially helpful for new faculty, often closer to students in age and identity, to whom some students may turn first, but who are least experienced in their role as "faculty as helper," and the more likely to experience inappropriate boundary crossings.

Ethical Guidance

The area of ethics and working with students in need deserves all of the serious thought faculty can give it. We applied the American Psychological Association's five aspirational principles (APA, 2002) to issues that in our experience are related to helping such students. If readers have examples and ideas for us, we would appreciate hearing from you. (Perlman@uwosh.edu).

Beneficence and Nonmaleficence: Do Good and Avoid Doing Harm

Teachers must avoid doing harm and be helpful, if possible. They must avoid misusing their influence and power and safeguard the welfare and rights of their students. Faculty need to act with integrity — being honest and truthful with students, but in ways that are not harmful. Total honesty can be inappropriate; for example, advising a student to "dump" an abusive boyfriend. When a student approached one of the authors about pressures to come home on weekends versus academics and studying, he was honest that 1) he did not know her home situation well enough to give her advice with confidence; 2) that in his experience students who spent weekends on campus did more studying and seemed to do better in their coursework; 3) that a compromise would be to return home less often; 4) this was a decision that she had to make for herself (self determination, see below), but one she could revisit; and 5) he was very interested in what she decided and how it worked out.

Many faculty members are unaware of the power they possess over students. Students may be worried that if a teacher asks them to stop by their office, and they do not, their course grade could suffer. Students see faculty as knowing a great deal. They may have unspoken high expectations for the help they will receive from this "wise" person teaching their class. Our observation is that psychology faculty may be more likely to have students approach them because of the discipline and course content they teach, and psychology faculty, more than colleagues in other disciplines, also may be more tempted to think they know what to do. Faculty members need to be aware that it is not their responsibility as teachers, even if a trained clinician or counselor, to work with students in need. Others in the institution, such as the Counseling Center, have that responsibility and probably have more relevant training and experience. Faculty need to take themselves off pedestals and be honest with students about their life experiences and abilities to help. They need to learn to say:

- My experience with that is limited, and I am not very knowledgeable about what you are going through.
- When my son or daughter had trouble with that, this is what helped, but I do not know if it applies to you.
- That sounds difficult. You are clearly in distress. But I do not know what to advise or what you should do. Do you have any ideas?
- I have no good advice for you except that you seek out someone more experienced than I.

Faculty Members Must Remain Aware of Their Personal Limitations

For example, faculty have personal experiences with, but probably little professional expertise regarding relationships, medical or legal advice, and so on.

Fidelity and Responsibility

Faculty members must keep their promises to students. Faculty are role models for students and are more important to students than teachers may realize. As role models, faculty members need to follow through on promises they make to students: you can take the exam early, you can turn in your term paper a day or two late, I will bring you a book or two about that topic for your reading. A colleague spent some time talking with a student who was going overseas for the first time. The student was both excited and anxious. The faculty member told the student he would bring some travel books that might prove useful but got busy and never did. The student felt let down and unimportant, and the teacher heard from other students that his relationship with this student was harmed.

Faculty must act responsibly, value consultation, and refer students when appropriate. One of the authors, a clinical psychologist, was approached by a student about treatment decisions for a client living at a residentially based facility where the student worked. The author listened, and referred the student back to the agency's director. Despite the fact the faculty member had expertise in this area, the student needed to talk with the person who had legal and moral responsibility for the client and the student's clinical work. Going too far with advice raises the risk for faculty members that students, their parents, administrators, and in this case, the student's supervisor and boss may complain.

Listen Closely

The process of listening can be as important as whether teachers really understand what their students are saying. Students need to feel valued and attended to in such situations. Do not answer the telephone or respond to e-mail signals while talking to this student. Often all students want and need is for someone to listen to what they are saying, so learn to listen with silence. Simply listen. Then faculty need the ability to respond, to become practiced with language such as:

♦ Let me see if I am hearing you accurately. Are you saying that ____ is the problem?

♦ It sounds like you are really in distress. Is that so?

♦ You sound worried.

♦ I'm not sure I understand. Can you tell me more?

Part of listening well — something rare in our society — is to look at someone without interruption. Eye contact in a quiet setting can be helpful in its own right.

Give Students the Time They Need

Part of helping is the time to be patient and explore what is troubling a student. Let students know how much time you have to meet with them (30-45 minutes may be needed) and let them know how much time is left ("I want to let you know we have about 20 minutes left"). Knowing how much longer they can meet with you helps students decide what to talk about and focus the meeting. Diagnostically, students who require a lot of time or who ask for multiple meetings are communicating that they need expert assistance. Refer them to a designated agency so a trained professional can deal with their needs and dependency. They always can report back to you about how things are going. The issue of time is difficult because some students simply see no boundaries and their problem can be (or seem) trivial to the faculty with whom they are talking. Also, colleagues may resent students who take up too much time and may, consciously or unconsciously, work against the student when it comes to grading or, especially, letters of recommendation later.

Integrity (Trust)

Be respectful and treat all students with dignity. Students must never feel as if they are bothering faculty members or taking up their time unduly, although some need limits. Regardless of how the student "presents"— whether articulately or with great emotion, organized or disorganized — faculty members must be respectful and never diminish or demean what the student is presenting. Teachers can be caring and at the same time communicate to a student that they are not available right now. If faculty members are having a stressful day, and have a scheduled meeting with a student, they need to take a deep breath before the meeting. If students have been difficult in the past (demanding, making excuses for poor course work) separate this fact from the problem at hand. Faculty members should never humiliate students or discount their problems as trivial even when they feel that way; total honestly and truthfulness (see beneficence and nonmaleficence above) is not always ethical intervention. One colleague tells the story of a sobbing, devastated coed who came to talk about a young man who did not call her for a third date. The faculty member told her that "Men come, men go. Get used to it." That same young woman went to see another faculty member, even more upset. This second teacher let her talk for a while, and that is what she needed.

Justice

Be equally helpful to all students. Take whatever problems students bring you as important to them. An embarrassing moment at a party can seem like the end of the world to an 18-year-old. Students with roommate problems may be experiencing the most difficult times they have ever had and such situations not only can be stressful, but also offer potential for learning life-long skills (problem solving, confronting others appropriately, standing up for oneself, etc.). One of the authors greatly contributed to a student's life quality and commitment to college by providing her information on how she could obtain a different dorm room and separate from a difficult roommate.

Respect for People's Rights and Dignity

Treat the content of discussions with students-in-need in confidence. Faculty are not to disclose student information unless they have serious concerns about students' personal safety or their risk to others (see below). Never walk down the hall to talk with a colleague about a student and disclose that student's identity or disclose information from a meeting with a student to anyone (spouse, best friend, or colleagues) unless you can camouflage students so that identifying them is impossible. When a student approached one of the authors about her shyness and her growing tiredness with this part of her personality, he listened, and recommended she see someone at the Counseling

Center and keep in touch with him about how she was coping with her shyness if she felt comfortable doing so. Even though she was enrolled in two of his colleagues' classes, he spoke to neither about his interaction with her.

Meet with students in private. Often students walk with teachers back to their offices. Avoid talking with students about substantive issues until the office door is closed or ajar. If you share an office or have a cubical you must find a private place to meet. Hang a "Do not disturb" sign on your door during such meetings. Typically faculty members leave their door ajar to avoid a false harassment claim. However, students-in-need may not talk with a faculty member unless the door is closed. Our advice would be to close the door if the student requests it and your judgment and experience tells you doing so is okay. (P. Keith-Spiegel, personal communication, March 1, 2005). On occasion, students self disclose personal issues to everyone in class. Sometimes these self-disclosures add to the depth and relevancy of course content and are beneficial for students and teacher alike. At other times, students go too far, potentially embarrassing their classmates with personal information or problems best discussed in private. Teachers must monitor students' statements, make decisions as to whether the self disclosure is appropriate, and move the class discussion and content on to other students and other topics if necessary. A simple, "Talk with me after class about that when I can give you more attention and time" often is an appropriate intervention.

Allow self-determination. Faculty members must allow students to make their own decisions. It is the student's life, even if, at times, youth appears to be wasted on the young. Faculty members meeting with and working with students-in-need must allow them to proceed as they decide. Faculty members can lay out a smorgasbord of choices and point out the pluses and minuses of each, but the student chooses. A faculty member would not openly agree with a student, for example, that an abortion is what she needed or that they should move out of the house despite their parent's strong objections.

Faculty need to be sensitive to the fact that how they frame and describe various courses of action can make some choices more attractive than others, thus undermining students' self-determination. Students are free to not choose — that is a choice.

Sometimes situations heal themselves; sometimes they must worsen before they get better.

Students With the Most Serious Problems

Faculty members are probably most concerned about how to respond to students who are seriously in need (e.g., suicidal or talk about suicidal thoughts and feelings, appear severely depressed, or seem psychologically disorganized). Other students may be dealing with serious grief and loss, alcohol and drug problems, or severe distress or anxiety caused by career decisions; or be in abusive relationships; struggling with sexual identity or orientation; or facing what they perceive as unsolvable problems (e.g., dropping out of school and disappointing parents versus staying in school when they know it is not a good time to do so).

Our advice is simple and direct: Never be the primary helper for students with serious problems. Listen, express concern and a sense of caring, and refer them to professionals (Nilson, 2003). Simply tell students: "Your problem is beyond the scope of what I can ethically do for you. I respect you for trusting me enough to share this problem with me, and it is because of my concern and respect that we need to find someone professionally trained with whom you can meet." One of the authors teaches Abnormal Psychology and has students do some writing, applying course content to their own lives. He refers at least five to seven students a semester to the Counseling Center.

If a student threatens to commit suicide or to harm another individual, teachers are obligated to breach confidentiality and call the police or some emergency intervention office and not leave the student alone. Err on the side of their safety. One would simply tell a student, if the circumstances are appropriate for it, "I know you have not directly asked for help and what I am about to do may seem intrusive, but I am extremely concerned about what I have heard and I think it would be best for both of us for me to _____." If a student is extremely angry or agitated in a faculty member's office, you may choose to call someone from the office next door or down the hall. Another piece of direct advice: If students' problems worry you, refer them to someone. Be honest and clear with students that support services exist for their well-being and that although students may not know any of the professionals who work there, these are the settings in which they will get the help they need and that you will assist them in getting this help. Exact rules for how faculty members are to behave in such a situation are impossible to delineate.

Conclusion

Students-in-need are best served if faculty members have a framework that guides professional and ethical behavior. We have suggested that the aspirational principles of the APA's Ethical Principles and Code of Conduct can provide that framework. Even if a referral is the desired and typical outcome of an interaction with a student in serious need, a lot goes on in such interactions. Society entrusts faculty to effectively navigate these difficult interactions, and they need to uphold that trust in their abilities and judgment. Faculty members can suggest options for students that are directly related to a course, school-related activity, academics, and career advising. Faculty members meeting with students with day-to-day problems can listen and lay out some alternative courses of action. When students have serious needs, professional and ethical practice calls for faculty to refer them to those with the expertise and responsibility to help them.

Thanks to Patricia Keith-Spiegel for her ideas and contributions.

References and Recommended Readings

American Psychological Association. (2002). Ethical principles of psychologists and code of conduct. *American Psychologist, 57,* 1060-1073.

Curzan, A., & Damour, L. (2000). *First day to final grade: A graduate student's guide to teaching.* Ann Arbor: University of Michigan Press.

Davis, B.G. (1993). *Tools for teaching.* San Francisco: Jossey-Bass.

Francis, P. (2003). Developing ethical institutional policies and procedures for working with suicidal students on a college campus. *Journal of College Counseling, 6,* 114-124.

Haney, M. (2004). Ethical dilemmas associated with self-disclosure in student writing. *Teaching of Psychology, 31,* 167-171.

Keith-Spiegel, P., Whitley, B., Balogh, D., Perkins, D., & Wittig, A. (2002). *The ethics of teaching: A casebook* (2nd ed.). Mahwah, NJ: Erlbaum.

Koocher, G.P., & Keith-Spiegel, P. (1998). *Ethics in psychology: Professional standards and and cases* (2nd ed.). New York: Oxford.

Nagy, T.F. (2000). *Ethics in plain English: An illustrative casebook for psychologists.* Washington, DC: American Psychological Association.

Nilson, L.B. (2003). *Teaching at its best: A research-based resource for college instructor* (2nd ed.). Bolton, MA: Anker.

Vickio, C. (1990). The goodbye brochure: Helping students to cope with transition and loss. *Journal of Counseling & Development, 68,* 575-577.

Part VII

Coda

Observations on Teaching: Fifteen Years of Teaching Tips

BARON PERLMAN
LEE I. MCCANN
SUSAN H. MCFADDEN
University of Wisconsin-Oshkosh

Whatever is rushed to maturity will surely break down early. Whatever is accomplished in a hurry will surely be easily destroyed.
(Zen Lessons, 1989, p. 33).

This final Teaching Tips column under our editorship looks back and seeks to summarize the important, prevailing ideas in Teaching Tips over the last 15 years. We read Teaching Tips from its inception to the conclusion of our editorship, 107 writings. What did they tell us? What is left unsaid? We sought substantive ideas that would withstand the test of time. Our observations emphasize the paradoxes that infuse the practice of teaching; they reveal why good teaching can be so difficult, but that at the same time, understanding them can assist us in teaching well.

Be Intentional in Your Teaching

As we read our columnists' work it became evident that teaching is a craft with many nuances. Decisions on planning our courses, what to teach in today's class, and how to teach it, all have as their goal positive outcomes for both students and teachers. We should be, but are often not, intentional about how and why we teach the way we do. Good teachers plan and are mindful of the decisions they make and what they do, and do not do, in their teaching. That is the theme of Teaching Tips:

assisting teachers in careful consideration of ideas about teaching and in deciding deliberately whether to integrate and adopt them. Ideally, we have a well-considered reason for everything we do in the classroom and with our students.

Our actions, teachable moments and the spontaneity in the present notwithstanding, should be planned, the result of thoughtful consideration and, when possible, rehearsal or practice. For example, syllabus preparation starts with a consideration of what material will be covered and with the tough choices about what it will not be possible to include. Our lectures should be well organized with thoughtful, real world examples that will hold student attention and facilitate retention. Our discussion topics should be relevant to course content and interesting (we hope) to our students, and our exams should be carefully constructed. We should be aware that much teaching and student learning takes place outside of the classroom and be available to our students, urging them to talk with us in other environments like our offices or laboratories.

There are many things we can do to move us closer to these ideal levels of course preparation. Seeking the advice of other instructors who do a good job in the classroom is a natural place to start and has the benefit of helping teachers develop the sense of community that is so important in sustaining them. There also are many other sources of useful ideas, including various books, journals, and conferences that focus on teaching.

Undergraduate Psychology Is Part of a Liberal Education

One of the most striking themes we noted in reviewing all the TIPS columns is the way the teaching of psychology exemplifies the ideals of a liberal education. According to a statement by the American Association of Colleges and Universities (AAC&U):

> Liberal education requires that we understand the foundations of knowledge and inquiry about nature, culture and society; that we master core skills of perception, analysis, and expression; that we cultivate a respect for truth; that we recognize the importance of historical and cultural context; and that we explore connections among formal learning, citizenship, and service to our communities (AAC&U, 1998).

To teach and study psychology is to stand at the crossroads of these facets of a liberal education: acquiring knowledge, mastering skills, testing truth claims, understanding contextual influences, and making connections to the world outside the academy. Several TIPS authors addressed the teaching of scientific methodology and offered suggestions on how to help students grasp the meaning of the scientific enterprise as applied to behavior and mental processes. In addition to discussing how to teach the methods of science, some columns provided advice on teaching students skills like writing and quantitative thinking. Others focused on content, relating how psychology courses invite the integration of other disciplines, such as biology, mathematics, and even law.

TIPS authors also showed there are many ways to draw connections among various domains of knowledge. For example, cross-cultural psychology can be taught as a stand-alone course, or it can be incorporated into nearly every other course typically taught to undergraduates. Likewise, many institutions require psychology majors to take a course on the history of the discipline, although Michael Wertheimer argued that "history belongs in every course" (Wertheimer, 1999). The arts are the only subject area of liberal education not addressed in any TIPS columns and we leave that rich area of psychological research and practice for future authors. It is worth noting, however, that Henry Gleitman, one of the most widely respected authors of an introductory textbook in the last decades, insisted on incorporating the arts into his presentation of the field to new students of psychology.

As noted in the AAC&U statement, a liberal education not only provides foundations for knowledge and methods of inquiry, but also recognizes the ethical principles that are essential to gaining knowledge and using it wisely. Again, our review of TIPS columns shows how seriously psychologists take their ethical responsibilities as they teach and supervise student research. Finally, in addition to providing knowledge and skills for inquiry, writing, and statistical analysis, teachers of psychology increasingly structure service learning into their classes as a way of helping students make meaningful "connections among formal learning, citizenship, and service to our communities" (AAC&U, 1998). Several TIPS columns described innovative ways of helping students make those connections.

Psychology teachers have wonderful opportunities to assist students prepare for an educated life. Teachers must accept, however, that we often do not know if and how our efforts and values influence students in their future lives. This is a form of uncertainty that faculty need to learn to accept.

Teaching Needs Both the Intellectual and the Emotional

Part of what we describe above is intellectual, the cognitive processes of designing courses, working with students, presenting theory, research findings, biography, and example. Reason is not enough, however. Good teaching requires passion, enthusiasm, and joy; it is these that provide the bridge from the intellectual to students' understanding and open the door for students to step over the threshold to confront and understand psychology.

Teaching Requires Compromise

As we lay out our courses and choose from a wide array of possible themes and important skills for students, we make a thousand reasoned decisions. TIPS authors would each have us choose their ideas and approaches to teaching, ones in which they believe deeply and passionately. We cannot, however, choose them all. We must engage in what we call "the compromises of teaching." Teachers are faced with decisions about what content makes up the core in a course, how much is necessary to give a course validity, and how students will learn this content. At the same time, a myriad of other learning experiences and skills exist for students (e.g., writing, group work, ethics, history, classic research, knowledge of the people who are psychologists). Time is finite in teaching any course, but the options are almost infinite.

Teaching compromises are one reason that teaching is hard work, and all teachers feel they come up short. Many teachers lament the losses that result from these compromises ("I had to leave out the chapter on _____," "I wanted to have students do _____ but they are doing enough as it is."). Compromises of teaching need to be made wisely.

Emotion

As amply revealed in TIPS columns over the last 15 years, teaching psychology is not simply about information transfer from teacher to student. Some time after we started editing these columns, the internet revolution burst widely upon intellectual life with an enormous, and sometimes confusing, array of information, along with a proliferation of strategies for accessing that information. Although most of us now celebrate the manifold intellectual resources we mine though the internet, we have not yet concluded that teachers are irrelevant to the learning process. It is emotion — our passion and enthusiasm — that motivates students to stretch themselves intellectually. Recognizing the important place of emotion in teaching does not mean that a teacher needs a demonstrative style; even the quietest teachers can be passionate about their subject matter, and about what they expect from the time they spend with their students. This exultation in learning is contagious, seductive, and enrapturing, all good things in teaching.

Passion for our subject and the pursuit of knowledge enables us to cope with the inevitable frustrations of the professoriate. Enthusiasm and even joy in teaching and learning not only give us the stamina to slog through the occasional bad class session, but these positive emotions "broaden and build" our "thought-action repertoires" (Fredrickson, 2001, p. 221), producing creativity in how we think about teaching, willingness to try new approaches to teaching, and openness to the "individual growth and social connection" (Fredrickson, 2001, p. 224) that can arise from being intentional about teaching and sharing that intentionality with others.

Teachers Need to Think About Teaching and Develop Over Time

We frequently talk about teachers as if they are all the same. We all know this is not the case. For example, in our Teaching Tips columns, we have senior faculty presenting ideas for their colleagues and junior faculty doing the same. As teachers age, they represent different cohorts to their students, and students may teach teachers with their questions, ideas, and passions. As one would expect, teachers change as they age and as they teach more, often because of self critical reflection, facing the challenges of staying intellectually alive, or due to changes in the nature of our students as new generations appear in our classes.

Taking Time to Reflect About Teaching

Our tightly structured lives are filled to the brim with activities that include teaching both inside and outside the classroom, conducting and supervising research, doing administrative work, serving on committees, writing grant proposals and journal articles, etc. Amidst all the "busy-ness," faculty members often feel little leeway to read and think without an immediate goal, or to structure critical self-examination into their schedules. We know from the stress and coping literature how important it is to feel in control of one's life, and yet often faculty feel anything but in control. Recognizing this, several TIPS columns through the years have specifically addressed the importance of faculty taking care of themselves, making time for intellectual growth, and monitoring their teaching attitudes and behaviors. For example, in Volume 2 of *Lessons Learned* (Perlman, McCann, & McFadden, 2004), authors emphasized the importance of taking time for reflection and renewal, making the effort to talk with others about teaching, doing scholarship of teaching research to improve student learning, and constructing a course portfolio to produce a comprehensive audit of how a particular class is taught. These columns plus assorted others published through the years show the multi-faceted nature of teaching psychology.

Teaching is, after all, a profoundly human enterprise, engaged in by people who have developed particular professional skills in order to discover and communicate knowledge about behavior and mental processes. These skills are essential, for sometimes we teach when we are tired, ill, grieving, worried, or distracted. Most of the time, our professionalism carries us through the hour's lecture on Pavlov when we are also thinking about the baby's temperature. Sometimes, we are acutely aware the class did not go well, whereas on other days we leave the lecture hall with a powerful sense of pride and accomplishment, particularly when students walk out with us, asking questions and probing for more insight into challenging issues.

Development as Teachers

Eventually, we learn the rhythms of the academic year and the way the best and worst of classroom experiences fall onto a normal curve. This kind of learning reflects our development as teachers, both in terms of mastery of new teaching techniques but also in processes of personal maturing. The two cannot be easily separated. For example, TIPS columns offer numerous, detailed suggestions for incorporating new approaches to teaching psychology. These include various active learning techniques like demonstrations, role-playing, and small group discussions. Other columns address the challenges of writing good tests and giving feedback to students on their writing. If, however, we come to believe early in our careers that we know how to teach well enough and have no need to revise or change our approaches to teaching, then we reach a dual developmental stasis: avoiding critical reflection about the self and possibilities for personal development as a teacher, and rejecting opportunities to learn new approaches to teaching.

We assume that the readers of the TIPS columns recognize the multiple forms of development that teachers can experience. Some of this development is prompted by working with colleagues and students of different ages and cohorts. As editors of this column, we understand this well; although each of us has taught for more than three decades, we are delighted to discover what we can learn from younger colleagues and the columns they have written. Being in conversation with colleagues at different points in their careers is yet another stimulus to critical reflection about teaching. Typically, cultures assume that novices learn from experts; however, in our rapidly changing world, replete with multiple forms of expertise, experts can learn from novices. This is why some colleges and universities are exploring the idea of reciprocal mentoring. For example, the newly appointed assistant professor might work with a more experienced colleague on incorporating interactive technologies into lecture hall teaching, whereas the tenured full professor just a few years from retirement might help a younger faculty member think through an ethical challenge encountered in the classroom.

Some Realities of Teaching Are Rarely Discussed

In our review of Teaching Tips, we noted that while many useful topics have been discussed, some well-researched principles that deserve consideration in our efforts to improve teaching and student learning receive little attention.

Repetition

Repetition is an excellent example of a principle that applies to good teaching but is rarely discussed. The Law of Frequency has been well studied over the years, but the idea that simple repetition has a positive influence on learning does not come up often in our discussions of teaching and learning, nor is it a common subject in the columns we have published over the years or in the general literature on the teaching of psychology. With so much to cover during a semester, we are reluctant to spend much time repeating something already covered even when we add in the well known benefits of distributed practice. Alas, as anyone who has asked students in upper level courses to describe classical conditioning knows, the usually lengthy discussion of this topic in Introductory Psychology has not been retained as well as we might like. Our typical curriculum with its stepped sequence of prerequisites and lower- and upper-level courses should provide some repetition of major topics, but students still often seem to forget course material and ideas as soon as the test is over.

Overlearning

Even less likely to be addressed is the usefulness of Ebbinghaus' observations about overlearning, where learning material beyond mastery adds greatly to the degree of retention. Again, we have little time in our semesters to repeat material to this degree. If we were able to do more of this or our students practiced overlearning as they studied, especially for their exams, there is little doubt that performance and grades would improve.

The Role of the Student

The amount of energy good teachers spend assisting students in the learning process is inordinate. Much of the content of the Teaching Tips columns concerns ideas and techniques to make our teaching better, and that is as it should be. The vast majority of writings on teaching, as well as Teaching Tips, emphasize how teachers can better ensure student success. Recommendations on course design in which students can demonstrate mastery not only on exams, but in papers, group work, and so forth are but one example. The fact that students in the end must do their own learning (and that some will fail) is a universal truth far less discussed. Rather, we focus on the observation and reality that teaching is hard work and pay less attention to how learning requires hard work by students. Teachers should not overlook or underestimate the difficulty of the task. One of the best ways to remember this lesson is for teachers to be students themselves on occasion, at workshops, for example. The acknowledgement by teachers that their students are asked to work hard and that they (teachers) are aware of what they are asking of their students goes a long way to establishing rapport and building within a single course a learning community made up of both teacher and students.

All Students Cannot Be Reached

Whereas many teachers feel they have failed if their students fail, experience teaches that teachers cannot rescue or reach all students. Even good teachers can only do so much. Some students are ill suited to being in college when we teach them, and although it can be difficult, teachers must allow students to fail if they need do so. It is often challenging for teachers to talk with students getting Ds or Fs, to inquire simply and honestly if there are things they can do to assist, but also to point out that the student may have taken too many credits, illnesses may have a greater impact than they suspected, college is more difficult than they knew, they may not be studying enough, they may want to consider leaving college knowing that they can return at a later date, or they should consider alternative educational paths including other institutions, and the like. Often it is the student who teaches and rescues the teachers, telling them that they had too many part-time jobs, that they are leaving school anyway, or that the teacher should not worry, the student will retake the course. Many teachers want their students to take risks and to get out of their "comfort zone." Failing a course or doing poorly, if put in perspective and treated with respect and interest, may offer opportunities for students to find themselves.

Conclusion

Teaching is an honorable profession and it matters. We end with this basic theme, again widely understood but often unstated. The idea of teaching as an honorable profession has great meaning and needs to be understood and internalized if we are to sustain ourselves in the profession. It implies that what we as teachers do is characterized by principles of honor, that we are upright in our dealings with colleagues and students, and that we are ethical. It further implies that teachers carry themselves with dignity, that the profession has a distinguished history, and that we are standard bearers for all who have gone before us. From this perspective, what we do is worthy of respect although we must be credible to earn this respect. The title of "faculty member" and the responsibilities we accept in our role as teachers demand professionalism on our part—positive personal appearance and behavior, long hours, acceptance of teaching as a calling more than a job, and working with our students with patience and expertise.

What we do does matter. In our dealings with students and in our teaching, what we do has the potential to be substantive, to matter in their lives and ours, to make a difference. To ask for regular, demonstrable examples of such substantive difference making is to ask too much. Like parenting, teaching is at its core an act of faith that in the future what we do will be proven worthwhile. Also, we can teach about substantive issues in our students' lives or anyone's lives for that matter. We can teach about love, loss, death, choice, pathology, and in our examples illumine even neurobiology with ideas that matter to our students.

What we do can matter in our serving as role models for our students and in making overt the workings of a scholarly mind — our own. The belief that teaching matters and is honorable sustains one through a semester, an academic year, and a career and is the bedrock on which all of what we do must be built. All of our TIPS columns are, at their core, based on the idea that if done well, what the authors present will make a difference for students and improve the quality of their education. And when we fail as teachers — and we will and must — the grace, dignity, and honor we represent as teachers allow us to try again.

We wish our readers the very best in their endeavors of confronting and balancing the paradoxes and tensions of good teaching. Use your intellect to benefit your students, but be mindful of the place of emotion and passion. Enjoy and seek out the mix of novices and experts in your work. While striving to become experts in the particular, save time for the awe and reverence for the universal themes of teaching that cause us pain while at the same time giving us satisfaction and meaning.

References and Recommended Readings

AAC&U. (1998). Statement on liberal learning. Retrieved June 20, 2007, from http://www.aacu.org/About/statements/liberal_learning.cfm

Fredrickson, B.L. (2001). The role of positive emotions in positive psychology: The broaden-and-build theory of positive emotions. *American Psychologist*, 56, 218-226.

Perlman, B., McCann, L.I., & McFadden, S.H. (2004). *Lessons learned: Practical advice for the teaching of psychology* (Vol. 2). Washington, DC: Association for Psychological Science.

Wertheimer, M. (1999). History belongs in every course. In B. Perlman, L.I. McCann, & S.H. McFadden (Eds.), *Lessons learned: Practical advice for the teaching of psychology* (Vol. 1, pp. 129-134). Washington, DC: Association for Psychological Science.

Zen lessons: The art of leadership. (1989). Cleary, T. (translator). Boston: Shambhala.

Contributors

PAMELA I. ANSBURG is an associate professor of psychology at The Metropolitan State College of Denver. Her research interests include problem solving and pedagogy.

DREW C. APPLEBY received his BA in psychology from Simpson College in 1969 and his PhD in experimental psychology from Iowa State University in 1972. He is the director of undergraduate studies in the Indiana University-Purdue University Indianapolis psychology department, where he is professor. He is the author of *The Savvy Psychology Major*, has made over 250 presentations to a wide variety of audiences, and has received many local, regional, and national teaching, advising, and mentoring awards.

EMILY BALCETIS is an Assistant Professor of Psychology at Ohio University. She teaches Introduction to Psychology for undergraduates and graduate seminars in automatic social cognition. Her current research interests fall at the intersection of social and cognitive psychology. Specifically, she investigates what and how motivations constrain visual perception, social judgment, and decision-making.

ROBERT A. BARON received his PhD from the University of Iowa (1968) and has held faculty positions at several universities including Purdue, University of Texas, Princeton, University of Washington, and Oxford University. He is currently Wellington Professor of Management and Psychology at Rensselaer Polytechnic Institute, where he teaches a wide variety of courses. He actively exports psychology both in his teaching and in his research, which currently focuses on cognitive and social factors in entrepreneurship.

MARK E. BASHAM is an assistant professor of psychology at The Metropolitan State College of Denver. His research interests include neuroscience, learning and memory, language acquisition, motor learning, and neuron-pharmacology.

DENISE BORD is completing her BS in Education and her BA in Psychology and will soon be teaching in elementary school. After a stint as a teaching assistant she was lured into pedagogical research.

DENISE BOYD teaches psychology at Houston Community College. With Helen Bee, she is the author of *Lifespan Development and The Developing Child*, published by Allyn & Bacon. She is also co-author, with Samuel Wood and Allen Green Wood, of *The World of Psychology and Mastering the World of Psychology*, also published by Allyn & Bacon.

BRIAN L. BURKE is an Assistant Professor of Psychology at Fort Lewis College, a public liberal arts college in Durango, Colorado. Brian is a licensed clinical psychologist whose principal academic interests include motivational interviewing and college teaching. He regularly presents at teaching conferences on the scholarship of learning and teaching, winning the Doug Bernstein Poster Award for innovative teaching ideas twice (NITOP 2004 & 2005) and the New Faculty Teaching Award at Fort Lewis College in 2005. Brian originally hails from Montreal, Canada, and received his PhD from the University of Arizona in 2003. For more information, visit Brian's website at http://faculty.fortlewis.edu/burke_b.

WILLIAM BUSKIST is the Distinguished Professor in the Teaching of Psychology at Auburn University. He teaches courses in introductory psychology and the teaching of psychology. His research interests center on the qualities and behaviors of master teachers, development of student-teacher rapport, and assessment of effective teaching and student learning.

TAMI EGGLESTON is an associate professor of psychology at McKendree College in Lebanon, Illinois. She teaches introduction to psychology, social psychology, human sexuality, and sport and health psychology. She is a member of the Association for the Advancement of Applied Sports Psychology. She and her husband, Mike, campaign a drag car, and she assists McKendree College athletes with mental performance training. She also is a Green Bay Packers fan.

KRISTA FORREST is an Associate Professor of Psychology at the University of Nebraska at Kearney where she has taught General Psychology, Human Development, Adolescent Psychology, Group Dynamics, and Psychology and Law since 1997. Her current research interests include police interrogation strategies, factors contributing to false confessions, and pedagogical techniques in the college classroom.

REBECCA FOUSHÉE is associate professor and director of psychology at Fontbonne University in St. Louis, Missouri, where she teaches introductory, developmental psychology, research design and statistics, behavioral neuroscience, psychology of women, history and systems, and senior research seminar. In 2006, she won the Joan Goosetree Stevens Award for Excellence in Teaching and the Emerson Excellence in Teaching Award. She is a member of APS, APA, STP, and the International Society for Developmental Psychobiology. In addition to teaching psychology, advising students, and conducting research, she spends her time hiking, traveling, growing organic vegetables, and supporting live music, preferably in outdoor venues.

SOLOMON FULERO is professor and past chair of the psychology department at Sinclair Community College in Dayton, Ohio. He is both a psychologist and an attorney; he received his PhD and his JD from the University of Oregon in 1979. He is a past president of the American Psychology-Law Society.

LESLIE B. GOLDSTEIN is a Learning Support Coordinator and Instructor in the Freshman Math Program at Fort Lewis College in Durango, Colorado. Leslie was born in Ottawa, Canada, and received her MA in Teaching & Teacher Education from the University of Arizona in 2002. Leslie's chief academic interests include understanding student motivation, technology in teaching, and training teachers. She has done the latter via a three-year grant called the Southwest Colorado Math Initiative (http://scmi.fortlewis.edu) and as an official Texas Instruments (TI) presenter at various conferences on teaching with technology. For more about Leslie, visit her website at http://faculty.fortlewis.edu/goldstein_l.

RAYMOND J. GREEN is an associate professor of psychology and assistant department head of Psychology and Special Education at Texas A&M University-Commerce. He received his PhD in the area of Social Psychology from Rutgers University in 1997. The only semester he received a 4.0 as an undergraduate is the only semester where he did not miss a single class (but, it was his choice not to miss any classes). If you have any comments or ideas you can contact him at Raymond_green@ tamu-commerce.edu.

REGAN A. R. GURUNG is Associate Dean of Liberal Arts and Sciences and Assistant Professor of Psychology and Human Development at University of Wisconsin-Green Bay. One of his major research interests is the optimization of student learning and he is obsessed with how Introductory Psychology is taught. He can be contacted at gurungr@uwgb.edu.

JESSICA IRONS an Assistant Professor of Psychology at James Madison University. She earned her PhD in Experimental Psychology from Auburn University and an MS from Augusta State University. Her scholarship of teaching interests focus on empirically supported teaching methods, specifically methods for teaching critical thinking.

TAMMY L. KADAH-AMMETER received her MS degree with an experimental emphasis from the University of Wisconsin-Oshkosh and was senior author of the research, *Faculty Ethical Guidelines and Procedures for Dealing With Students in Need*, a poster presented at the January, 2006 annual meeting of the National Institute on the Teaching of Psychology.

JARED KEELEY is a fifth-year graduate student in the Clinical Psychology program at Auburn University. He is the past Chair of the Graduate Student Teaching Association of the Society for the Teaching of Psychology. Some of his scholarly teaching endeavors include examination of the high school psychology course and the development of an empirically validated teaching evaluation measure.

JUDITH E. LARKIN is a professor of psychology at Canisius College in Buffalo, New York, and teaches courses in industrial/ organizational psychology and leadership and motivation. Her research examines gender, affect, and risk in public performance. Pines is Koessler Distinguished Professor and chair of the psychology department. Besides introductory psychology, she currently teaches social psychology and forensic psychology and has also taught cognitive psychology. Both are committed to engaging undergraduates in authentic psychological research at all levels in the curriculum. She can be reached by e-mail at larkin@canisius.edu.

SCOTT O. LILIENFELD is associate professor of psychology (Clinical Program) at Emory University. He is founder and editor of the journal, The Scientific Review of Mental Health Practice and is a consulting editor for Skeptical Inquirer magazine. His book, *Science and Pseudoscience in Clinical Psychology* (2003, Guilford), co-edited with Steven Jay Lynn and Jeffrey M. Lohr, critically examines a broad spectrum of controversial and novel mental health practices. His research interests include the causes and assessment of psychopathic personality and the classification and diagnosis of mental disorders.

NEIL LUTSKY is professor of psychology at Carleton College in Northfield, Minnesota. Lutsky heads Carleton's Quantitative Inquiry, Reasoning, and Knowledge initiative. For additional information, contact nlutsky@carleton.edu.

LEE I. McCANN is a professor of psychology, a Rosebush and University Professor at the University of Wisconsin-Oshkosh; and a Fellow of the American Psychological Association and the Society for the Teaching of Psychology. He is the coauthor (with Baron Perlman) of *Recruiting Good College Faculty: Practical Advice for a Successful Search* (1996, Anker), coeditor (with Baron Perlman and Susan McFadden) of *Lessons Learned: Practical Advice for the Teaching of Psychology: Vol. 1* (1999, Association for Psychological Science), *Lessons Learned: Practical Advice for the Teaching of Psychology: Vol. 2* (2004, Association for Psychological Science), and the Teaching Tips column in the APS *Observer*, and coeditor (with Baron Perlman and William Buskist) of *Voices of Experience: Memorable Talks From the National Institute on the Teaching of Psychology* (2005, Association for Psychological Science).

SUSAN H. McFADDEN is a Rosebush and Endowed Professor, a University of Wisonsin System Distinguished Professor and a professor at University of Wisconsin-Oshkosh. She has taught psychology for 35 years, and is coeditor (with Baron Perlman and Lee I. McCann) of *Lessons Learned: Practical Advice for the Teaching of Psychology: Vol. 1* (1999, Association for Psychological Science), *Lessons Learned: Practical Advice for the Teaching of Psychology: Vol. 2* (2004, Association for

Psychological Science), and the Teaching Tips column in the APS *Observer.*

CATHY SARGENT MESTER is Senior Lecturer and Program Chair for Communication and Media Studies at Penn State-Erie, The Behrend College, specializing in public address education. In her 36 years of college teaching, she has taught over 250 sections of general education courses for undergraduates as well as advanced public speaking courses and numerous workshops for educators and managers. She created the course, Communication for Teachers, now a requirement for the college's education students. She is the recipient of the college's Excellence in Academic Advising Award and the Benjamin A. Lane Award for Service and is listed in *Who's Who Among America's Teachers.*

STEVEN A. MEYERS is Professor of Psychology at Roosevelt University in Chicago, Illinois. He received an AB degree in psychology from Brown University and MA and PhD degrees in clinical psychology from Michigan State University. He also holds a diplomate in clinical psychology from the American Board of Professional Psychology. His research interests include parent/child relations, effective college instruction, and faculty development. He can be reached by email at smeyers@roosevelt.edu.

CHRISTOPHER P. MIGOTSKY is the head of Measurement and Evaluation within the Center for Teaching Excellence at the University of Illinois at Urbana-Champaign. He received a BA degree in psychology and MA degree in counseling psychology from New Mexico State University (Las Cruces). Mr. Migotsky coordinates the Instructor & Course Evaluation System (student ratings) at the University of Illinois and conducts workshops on the evaluation of teaching and assessment of students. His current research area is student perceptions of student ratings of instruction.

JOANN M. MONTEPARE is an associate professor in psychology at Emerson College and teaches courses in social and developmental psychology and nonverbal communication. She is a member of the Communication Sciences and Disorders faculty and is the acting chair of the department of marketing communication.

DAVID G. MYERS is a professor of psychology at Hope College, where he devotes most of his energies to communicating psychological science to college students and the lay public. His scientific and magazine articles span five dozen periodicals, from Science to Scientific American. Among his fifteen books are four general audience trade books, including, most recently, *Intuition: Its Powers and Perils* (www.davidmyers.org/intuition). His current passion is his advocacy for "hearing aid compatible assistive listening," via articles, talks, community initiatives, and a website, hearingloop.org.

JEFFREY S. NEVID is Professor of Psychology at St. John's University and author of several psychology texts in such areas as introductory psychology, abnormal psychology, and psychology of adjustment.

RANDY OTTO is an associate professor in the Department of Mental Health Law & Policy, Florida Mental Health Institute, University of South Florida. He has served as President of the American Board of Forensic Psychology, the American Academy of Forensic Psychology, and the American Psychology-Law Society.

JOHN C. ORY is the director of the Center for Teaching Excellence and professor in the Department of Human Resource Education at the University of Illinois at Urbana-Champaign. He received a B.A. degree in psychology from Augustana College (Rock Island) and his MS and PhD degrees in educational psychology from the University of Kansas. Dr. Ory has written articles and books in the area of student, faculty, and program assessment, and he has conducted teacher/faculty workshops on testing and assessment at the secondary and post-secondary levels. He has also reviewed and developed testing and assessment programs for profit and non-profit organizations.

BARON PERLMAN is a Rosebush and Endowed Professor, a Distinguished Teacher in the Department of Psychology at the University of Wisconsin-Oshkosh, and a Fellow in APA's Society for the Teaching of Psychology. He has a long-standing interest and involvement in the development of faculty. He also is senior editor of Teaching Tips in the APS *Observer*, available in book form, *Lessons Learned: Practical Advice for the Teaching of Psychology* (Perlman, McCann, & McFadden, Eds., Volume

1, 1999; Volume 2, 2004) published by the Association for Psychological Science.

HARVEY A. PINES is a Koessler Distinguished Professor and chair of the psychology department at Canisius College in Buffalo, New York. Besides introductory psychology, he currently teaches social psychology and forensic psychology and has also taught cognitive psychology. His research focuses on topics in social perception and cognition. He is committed to engaging undergraduates in authentic psychological research at all levels in the curriculum. He can be reached by e-mail at pines@canisius.edu.

TED POWERS is a professor of psychology at Parkland College in Champaign, Illinois. While at the University of Illinois, where he earned both his undergraduate and graduate degrees, he was selected by the Alpha Lambda Delta National Honor Society as the 1998 Outstanding Teacher of Freshman. Ted may have also already won 10 million dollars in the Publisher's Clearinghouse Grand Prize Giveaway.

CHERYL E. SANDERS is an assistant professor of psychology at The Metropolitan State College of Denver. Her research interests involve college student development.

MICHAEL SCHULTE-MECKLENBECK is a post-doctoral researcher at the University of Bergen, Norway. His research interests are decision making, online research and research methods. He taught at universities in Austria and Switzerland. He has used computer programs and online methods (Web pages, e-mail) as teaching tools since 1998 and VLEs since 2000.

JOEL I. SHENKER is a clinical instructor and attending neurologist at the department of neurology at the University of Virginia. He has taught courses in introductory psychology and biological psychology and has lectured on neuron-psychology, neuroscience, and clinical neurology. He received a master's degree in psychology in 1991, a PhD in psychology in 1997, and an MD in 1998, all at the University of Illinois at Urbana-Champaign. His research focuses on how human brain damage alters mental representations of experience.

GABIE SMITH is an associate professor of psychology at Elon University in Elon, North Carolina. She teaches health psychology, empirical research, general psychology, human sexuality, and psychology of sex and gender. She and her husband, Brian, have two children who love soccer, tae kwon do, skiing, and tennis.

MARILLA SVINICKI received her PhD in experimental psychology from the University of Colorado in 1972 after which she taught psychology at Macalester College in Minnesota for two years. She then joined a group at the University of Texas at Austin researching the impact of computer-based instruction on learning. At the same time, the University opened a faculty development center and Dr. Svinicki became one of the consultants who worked with faculty on their teaching. After a few years, she started teaching classes on the implementation of psychological principles in educational settings as part of the Educational Psychology department at UT. She recently retired from the faculty development center and began teaching full time in Educational Psychology. She teaches courses in instructional psychology, college teaching, cognition, human learning, and motivation at the undergraduate and graduate levels.

JASON A. WILLIAMS received his BA from the University of California, Riverside, and PhD from the University of California, Santa Cruz. He is currently in his sixth year at Gonzaga University in Spokane, Washington, and was recipient of the Gonzaga University Exemplary Faculty Award in 2005-2006. Currently Chair of the Gonzaga Faculty Senate Committee on Academic Affairs, he frequently engages undergraduates in research both inside and outside the classroom and is constantly amazed at what his students come up with next.

TODD ZAKRAJSEK is the Founding Director of the Faculty Center for Innovative Teaching at Central Michigan University in Mt. Pleasant, Michigan, a centralized faculty development office providing resources in many areas of teaching, learning, and technology. Zakrajsek also was the Founding Director of the Center for Teaching and Learning at Southern Oregon University, where he taught as a tenured associate professor of psychology. Zakrajsek has written two introductory psychology instructor's manuals for McGraw-Hill and a student study guide for Addison-Wesley. He received his PhD in Industrial/ Organizational Psychology from Ohio University. Zakrajsek facilitates workshops and presents conference keynote addresses throughout the United States. He is also the recipient of a 2003 national innovation in faculty development award for the development of "The 5-Minute Workshop."

Index

Engaging students, 10-12

Enthusiasm, 4

Ethics, 152-153, 309-310, 321-322, 325-333

Evaluating and improving teaching, 163-172; advantages, 163-164; assessment process, 166-169; improvement process, 166-169; what to evaluate, 164-166

Exams, 102, 106; grading, 123; minimizing student-teacher disagreements, 8; missed, 151-160; review sessions, 131-138, self correcting multiple choice, 139-'49. *See also* Missed Exams by Students; Review Sessions for Exams; Self-Correcting Exams

Extra credit, grading, 126

Feedback, 3-4, 191-194; on student behavior 197-205. *See also* Student Behavior

Grades, 106-108, 121-130; curves, 127; final, 126-127; "fudge" factor, value of, 128; inflation, 122; motivate students, 121-122; student-faculty disagreements, 128-129; traditional versus pass/fail, 122; what can be graded, 123-126

Groups, 65-70, 73-80; accountability, 77-78; conflicts, 74-75; creating effective 73-76; "cross-training" members, 75; evaluating performance, 78-79; goals, 78-79; research, 239-240; shy/withdrawn students, 77; social skills necessary, 76-77; social loafing by students, 73, 238-239; tasks, 75-76; virtual learning environments, 114-115

Guest lecturers, 221-222

Habituation, students to faculty teaching, 18-19

Humor in teaching, 53-62; guidelines for use, 54-62

Introductory Psychology, 5

Laboratories, virtual, 116-117

Law, 263-271; curricular options, 264-269; in existing courses, examples, 264; resources available, 269

Learning, enhancing student, 81-89, 131-138. *See also* Review Sessions for Exams; Studying, Student

Lecture: diagrams and graphs, 186; effective, 181-187; engaging students, 184-185; evaluating student learning, 185; handouts, 185-186; monotone voice, 26-27; speed and pacing, 186; value of less, 10. *See also* Public Speaking

ASSOCIATION FOR PSYCHOLOGICAL SCIENCE

The Association for Psychological Science is the only association dedicated solely to advancing psychology as a science-based discipline. APS members include the field's most respected researchers and educators representing the full range of topics within psychological science. The Association is widely recognized as a leading voice for the science of psychology in Washington, and is focused on increasing public understanding and use of the knowledge generated by psychological research.

APS *OBSERVER*

The premier news publication for the field of psychological science, the APS *Observer* informs APS Members — as well as public policy makers and the media, — of noteworthy events, activities, news, and opportunities affecting, and affected by, psychological science.

The *Observer* offers a host of information that is invaluable to the academic, research, and applied psychological community. Informative news articles and opinion pieces discuss issues such as important national trends, public policy, and research related matters of direct relevance to the discipline of psychology and its application. In addition, the *Observer* profiles Members making headlines, offers an inside look at Member efforts with provocative, exploratory series, and distributes detailed and practical "how to" information (including the *Teaching Tips* columns that make up this book) to psychological scientists in all stages of their careers.

For more information on APS membership, publications, conventions and other programs, contact APS at:

Association for Psychological Science
aps@psychologicalscience.org
www.psychologicalscience.org